Media, Margins and Civic Agency

# Media, Margins and Civic Agency

Edited by

Einar Thorsen, Daniel Jackson, Heather Savigny and Jenny Alexander
*The Media School, Bournemouth University, UK*

First published 2015 by
PALGRAVE MACMILLAN

Palgrave Macmillan in the UK is an imprint of Macmillan Publishers Limited, registered in England, company number 785998, of Houndmills, Basingstoke, Hampshire RG21 6XS.

Palgrave Macmillan in the US is a division of St Martin's Press LLC, 175 Fifth Avenue, New York, NY 10010.

Palgrave Macmillan is the global academic imprint of the above companies and has companies and representatives throughout the world.

Palgrave® and Macmillan® are registered trademarks in the United States, the United Kingdom, Europe and other countries.

ISBN 978–1–137–51263–5

This book is printed on paper suitable for recycling and made from fully managed and sustained forest sources. Logging, pulping and manufacturing processes are expected to conform to the environmental regulations of the country of origin.

A catalogue record for this book is available from the British Library.

A catalog record for this book is available from the Library of Congress.

# Contents

# Figures and Tables

## Figures

## Tables

# Contributors

**Jenny Alexander** is Senior Lecturer in Media and Communication at Bournemouth University, UK. She previously worked for the Advertising Standards Authority in London, UK, where she was their environment specialist. Her research interests include gender, sexuality and representation, fan cultures, advertising semiotics, anarchism and environmental communication. She teaches media and popular culture, and a specialist final-year degree option in environmental communication.

**Stuart Allan** is Professor of Journalism and Communication in the School of Journalism, Media and Cultural Studies at Cardiff University, UK. His books include *Citizen Witnessing: Revisioning Journalism in Times of Crisis* (2013), as well as the edited *The Routledge Companion to News and Journalism* (revised 2012) and *Citizen Journalism: Global Perspectives*, Volume 2 (co-edited with Einar Thorsen, 2014). He is engaged in research examining the uses of digital imagery in news reporting, among other projects.

**Jen Birks** is Lecturer in Media in the Department of Culture, Film and Media at the University of Nottingham, UK. She is the author of *News and Civil Society* (2014) and has also written about media representation of publics and newspaper campaigning in journalism practice, discourse and society, and British politics.

**Lene Brennodden** is a researcher for 'Generation Falcone', a book project on the Sicilian mafia, alongside being a teacher at a school in Norway. She holds a Master's in Terrorism, International Crime and Global Security from Coventry University, UK, and a BA in International Journalism from Liverpool John Moores University, UK. She was awarded the Liverpool John Moores University research excellence award for her dissertation about news coverage, victims and the bereaved.

**Glenda Cooper** is Lecturer in Journalism at City University London, UK, and a PhD researcher at the university's Centre for Law, Justice and Journalism. She is co-editor with Simon Cottle of *Humanitarianism, Communications and Change* (2015) and the editor of *The Future of*

*Humanitarian Reporting* (2014). She was the 14th Guardian Research Fellow at Nuffield College Oxford (2006–7), Visiting Fellow at Reuters Institute for the Study of Journalism, Oxford (2007–8). Before that she was a journalist working at the national level for over a decade.

**John Downey** is Professor of Comparative Media Analysis in the Department of Social Sciences, Loughborough University, UK. He is Director of Research in the department and also leads the research challenge in communication, culture and citizenship, which is an interdisciplinary initiative drawing together researchers from across the university. He is principal investigator on an ESRC-funded project to provide advanced training courses to postgraduate and early career researchers, and co-investigator on a Horizon 2020-funded project investigating the use of social media in the context of 'terrorist' attacks.

**Deborah Gabriel** is a lecturer in the Faculty of Media and Communication at Bournemouth University, UK, where she brings a critical focus to degree programmes in marketing communications, advertising, public relations and politics. Her research centres on the political dimensions of media communication, principally media inequalities and how they are maintained and perpetuated through the lens of race, class and gender in terms of representation. She also has a keen interest in online political participation and how women and people of colour critique mainstream representation and challenge dominant discourses through alternative media channels.

**Anita Howarth** is Senior Lecturer in Journalism Theory at Brunel University London, UK. Her research on political communication explores the interactions between media and public policy in a range of areas, including food politics, protests and migration. She also researches campaigning journalism of food, risks and human rights, and conflicting discourses on social justice.

**Yasmin Ibrahim** is Reader in International Business and Communications at Queen Mary University of London, UK. Her research on new media technologies explores the cultural dimensions and social implications of the diffusion of information and communications technologies in different contexts. Beyond new media and digital technologies she writes about political communication and political mobilisation from cultural perspectives. Her other research interests include globalisation, Islam, visual culture and memory studies.

**Daniel Jackson** is Principal Lecturer in Media and Communication at Bournemouth University, UK, where he is also Head of Knowledge Exchange for the Corporate and Marketing Communications group in the Faculty of Media and Communication. His research broadly explores the intersection of media and democracy, including news coverage of politics, the construction of news, political communication and political talk in online environments. He is co-convenor of the Political Studies Association Media and Politics Group. He is co-editor of *The Media, Political Participation and Empowerment* (2013) and *Reframing Disability? The Media, (Dis)Empowerment and Voice in the London Paralympics* (2014).

**Lisette Johnston** is a journalism PhD student at City University London, UK. Her research interests include social media and citizen journalism, and how their use impacts broadcast coverage. She has been a journalist for 13 years, the past 5 with BBC TV News, and she is working as a senior broadcast journalist for BBC World News alongside her PhD study. This role gives her a unique insight into the workings of a major news organisation, and how it uses social media and user-generated content. This has helped inform her research, which focuses on the Arab Spring and the Syria conflict.

**Ann Luce** is Senior Lecturer in Journalism and Communication at Bournemouth University, UK. She is Programme Leader of the BA (Hons) Communication and Media, and she also teaches across the journalism and communication academic group, specifically on the BA and MA in Multimedia Journalism. Her research interests focus on the representations of suicide and mental illness, and, more recently, she has been working with disabled people via the charity Access Dorset. As part of this research she has taught disabled people journalism skills so they might become citizen journalists and report on issues that are of importance to them.

**Sarita Malik** is Senior Lecturer in Media and Communications at Brunel University London, UK, where she is also Director of Research for the Department of Social Sciences, Media and Communications. Her research is focused on the politics of media communication, representation and institutional frameworks within the contexts of media history, cultural policy and social change. Her research interests include cultural diversity and public service broadcasting, media genres and cultural representation, black and Asian British cinema, and the relationship between media regulation and public discourse. She has been the principal investigator on three Arts and Humanities Research Council Connected Communities projects looking at the relationship between communities and media culture. Her current project examines the relationship between 'disconnected communities' and the media.

**Monika Metykova** is Lecturer in Media Communications and Journalism Studies at the School of Media, Film and Music, University of Sussex, UK. Her research interests include media/journalism and democracy, migration and cosmopolitanism, and European media spaces and policy. She has recently edited a special issue entitled 'New Media and Democracy' of the journal *Cyberpsychology: Journal of Psychosocial Research on Cyberspace*. Her book provisionally entitled 'Diversity and the Media' is forthcoming (Palgrave Macmillan).

**Jackie Newton** is Programme Leader for Journalism at Liverpool John Moores University, UK, and a former newspaper editor. A psychology graduate with a master's in educational management, she is particularly interested in journalists' relations with the bereaved, and associated sensitive interviewing and media representations of violence. She has published about bereaved families' varying responses to news media intrusion and has written papers and a book chapter about death reporting and humanitarian reporting with Dr Sallyanne Duncan of the University of Strathclyde, UK. She has also worked on journalism education initiatives with the Merseyside branch of Support After Murder and Manslaughter.

**Olatunji Ogunyemi** has extensive teaching and research experience in both the UK and overseas, and he received his PhD in journalism from Moscow State University, Russia. A principal lecturer and the convener of the Media of Diaspora Research Group, he regularly publishes articles in journals and chapters in edited books. He researches journalism and diaspora, and he is the author of *What Newspapers, Films, and Television do Africans Living in Britain See and Read? The Media of the African Diaspora*.

**Katy Parry** is Lecturer in Media and Communication at the University of Leeds, UK. Her work focuses on visual politics and how 'frames of war' circulate in public culture. She is a co-author of *Pockets of Resistance* (2010) with Piers Robinson, Peter Goddard, Craig Murray and Philip Taylor, and *Political Culture and Media Genre: Beyond the News* (Palgrave Macmillan, 2012) with Kay Richardson and John Corner.

Along with Stephen Coleman and Giles Moss, she has recently co-edited a Festschrift for Jay G. Blumler, *Can the Media Serve Democracy?* (Palgrave Macmillan, 2015).

**Barry Richards** is Professor of Political Psychology in the Media School at Bournemouth University, UK. Prior to moving to Bournemouth in 2001, he was Professor and Head of the Department of Human Relations at the University of East London, UK. His books include *Images of Freud: Cultural Responses to Psychoanalysis* (1989), *Disciplines of Delight: The Psychoanalysis of Popular Culture* (1994), *The Dynamics of Advertising* (2000) with I. MacRury and J. Botterill, and *Emotional Governance: Politics, Media and Terror* (Palgrave Macmillan, 2007). He is a founding co-editor of the Sage journal *Media, War and Conflict*. He has written widely about popular culture and politics. His major interests are in the psychology of politics, particularly in the emotional dynamics of conflict and extremism, and in psychosocial dimensions of cultural change. His latest book is *What Is Holding Us Together* (forthcoming).

**Pollyanna Ruiz** is Lecturer in Media and Communication at the University of Sussex. The author of *Articulating Dissent: Protest and the Public Sphere*, she is interested in the media's role in the construction of social and political change. Her research focuses on the ways in which protest movements bridge the gap between their own familiar but marginal spaces, and a mainstream which is suspicious at best and downright hostile at worst. In doing so she looks at the communicative strategies of contemporary political movements, such as the anti-globalisation movement, the anti-war movement and coalitions against the cuts.

**Heather Savigny** is Associate Professor of Politics and Gender in the Faculty of Media and Communication at Bournemouth University. She researches and teaches in the broad areas of gender, media and politics. With Helen Warner she co-edited *The Politics of Being a Woman; Feminism, Media and 21st Century Popular Culture* (Palgrave Macmillan, 2015) and with Deirdre O'Neill she published in the *AJE* journal and the *New Statesman* on the representation of female MPs in the press. She also writes more widely about heavy metal and feminism.

**Einar Thorsen** is Principal Lecturer in Journalism and Communication at Bournemouth University, and Associate Director of the Centre for the Study of Journalism, Culture and Community. His research focuses on online journalism, particularly during crisis and conflicts, and in response to political and environmental change. He has co-edited two volumes of *Citizen Journalism: Global Perspectives* with Stuart Allan (Volume 1: 2009, Volume 2: 2014), and has also published journal articles and book chapters on public service media online, crisis reporting, WikiNews, whistleblowing and WikiLeaks.

# Introduction

Daniel Jackson, Jenny Alexander, Einar Thorsen and Heather Savigny

This juncture in history finds Europe in an uncertain and unstable position. There are several reasons for this: a zombie echo of the Cold War in the annexation of part of Ukraine by Russia; the long shadow of the Israel–Palestine conflict; the worst economic depression since the 1930s (following the international banking crisis of 2008); and the ever-widening income and wealth gaps between rich and poor. Geopolitical and economic power is shifting, resulting in a reactionary retrenchment of national identities. Thus, definitions of citizenship – who is inscribed at the centre and who at the margins – are presently being subjected to ideological pressures from a resurgent xenophobia in many quarters. The UK Independence Party, the Jobbik Party in Hungary, Golden Dawn in Greece, Pegida (Patriotic Europeans Against the Islamization of the West) in Germany and Marine Le Penn's Front Nationale in France, for example, all rely on anti-immigration rhetoric to fuel their growing popularity. Rising anti-Semitism is driving significant numbers of France's Jewish population to emigrate to Israel (Beaumont, 2015), and jihadist Islamism is proving attractive to many young European Muslims, perhaps searching for identity between the conservatism of their parents and the Islamophobia of their neighbourhoods. The grander 'realpolitik' – that Europe has consumed far more than its fair share of global resources for several hundred years, that its place in the world order is no longer secure – is not a message any of the self-preservationist political classes wish to bear to their electorates. Instead, the cultivation of fear and hatred for the 'other' – migrants, diasporic communities, ethnic minorities, and the 'feckless' poor and disabled – has become an easier (and more convenient) narrative to sell.

This could also be said to be part of a broader shift in approaches to citizenship in Europe, with renewed critiques of multiculturalism being voiced by mainstream political leaders from Germany's Angela Merkel to the UK's David Cameron. There has been a swing away from a politics of difference where 'the unique identity and practices of individuals and groups are recognised and accorded respect within a national body politic' (O'Cinneide, 2004: 47) towards an older 'unitary model' emerging from the Enlightenment, which 'requires minorities to adopt dominant Eurocentric norms of conduct if they wish to be treated as full and equal citizens' (O'Cinneide, 2004: 46). This 'unitary model' inscribes an assimilationist centre and separatist margins which, one might argue, further reproduces incommensurate realities. This has been starkly illuminated by events in contemporary France with the 2015 shootings of cartoonists, journalists and others at the Parisian offices of the satirical French magazine *Charlie Hebdo* by French Muslims claiming to be affiliated with Al Qaeda Yemen, in retaliation for the publication of scatological cartoons of the prophet Muhammad. The freedom of expression upheld by the innumerable French citizens who wore the slogan 'Je suis Charlie' in street vigils of solidarity for the dead might seem incommensurate with the 2010 French law prohibiting the covering of the face in public space, which effectively banned the Muslim female face veil, the niquab.

The mainstream media are, of course, discursively active in this arena, remaining a powerful force in the shaping of popular understandings of citizenship (its insides and outsides). In this collection we explore the discursive and structural (re)production of social, cultural and political marginality via constructions of voiced and silenced, 'orderly' and 'disorderly', 'normative' and 'non-normative', citizens and 'non-citizens' in mainstream media and media policy. Those who find themselves marginalised by political rhetoric, mainstream media representation, or lack of representation, sometimes find the means to push back. When the UK TV station Channel 4 ran advertising for its entertainment show *My Big Fat Gypsy Wedding*, which depicted traveller children in aggressive and sexualised poses, the Irish Traveller Movement in the UK successfully complained about stereotyping to the Advertising Standards Authority and the adverts were removed (BBC, 2012). When Sue Marsh, a sufferer of Crohn's disease, found UK Government (and associated press) oratory about disabled people vitriolic, she became a disabled rights activist and her blog, *Diary of a Benefit Scrounger*, coalesced as a powerful voice for disabled people struggling with Department for Work and Pensions 'work capability assessments'.

The second of these examples speaks to one of the key questions for the new century, and one addressed by this collection: the relationship between social media as a platform for counterhegemonic citizen voices and mainstream media's engagement (or not) with those voices. If mainstream media do not engage, as media owners are well aware, they run the risk of watching their audiences dissolve as a younger generation turns to peer-to-peer content-sharing. Indeed, news sites such as Upworthy and Buzzfeed have already sprung up to cater to 'digital natives', their informal tone and layout savvy for (re)sharing via Facebook, Tumblr and Twitter. Established newspapers have also migrated online and become multimedia platforms, including embedded video, users' photo galleries and reams of readers' comments (Allan, 2006). No radio or TV news programme is now complete without the invitation to audiences to engage with the programme or its themes via Twitter.

There are, of course, a range of idealistic, optimistic, critical and realist perspectives on the contribution of social media to the public sphere, on its potential to allow the intervention of marginalised voices into the mainstream (see e.g. Curran et al., 2012; Dahlgren, 2012; Shirky, 2011). The position adopted on this depends in part on the role played by specific actors within mainstream media (which is not, after all, unitary) as gatekeepers, as a filter checking the accuracy of social media sources and/or as an ideological narrator serving vested interests. There is certainly the potential for mainstream news accounts to be significantly called into question by peer-to-peer networks speaking 'from the margins'. This is happening in the US with, for example, citizen protests (and associated social media activities) against institutional racism in neighbourhood watch schemes and police forces, following a number of 'law enforcement' shootings of young African Americans, including those of Trayvon Martin in 2012 in Sanford, Florida, and Michael Brown in 2014 in Ferguson, Missouri.

On the other hand, despite Clay Shirky's optimistic manifesto for plurality in the digital age (Shirky, 2008), all voices are not equal. Mainstream media continue to enjoy a wellspring of social legitimacy (propped up by capital, historic reputation and entrée to the corridors of power), which means that its (often highly ideological) ways of framing news agendas remain powerful. Grassroots activists know that for their narratives to gain traction, their tweets, videos and protest photos still need to be picked up by mainstream media organisations in order to be amplified and accorded gravitas.

In today's cacophonous media, we know that certain voices continue to be bolstered by social, cultural and economic capital. That is why Islamic State release videos of hostage beheadings. They understand that to compete with these forms of capital it must bring spectacle. To succeed in entering public consciousness, all activist movements must now cultivate a spectacular wing. However, to create a simple dichotomy, pitting conservative established media hegemony against the activist voices of the marginalised on social media (one managerialising the public sphere, the other calling it to account) would be reductive. Not all marginalised voices post messages in the language of social justice (hate speech on social media is endemic, as we know), and grassroots activists often still require allies in the mainstream media. The public is aware of the US and UK intelligence services' mass electronic surveillance programme, PRISM, thanks to whistleblower Edward Snowden's collaboration with *The Guardian* newspaper and *The Washington Post*, as well as his connection to Wikileaks.

Yet a broader challenge still remains. To create something beyond competing claims for recognition in the polity, to resist calls for citizenship based in absolutism and 'purity' (be they fascist or jihadist), we need a new narrative of the commons. For some, Marxism has failed, Europeanism is creaking at the seams, liberal multiculturalism is faltering (mired, among other things, in the classism and tokenism of which some post-colonial thinkers have long accused it [Spivak and Gunew, 1986]) and party political democracy has, as Frank Zappa rather cynically said, become 'the entertainment division of the military-industrial complex'. To steer a course through these times of gathering clouds, we must, as scholars and as citizens, call injurious media narratives to account, whether they be Islamic State videos depicting the (forced) conversion of Yazidis or UK newspaper headlines dehumanising migrants. Derrida, in his tribute to Levinas, speaks of 'the welcoming of the other' (Derrida, 2002: 21) as *the* ethical relation; Chimamanda Ngozi Adiche, musing on love, notes: 'It is not easy to see another person' (Kellaway, 2013); Thoreau (the author of *Civil Disobedience*) reminds us that 'It takes two to speak the truth, one to speak and the other to hear' (1849). Social media may permit many more citizens a platform for speech in the mediated public sphere, but welcoming, seeing and listening require us to truly engage in social relations.

## Civic agency and social change

The purpose of this edited collection is to bring together some of the leading research on media, power and the margins. The book will therefore include both theoretical and empirical chapters that draw specific attention to a reappraisal of the theories, methods and issues that inform our understanding of citizens and publics in contemporary society. Here we put the activities of groups and practitioners traditionally seen at the margins at the centre of our focus. This means examining the power relations at play in mediated environments at the margins, by the margins and for the margins.

Here, various operationalisations of 'marginal' citizen voices emerge: as audiences for diasporic media; as sources for mainstream media, as bloggers providing alternative spaces for 'counterpublics'; as citizen narrators and citizen journalists (Warner, 2002). A further perspective is provided by reflections on mediatised protest, activism and counternarratives 'from the margins'. We focus on the ways and means through which (all and any) media can and do empower or disempower citizens at the margins – that is, how they act as vehicles of, or obstacles to, a sense of civic agency and social change.

In mature Western democracies, civic agency is at the centre of social change. It drives the ongoing (re)formation of civil society and challenges authority. For Dahlgren (2012), a robust civic identity implies an empowered political agent, one equipped to confront structures of power: 'Engagement in issues becomes meaningful, citizens feel that they, in concert with others, can in some way make a difference, that they can have some kind of impact on political life, even if they do not win every battle' (Dahlgren, 2012: 40). It is thus important to note that a sense of civic agency by no means guarantees any kind of social change, but that the latter still needs the former. In this collection, our concern is those who have (or at least seek) a sense of civic agency and want to elicit change.

For too long, discussions of civic agency and social change have been the domain of the political sciences, public sphere theory, deliberative democracy and political communication (see Dahlgren, 2006). Only relatively recently have media and cultural studies begun to contribute to debates about civic agency, despite the natural tendency of such scholars to talk compellingly of issues of mediated (dis)empowerment and democratic renewal. This collection is a modest attempt to continue this important work. In the chapters that follow we provide a vibrant snapshot of both established and emerging concerns around media, margins and social change. From the appropriation of user-generated content (UGC) in BBC newsrooms, to disabled people taking up citizen journalism, to the mainstream mediation of 'aliens' living in migrant camps at the margins of society, we take a fresh and contemporary look at questions of marginalised representations in, and activism through, the media.

## Chapter overview

Part I of this collection begins with a focus on citizen voices. It asks how citizens at the margins of society use media – particularly through self-representation – to gain voice, challenge the mainstream and cultivate symbolic power? In Chapter 1, Deborah Gabriel examines how African Caribbean people use blogs as a discursive medium through which raced and gendered identities are contested, reconfigured and enacted within the blogosphere. She highlights how the motivations and gratifications of African Caribbean bloggers are driven by a complex set of factors linked to issues of race and representation that stem from feeling voiceless, invisible and marginalised within UK society. While recognising the blogosphere as a potentially democratic space, she argues it maintains raced and gendered inequalities found offline and reproduces unequal power relations. Despite such limitations, African Caribbeans still appropriate the blogosphere as a medium for self-representation to cultivate symbolic power through their own constructions of Black identity.

It remains the case that the historical legacies of colonialism still impact on Western media's construction and representation of the West as the centre and 'the rest' as peripheral. Disaster experience and response encounters, between the global North and the global South in the mediasphere, are still profoundly materialised by and through structural, economic and historical power relations. These relations shape the representation and conceptualisation, in other words the imaginary, of disasters and disaster relief. That is so even with the advent of the greater plurality of voices occasioned by social media, as Jenkins et al.'s (2012) analysis of the Stop Kony 2012 campaign illustrates. In Chapter 2, Glenda Cooper speaks to these issues of aid, media communication and unequal power relations by looking at the ways in which international non-governmental organisations (NGOs) marshal the voices of citizen witnesses to humanitarian crises, in particular via social media. She considers the tensions between the search for 'authentic voices' (from the margins) to be message bearers from recipients of aid (the citizenry of one region) to donors of aid (the citizenry of others), and the desire of mediating NGOs to control those voices as part of their public relations work. Social media may be more communicatively horizontal than broadcast media but it too is hierarchical in terms of access, reach and narrative control, in ways which replicate already existing power structures, the presence and follower command of Hollywood celebrities being illustrative.

Chapter 3 follows a similar theme of access to the media, voice and empowerment, but in a case where the citizens have created their own media platform. Here, Einar Thorsen, Daniel Jackson and Ann Luce document a citizen journalism project initiated by a charity representing older and disabled people in the south of England. Through interviews with the citizen journalists, they examine whether and how citizen journalism acts as a facilitator of citizen empowerment and a catalyst of social change. Here, the contradictory nature of citizen empowerment becomes apparent. For instance, of all the barriers to having their voice heard explored in the interviews, physical and mental disability were virtually absent. However, the fear of publically criticising the government was a genuine barrier for many, who felt vulnerable in the face of the government 'assault' on welfare and benefits. Furthermore, there was not a straightforward relationship between becoming confident as a citizen journalist, and feeling empowered as a disabled or older person.

Barry Richards' Chapter 4 takes a different approach by addressing a margin where tyrannical and violent voices prevail, and are at the present time increasingly able to recruit to their cause. It presents the argument that via the web, extremist ideologies which demand violence are now providing psychologically damaged persons with new ways of trying to manage their inner turmoil, through their promises of respect and enfoldment within a millenarian community and their legitimation of murderous impulses. It examines the similarities between many terrorists and non-ideological 'rampage' killers, and finds a major mental health factor in both groups, often centring upon an experience of the self as humiliated. With crucial online input (the virtual 'host', which reduces or obviates the need for face-to-face conversion), this inner turbulence is recast as ideological mission, and stabilised in a fundamentalist purity of mind. The need is stressed for any 'counternarratives' to address the importance of the mental health factor, and to take on the powerful appeal which absolute messages can make to some individuals.

Part II takes a more media-centred approach to margins and marginality, examining how media organisations and policy frameworks support (or hinder) the representation of marginalised groups. This starts with a focus on policy-making at the European level. In Chapter 5, Monika Metykova examines how European/European Union (EU) media policy-making addresses the margins. She argues that media policy-making in European countries tends to be restricted to nation-centric frameworks, and shows that pan-European agents are not empowered to work with transnational approaches to cultural diversity when it comes to media regulation. The nation-centric approach is particularly striking when we take into account the 'new' complexity of contemporary Europe, which is linked particularly to migration that has been a major factor in the social (as well as the cultural and demographic) transformation of contemporary societies – which call for new approaches to media policy-making. The underlying principles and approaches that characterise European media policy are largely ignorant of these developments on the ground in Europe and remain caught up in the 'national container' approach. The largest (transnational) ethnic minority group in the EU – the Roma – is a particularly problematic example of this. Through an examination of media catered towards Roma minorities in the Czech Republic, Metykova finds that Roma figure in national media policies in a marginal way and there are no policy interventions related to their media at the transnational level.

Retaining a policy focus but at the UK level, in Chapter 6, Sarita Malik puts together history and analysis to consider the relationship between 'race' and UK public service broadcasting (PSB). Building on earlier work that recognises a paradigmatic shift from 'multiculturalism' to 'cultural diversity', she identifies a third phase: 'creative diversity'. This provides a further incremental depoliticisation of 'race' in PSB contexts. Here, ideas of 'quality' and 'creativity' are foregrounded over (structural) questions of (in)equality or the positive recognition of social and cultural difference. The chapter situates the rapid rise of 'creative diversity' alongside parallel developments in the 'crisis of multiculturalism', UK equality legislative frameworks and creative industries policy. It is argued that 'creative diversity' shifts the paradigm of the multicultural problem (in PSB), enables the 'marketisation' of TV and multiculture, and ultimately continues to safeguard the interests of PSB. Therefore the social and political basis of the diversity agenda has been diminished through the discourse of 'creative diversity', which in turn has serious implications for PSB and society.

Inasmuch as Europe is in denial, lamenting that its children are enduring living standards less replete than their parents, struggling to accommodate a desire for cheap immigrant labour alongside high unemployment, refusing to perform the 'work of mourning' (Derrida, 2001) for the old order passing away, this can be connected, in part, to a 'death phobic' (Baker and McPherson, 2014) image cult of (predominantly white) youth in contemporary Western media. Some 50 years after her death, an eternally youthful Marilyn Monroe is the 'new' face of Chanel perfume advertising (2013), and Ebola is framed as the encroachment of death itself from the 'dark continent' (Spencer and Parry, 2014). The UK's National Crime Agency cannot prosecute all those known to regularly download child pornography because the numbers are too great (Peachey, 2014). In the Western public sphere, youth has become overdetermined by desire, and death has been banished. In Chapter 7, Jackie Newton and Lene Brennodden consider the voices of mourners in a cross-cultural comparison of Norway and the UK, and the way in which these voices (in this case the friends and family of those killed in road accidents) are gate-kept and/or marginalised by mainstream journalists. Their findings pose challenging questions about the comparative ethics of death reporting and whether Norwegian journalists' well-intentioned desire to avoid intruding on grief can have the less desirable effect of excluding families from stories of their loved ones' deaths.

In Chapter 8, Ola Ogunyemi looks at the case for considering diasporic media as fulfilling public service functions, in filling the representational gap for particular, often marginalised, audiences. Through a case study of the diasporic newspaper *Nigerian Watch*, his analysis reveals that it appropriates public service in articulating its rationale, and journalists allude to it to justify their role perceptions. These lead to the allocation of more space to public service content and to a tendency to embed semantic elements related to public service in frame packages. These have implications for the way we perceive the role of the diasporic media, especially in bridging the divide between mainstream and diasporic audiences.

In recent years, migrants have often found themselves voiceless in the face of negative news representations in the UK. In Chapter 9, Anita Howarth and Yasmin Ibrahim focus on how the online versions of the UK's two mid-market newspapers framed the migrant camps or 'jungles' on the French sea border as marginalised spaces. They examine discursive and material space constructions in framing human migration, and how borders as interstitial spaces become continually redefined and reconstructed through the interactions of the corporeal body with the physical environment, policy enactments and cross-border patrols. Spaces at the margin functioning beyond metaphors become heuristic entities where their material and intangible construction and destruction have consequences for shaping human empathy and engagement, as well as distance and detachment with the migrant as a human and with immigration debates.

While some marginalised groups continue to suffer in relative silence, Armando Salvatore reminds us that 'the substantial definition of the common within European modernity has been often a specific task of radical movements' (2013: 218). In other words, the democratic ideal of the European public sphere, historically, has many rebellious roots, from Catharism to the French Revolution, from Quakerism to Chartism, through abolitionism and successive waves of feminism. In Part III we document the counternarratives that emerge in the public sphere, often driven by marginalised people themselves.

In Chapter 10, Katy Parry explores the coverage of the 2013 Margaret Thatcher funeral protests in mainstream online news galleries, with a focus on the 'image politics' (Deluca, 1999) of those who chose to line the streets alongside the mourners and to quietly express their outrage at the ceremonial event. She explores the performance, visibility or invisibility, and framing of these protests, and their intervention into (or containment by) mainstream media narratives. Here the innovative, heartfelt and often humorous forms of expression were able to attract media attention and subsequent circulation across varied media forms, and hence placed contentious politics at the margins of a national media event.

Also examining how counterhegemonic discourses enter the public sphere are Jen Birks and John Downey in Chapter 11. Drawing on Bernhard Peters' metaphor of 'sluice-gates', they consider how flows of discourse pass between and through institutions within the public sphere, and how relatively resource-poor groups can, on occasion, influence public discourse in more powerful institutions such as media and legislatures. Their case study is UK Uncut, a resource-poor anti-austerity group formed in 2010 that campaigns energetically on the issue of tax avoidance by corporations and wealthy individuals in the UK. Through an innovative process-tracing methodology, they examine the complex recipe of causal conditions that explain its emergence out of the margins and into the centre of the public sphere.

In Chapter 12, Lisette Johnston turns the focus of counternarratives to inside the newsroom during the Syria crisis, when the BBC was compelled to engage with a new type of 'correspondent' – the media activist. She examines how UGC has become a tool to help BBC newsrooms understand developments surrounding the conflict. This in turn has led to greater interaction and engagement with citizens and activists within Syria. She also considers how BBC journalistic practices have changed to incorporate this content and these voices, which were marginalised at the start of the conflict in March 2011. For BBC journalists, assimilating activist content into mainstream news represented a steep learning curve in developing new practices and verification measures to ensure non-BBC content can go on air. However, editorial structures remain hierarchical, hence BBC journalism cannot be said to be truly collaborative or 'networked'.

The contemporary media landscape is characterised by a fractured unevenness that unsettles the clearly demarcated boundaries, which constituted classical models of the public sphere. Police and protesters are traditionally represented in mainstream news coverage as occupying a binary in which the police are trusted and law-abiding and the protesters are not. In Chapter 13, Pollyanna Ruiz examines emerging counternarratives to this binary by analysing broadsheet coverage prompted by the death of Ian Tomlinson to argue that the police's ability to frame protest is being undermined by technological, cultural and structural changes. She concludes by suggesting that these changes are impacting upon the representation of the police in such a way as to unsettle the 'citizenship line' (Waddington, 1999: 61) that exists between protesters and publics.

The Afterword to this collection is provided by Stuart Allan. He takes a long-lens view of the role of media and technology in social change. At the centre of his analysis is the idea – indeed hope – that the centre cannot hold; that it can be broken apart. In the pages that follow, our contributors document how those at the margins are doing such work. This means exploring the innovations and mutations of technology-facilitated civic agency; the opportunities, successes, failures and barriers to empowerment experienced by marginalised people; and the ongoing tension between the mainstream (be it mainstream media, culture or political institutions) and the margins. As history continues to show, achieving equality and progressive social change can be painfully slow, yet punctuated by intense moments of breakthrough. In this book our focus is on how the media and technology can both help and hinder those who wish to achieve such goals.

## References

Allan, S. (2006) *Online News: Journalism and the Internet.* Maidenhead, UK, and New York, US: Open University Press.

Baker, C. and McPherson, G. (2014) *Extinction Dialogues: How to Live with Death in Mind.* San Francisco and Montreal: Tayen Lane Publishing.

BBC (2012) My Big Fat Gypsy Wedding show poster complaints upheld. *BBC News*, 2 October 2012. Available at: http://www.bbc.com/news/uk-19809721 (accessed 18 February 2015).

Beaumont, P. (2015) Why are French Jews heading to Israel in such numbers. *Guardian*, 16 January Available at: http://www.theguardian.com/world/2015/jan/16/french-jews-israel-exodus-reasons (accessed 18 February 2015).

Curran, J., Fenton, N. and Freedman, D. (2012) *Misunderstanding the Internet.* London: Routledge.

Dahlgren, P. (2006) Doing citizenship: The cultural origins of civic agency in the public sphere. *European Journal of Cultural Studies.* 9(3), 267–286.

Dahlgren, P. (2012) Reinventing participation: Civic agency and the web environment. *Geopolitics, History & International Relations.* 4(2), 27–45.

DeLuca, K. (1999) *Image Politics.* New York: Guilford Press.

Derrida, J. (2001) *The Work of Mourning.* Chicago and London: University of Chicago Press.

Derrida, J. (2002) *Goodbye to Emmanuel Levinas.* Trans. Michael Naas and Pascal-Anne Brault. Stanford: Stanford University Press.

Jenkins, H., Vichot, R. and Zhan, L. (2012) A brief outline of Kony 2012 and initial reactions to the campaign. *Confessions of an Aca-Fan: The Official Weblog of Henry Jenkins,* 12 March 2012. Available at: http://henryjenkins.org/2012/03/ a_brief_outline_of_kony_2012_a.html (accessed 16 February 2015).

Kellaway, K. (2013) Chimamanda Ngozi Adichie: 'My new novel is about love, race...and hair', 6 April 2013. Available at: http://www.theguardian.com/ theobserver/2013/apr/07/chimamanda-ngozi-adichie-americanah-interview

O'Cinneide, C. (2004) Citizenship and multiculturalism: Equality, rights and diversity in contemporary Europe, in Gavan Titley (ed) *Resituating Culture.* Strasbourg Cedex: Directorate of Youth and Sport, Council of Europe Pub.

Peachey, P. (2014) National crime agency says system realistically can't prosecute all 50,000 child sex offenders. *Independent,* 20 October 2014. Available at: http: //www.independent.co.uk/news/uk/crime/national-crime-agency-says-that-realistically-the-system-cant-persecute-all-50000-child-sex-offenders-9806790. html (accessed 16 February 2015).

Salvatore, A. (2013) New media, the 'Arab Spring' and the metamorphosis of the public sphere: Beyond Western assumptions on collective agency and democratic politics. *Constellations: An International Journal of Critical and Democratic Theory.* 20(2), 217–228.

Shirky, C. (2008) *Here Comes Everybody.* London: Allen Lane.

Shirky, C. (2011) The political power of social media: Technology, the public sphere, and political change. *Foreign Affairs,* January/February. Available at: https://www.foreignaffairs.com/articles/2010-12-20/political-power-social-media (accessed 16 February 2015).

Spencer, B. (2014) Global threat of Ebola: From the US to China, scientists plot spread of deadly disease across the world from its West African hotbed. *Daily Mail,* 5 October 2014. Updated 15 October 2014. Available at http://www.dailymail.co.uk/health/article-2781667/Ebola-hit-UK-three-weeks-Scientists-warn-50-chance-virus-spread-here.html (accessed 16 February 2015).

Spivak, G. C. and Gunew, S. (1986) Questions of multiculturalism. *Hecate.* 12(1/2), 136–142.

Thoreau, H. D. (2003) [1849] A Week on the Concord and Merrimack Rivers. Project Gutenberg. Available at: http://www.gutenberg.org/cache/epub/4232/ pg4232.html (accessed 19 February 2015).

Waddington, P. A. J. (1999) *Policing Citizens.* London and New York: Routledge.

Warner, M. (2002) Publics and counterpublics. *Public Culture.* 14(1), 49–90.

# Part I
# Citizen Voices

# 1

# Alternative Voices, Alternative Spaces: Counterhegemonic Discourse in the Blogosphere

*Deborah Gabriel*

In 21st-century Britain, racial inequality remains deeply embedded in the fabric of society (Institute for Public Policy Research, 2010) and the media is a key site for ongoing struggles against hegemony (Bailey et al., 2008; Cammaerts, 2008; Downing, 2001). Women and people of colour remain at the margins of the mainstream media that often perpetuate inequalities through misrepresentation or exclusion. Black women are frequently constructed through the dominant discourse of 'the angry Black woman' (Isokariari, 2013) and measured by European standards of beauty (Collins, 1990) that render them invisible. Black men continue to be associated with criminality and are rarely represented beyond the stereotype of sporting hero (Ferber, 2007). This chapter examines how blogs are used by African Caribbean people as an assertive strategy, tool of resistance against racial oppression, and resistance to misrepresentation and exclusion in the mainstream media. It reveals how the motivation and gratification of African Caribbean bloggers are driven by a complex set of factors linked to issues of race and representation that stem from feeling voiceless, invisible and marginalised within UK society. While hailed as a revolutionary, democratic space, the blogosphere maintains raced and gendered inequalities that exist offline and reproduces unequal power relations (Cammaerts, 2008; Kellner, 2000; Papacharissi, 2002; Schradie, 2012). However, as this chapter reveals, African Caribbeans still appropriate the blogosphere as a medium for self-representation to cultivate symbolic power through their own constructions of Black identity. While there is a growing body of research on the blogosphere, the use of blogs by people of colour in the UK is an underdeveloped area of inquiry. This chapter expands the current literature by highlighting how Black Britons engage with blogs in ways that differ from the White majority population.

## Methodology

The research on which this chapter is based is approached through the theoretical frameworks of alternative media and critical race theory (CRT), and the conceptual framework of uses and gratifications theory. Alternative media practice can be defined as non-mainstream, radical and participatory (Atton, 2001; Hamilton, 2000), while a key purpose of CRT is centring the Black voice and the Black experience (Delgado and Stefancic, 2001; Hylton, 2012). In this study this is achieved through the constructed narratives of the bloggers in their in-depth interviews, which allows them 'to speak in a culturally authentic, socially meaningful and politically powerful voice' (Aldridge, 2000: 103). As Milner (2007: 391) argues, 'From critical race theory perspectives, knowledge can and should be generated through the narratives and counter-narratives that emerge from and with people of colour.' Uses and gratification theory aims to explain why people use certain types of media and the psychological needs that motivate their media use (Chung and Kim, 2008), although it is not without limitations. There is a tendency to assume the existence of a universal mass media with common values, rather than acknowledge the diversity of media audiences in terms of class, race, gender and other factors (Morley, 1992).

This chapter is based on a study involving in-depth interviews with 30 African Caribbean bloggers based in the UK, of which 26 are women and 4 are men, sourced through accidental and random sampling. The interviews were conducted in 2012 both face to face at the British Library and via telephone. Thematic data analysis was used as an inductive approach to identify key themes emerging from the data which will be discussed in this chapter.

## Motivation

Previous studies have found that bloggers are motivated by both intrinsic and extrinsic factors (Nardi et al., 2004), and that motivation for blogging is strongly linked to the gratification from writing blogs (Liu et al., 2007). The findings of this study confirm that bloggers are motivated by a combination of intrinsic and extrinsic factors. While consistent with other studies, the uniqueness of the findings lie in motivations linked to identity and life experiences as a racialised minority group in UK society. These have been conceptualised within the emerging themes of voice, visibility and empowerment.

## Voice and visibility

For some of the bloggers, the desire to have a voice in the public domain is an intrinsic motivation linked to a love of writing and sharing views, perspectives and experiences with an audience. However, for some of the participants, the motivation to blog is driven by a complex set of extrinsic factors linked to issues of race and representation that fuel a desire to be seen and heard in the public domain through their own constructions of identity. Isaac, a 35-year-old sports blogger explains his frustrations with the media as a major motivation for starting a blog:

> The media wants to cover what they want to cover about a certain race, portray a race as dumb or stupid or ignorant or illiterate or incapable of putting two words together or just complete criminals.

He turned to the blogosphere as an alternative space to challenge what he perceives as negative representations of African Caribbean people: 'I'll create my own audience and I'll create my own sort of media and through that I'll build up supporters along the way. That's how I got inspired, by being marginalised.' For Isaac, people with racialised identities are subject to negative stereotyping in the media, and there is little interest among journalists in reporting the positive activities of ordinary Black men who do not fit a particular stereotype: 'Unless I'm a gangster or some sort of superstar they're . . . not interested in what the man on the street has to say.' In using his blog as a medium to develop his own audience whom he cultivates as 'supporters', he adopts an approach that is radical in orientation; centred on challenging negative stereotypes of Black identity; and is a process of self-representation that denotes a 'new politics of representation' (Gabriel, 1998: 17). In this regard, blogs can be viewed as a tool of resistance against racial oppression.

The perception of being excluded from the public domain is articulated by some of the female participants, for whom voice and visibility are powerful motivations for blogging. Nancy, a 33-year-old career and lifestyle blogger explains:

> I was really fed up with what I thought was the misrepresentation of Black people in the mainstream. I just felt as a mum of three . . . where

are all the positive role models; where is the inspiration, where is the voice really?

For Nancy, the exclusion of Black mothers as positive role models and her perception of 'misrepresentation' in the mainstream media lead to a sense of invisibility and voicelessness. These feelings motivated her to start a blog: 'My initial aim was to inspire, to show that Black people do more than what the mainstream likes to present.' Similar sentiments are expressed by Chioma, a 48-year-old woman who writes about race, gender and politics:

> I'm a UK African woman. I felt very invisible and a sense of voiceless-ness ... voiceless in a society that doesn't hear me. I guess that having the blog was part of me using my voice. That's the reason I wanted to go with it really, to have that UK African womanist presence on the web.

It is important to note the self-identification in demographic, eth-nic, cultural and social terms. African womanism is an African-centred strand of feminist ideology that rejects Black feminism as an offshoot of (White) feminism and which does not regard Black men as adversaries but subject to the same oppression as Black women (Hudson-Weems, 2004). Chioma's reference to being voiceless and invisible therefore relates to her self-defined identity as an African womanist in the UK. Her extrinsic motivation is self-representation, and her blog allows her to negotiate and reconfigure her identity. The invisibility of Black women has been raised by many feminist writers, including Collins (1990) and hooks (2000), articulating the marginalisation of Black women. More recently, the term 'intersectional invisibility' has been discussed in relation to Black women as individuals with multiple subordinate iden-tities not regarded as being emblematic of women (a status reserved for White women), or of Black people, a status conferred upon Black men (Espinosa, 1994).

Black women are also rendered invisible in the mainstream media by being excluded from everyday representations of women. Nadine, a 31-year-old wedding and bridal blogger, as a bride to be felt that Black women were absent as brides both in print magazines and on the web, and this invisibility was her main motivation for starting a blog: 'I don't think I saw one Black model in the magazines ... I would flick through pages and pages and not see one Black bride to be.' The exclusion of particular groups within the public sphere has been conceptualised as 'symbolic annihilation' (Gerbner, 1972). Tuchman (1978) argues that symbolic annihilation of women occurs through the media's constant exclusion, trivialising and devaluing of women, diminishing their status in society. More recently, Coleman and Yochim (2008) have explored the 'symbolic annihilation of race'. The symbolic annihilation of Black women in the mainstream media as a consequence of intersectional invisibility is not necessarily remedied in the blogosphere as gender inequalities in the blogosphere do exist (Chen, 2011; Gregg, 2006; Harp and Tremayne, 2006; Herring et al., 2004; Pedersen, 2008). However, by utilising blogs as a strategy for voicing, Black women are able to experience discursive power on the internet.

Extrinsic motivations for blogging linked to issues of race and representation demonstrate how blogs are used as a socially interactive medium through which racialised and gendered identities are contested, reconfigured and renegotiated. The concept of voice and visibility in terms of the motivations of these participants represents a desire to harness the discursive power of the internet to facilitate self-representation and participation within the public sphere.

## Empowerment

Empowerment refers to 'a multi-dimensional social process' that 'fosters power in people for use in their own lives, their communities and in their society by acting on issues they define as important' (Page and Czuba, 1999). As a motivational construct, empowerment can emanate from a sense of powerlessness, 'an intrinsic need for self-determination' (Conger and Kanungo, 1988: 473) or self-efficacy (Bandura, 1977). Blogs can act as a medium for self-representation and a mechanism for constructing an assertive voice, generating visibility and engendering empowerment through enhanced self-efficacy. Psychological empowerment through blogging can emerge from feeling part of a community that has a strong collective voice leading to increased confidence and assertiveness (Stavrositu, 2007). Women can gain psychological empowerment via blogging through a sense of community and a sense of agency, defined as the perception of a 'competent, confident and assertive voice' (Stavrositu and Sundar, 2012: 371). Previous studies suggest that African women use the blogosphere to promote women's equality and empowerment through personal expression and social interaction (Somolu, 2007), and that the internet functions as a discursive space where marginalised groups can gain a sense of empowerment by developing successful voicing strategies (Mitra and

Watts, 2002). A small number of female participants use blogs as a medium for promoting business and enterprise. Jennifer, a 28-year-old business blogger, runs a marketing agency and was motivated to start a blog 'to constantly have that voice' and 'to connect with other people'. The desire to have an assertive voice can be seen as a tool for generating a sense of authority and credibility as a business woman in a competitive marketplace.

A small number of female participants express a clear motivation for empowering others. Nadine devotes part of her blog to promoting small businesses, and, though not exclusively owned by Black proprietors, the majority featured mostly serve Black communities: 'It's giving them a voice, free promotion and one of my most popular posts is where I've listed loads of African Caribbean wedding caterers.' The desire to showcase Black businesses denotes a motivation to empower others and self.

## Gratification

Previous research suggests that gratification from writing blogs is linked to factors such as emotion management, life documenting and discussion within overall themes of process, content and social gratification (Sepp et al., 2007). Other studies have linked self-expression as a major gratification and social interaction to a lesser degree (Papacharissi, 2007). The findings of this study reveal that voice, knowledge-sharing, knowledge acquisition and social interaction are the primary gratifications from blogging.

## Voice

For some of the participants, gratification is linked to complex forms of cultural expression. For example, Grace, a 35-year-old creative writing blogger, confirms that what she most enjoys about blogging is

> Definitely getting my voice across, whoever cares, but I think I've got an opinion on something that I feel should be shared. It's kind of educating through humour; it's kind of getting points across with a bit of tongue-in-cheek.

Voice is explicitly expressed here, but also implicit in the above statement is self-expression – giving her opinion on issues, and educating readers. Later in the discussion she reveals that her sense of gratification is directly linked to the nature of the content she posts, described as

Our experiences in Britain and being Black people. I think there are things we need to know about our history and culture and instead of beating people over the head with it, which sometimes I feel like I do, letting people laugh along with it as well as learning something.

The sense of gratification is further increased through receiving positive feedback, either through comments directly on the blog or where the article is shared on social media platforms as articulated through her narrative: 'What I relish most is when posts get a reaction and people start talking and take it off on their own. I think that's the best reward, then it's doing what it's meant to do.'

These examples demonstrate the interconnectedness between motivation and gratification in relation to voice as the primary factor. Although not explicit in their narratives, it is evident that positive affirmation of the blogger's efforts to represent the interests of African Caribbean people within the blogosphere leads to increased self-efficacy. This is particularly the case when the content is centred on issues around being Black in UK society. Increasingly, citizen engagement is directed more towards issues that affect the everyday lives of individuals and less influenced by formal political processes (Breindl, 2010). Consequently, the African Caribbean bloggers in this study engage in political thought and action through the pursuit of personal interests and lifestyle choices rather than through traditional political structures.

## Knowledge-sharing

Knowledge-sharing has been subdivided into three distinct areas: experiential knowledge, professional knowledge and 'Black knowledge', defined here as the dissemination of information that highlights the contribution of African Caribbean people to the knowledge economy. The term 'experiential knowledge' is used here in relation to experiential learning theory, defined as 'the process whereby knowledge is created through the transformation of experience' (Kolb, 1984: 41). A dimension of experiential knowledge that has emerged from experiential learning theory that has particular relevance to blogging is 'conversational learning' (Baker et al., 2002). This is based on the premise that people learn from each other to create new knowledge through the medium of conversation. Conversations are conceptualised as social experiences that generate new ways of seeing the world. The two dimensions of conversational learning involve personal knowledge, acquired through personal experiences, and social knowledge, which emerges from ideas generated through texts and experiences, and is shared in conversations. Blogs, with their interactive elements of commenting, linking and sharing via social media and orally, can function as a conversational space and medium for learning and generating new knowledge. Odera, a 27-year-old fashion blogger, makes an observant distinction between professional knowledge and experiential knowledge:

> For me it's not so much about expertise but experiences. When I say I share my knowledge and expertise it's more about me sharing my experiences and hoping that it will help other people who are going through the same thing.

Lisa, a 33-year-old who blogs on social issues, is a qualified counsellor and, although she no longer works in this profession, she uses her blog as a platform 'where I can use my knowledge in counselling to intertwine and weave with social issues and current trends'. The knowledge she imparts on her blog is self-defined as professional:

> I class myself as a counsellor not confined to the counselling room. Just because I'm not counselling one-to-one does not mean I'm not a counsellor. I've got a bag of knowledge and I'm still using it in an everyday way.

For some participants, gratification is linked to sharing Black knowledge. Tracy, a 50-year-old creative writing blogger, works as a marketing director and writes a blog focused on books and literature. She says: 'All the books that I write about are Black fiction, Black writers, whether they're from Africa or the USA, Europe or the continent itself.' The purpose of the blog is to encourage and stimulate engagement with African and Caribbean literature, and to promote the work of Black writers. Describing her level of gratification, she explains:

> I like sharing what I've found out with other people, I think that's the main thing. People do tell me they enjoy it; now and then I get comments and things. It's nice to know that people like what I have to say about XY book or be interested in the interviews.

Luther, a 43-year-old former journalist, has carved a niche within the blogosphere as a social commentator and uses his blog to '[show] off my knowledge and expertise on the topic of Black music and popular culture'. Artistic freedom, feedback and interaction contribute to the sense of gratification:

> I actually prefer blogging now to the journalism I used to do because I have a lot more freedom, I can write about whatever I want. The other great thing about blogging is the feedback. I very rarely got feedback when I was doing print journalism but now with the blog I get online feedback.

It can be argued that sharing Black knowledge is a political act, even if the content is not a direct critique of racism but focused on celebrating and promoting Black literature and music. Power can be defined as having an effective voice – the capacity to advance one's view of the world and to define one's place within it as an active participant (Aldridge, 2000; Couldry, 2010). By promoting Black music and literature, these bloggers are claiming a representational space within the public sphere and fulfilling a basic human need to be seen and heard (Couldry, 2010).

## Knowledge acquisition

The acquisition of knowledge gained through the process of constructing a blog post is part of the cycle of experiential (Kolb, 1984) and conversational learning (Baker et al., 2002). While bloggers generate knowledge within and beyond the blogosphere that informs others, they simultaneously undertake research for particular topics they write about. For some participants, gratification is produced through the act of informing and educating others, while on another level it occurs through the process of learning and conducting research. Mitchell, a 44-year-old who blogs on current affairs and race, is 'very interested in the media, in journalism and current affairs' and gets a sense of satisfaction from the research process:

> Researching can be quite interesting because I think there's an onus on you to do a little bit of homework when you write a blog. I think there's a duty to add a bit of research where you can because I think when people read a blog they expect a certain degree of expertise. Personally I find that interesting and fascinating in itself.

For Gloria, a 27-year-old arts and culture blogger, who seeks to highlight Black designers on her blog, the acquisition of knowledge relates to personal knowledge – one of the dimensions of conversational learning

(Baker et al., 2002). In this instance, knowledge represents a journey of self-discovery:

> I found it difficult to place myself one, as a designer and then two as a Black person. I think the blog is kind of hinting to the fact that what is being Black? That you wear African clothes and you speak with an accent?

Her gratification occurs through acquiring the knowledge that

> It's discovering or almost promoting that Black isn't necessarily one thing even though we all come from the same place we're all dispersed around the world so all our influences, even though they're inherently African they all have different meanings.

## Social interaction

Fumi, a 29-year-old creative writing blogger, began writing blogs as an online journal, which eventually developed into a fictional series featuring Nigerian characters. In terms of gratification, feedback is the primary factor:

> Just getting that feedback, getting the response, getting comments, that's something blogging does that nothing else can do...that's a very good buzz I get from blogging.

While feedback is explicitly stated, there is an underlying link to social interaction through engagement between blog authors and their audiences. Expressing similar sentiments, Isaac says:

> Some of it is ego-driven. When you're blogging and you see one person following you, two people following you, three people following you and it goes on it encourages you to write more. When you blog and push that one button and it's going all around the world. Nothing more fulfilling than to see that someone says well done.

Charmaine, a 32-year-old dating and relationships blogger, writes posts about her dating experiences as a Black woman in the UK and also cites interaction as the main form of gratification:

> I enjoy the interaction directly with the readers. Mine tend to be dating stories so people tend to connect more with them and they

relate their stories back so there's a lot more interaction in my type of blogging than other types of blogging.

These narratives, while demonstrating the importance of social interaction to the bloggers, also connect to the overarching themes of voice and visibility. Feedback and followers provide a form of validation that their blogs serve a useful purpose in informing and engaging audiences within and beyond Black communities.

## Conclusion

Existing research acknowledges a cultural shift towards personalised political activity (Breindl, 2010; Bennett and Segerberg, 2011) and the use of blogs for discursive activism (Moyo, 2011; Shaw, 2011; Steele, 2012). While this chapter complements current literature on the use of blogs as counterhegemonic practice, it offers new levels of understanding within a Black British context of the ways in which African Caribbeans use blogs to mediate against racism and marginalisation within UK society. The findings demonstrate a common understanding among the participants that race influences their worldview based on their histories and experience. In addition to the use of blogs as counterhegemonic practice, they function as a medium for developing subjectivity by exploring what it means to be an African Caribbean man or woman in UK society.

The blogosphere is a contradictory space that reproduces inequalities that exist within traditional media (Kellner, 2000) and helps maintain corporate media power while providing a platform for counterhegemonic practice (Fuchs and Sandoval, 2010). Despite these limitations, the blogosphere remains an important medium for discursive activism and discursive empowerment. The significance of voice in the findings links to Bourdieu's (1989: 20) concept of symbolic power. Thus it can be argued that the blogosphere provides a platform 'for symbolic struggles over the power to produce and to impose the legitimate vision of the world' which can take the form of 'representation, individual or collective'.

## Bibliography

Aldridge, D. (2000) On race and culture: Beyond Afrocentrism, Eurocentrism to cultural democracy. *Sociological Focus*. 33(1), 95–107.
Atton, C. (2001) *Alternative Media*. London: Sage.
Bailey, O., Cammaerts, B. and Carpentier, N. (2008) *Understanding Alternative Media*. Maidenhead: Open University Press.

Baker, A., Jensen, P. J. and Kolb, D. A. (2002) *Conversational Learning: An Experiential Approach to Knowledge Creation*. Westport, CT: Quorum Books.

Bandura, A. (1977) Towards a unifying theory of behavioural change. *Psychological Review*. 84(2), 191–215.

Bennett, W. L. and Segerberg, A. (2011) Digital media and the personalisation of collective action. *Information, Communication and Society*. 14(6), 770–799.

Bourdieu, P. (1989) Social space and symbolic power. *Sociological Theory*. 7(1), 14–25.

Breindl, Y. (2010) Critique of the democratic potentials of the internet: A review of current theory and practice. *TripleC: Cognition, Communication, Co-Operation*. 8(1), 43–59.

Cammaerts, B. (2008) Critiques on the participatory potential of web 2.0. *Communication, Culture and Critique*. 1(4), 358–377.

Chen, G. M. (2011) Why do women write personal blogs? Satisfying needs for self-disclosure and affiliation tell part of the story, *Computers in Human Behavior*. 28, 171–180.

Chung, D. S. and Kim, S. (2008) Blogging activity among cancer patients and their companions: Uses, gratifications, and predictors of outcomes, *Journal of the American Society for Information Science and Technology*. 59(2), 297–306.

Coleman, R. R. and Yochim, E. C. (2008) The symbolic annihilation of race: A review of the "Blackness" literature. *Perspectives*. 1–11.

Collins, P. H. (1990) *Black Feminist Thought: Knowledge, Consciousness and the Politics of Empowerment*. New York: Unwin Hyman.

Conger, J. A. and Kanungo, R. N. (1988) The empowerment process: Integrating theory and practice. *The Academy of Management Review*. 13(3), 471–482.

Couldry, N. (2010) *Why Voice Matters: Culture and Politics after Neoliberalism*. London: Sage.

Delgado, R. and Stefancic, J. (2001) *Critical Race Theory: An Introduction*. USA: Temple University Press.

Downing, J. (2001) *Radical Media: Rebellious Communications and Social Movements*. Canada: Sage.

Espinosa, L. (1994) Multi-Identity: Community and culture. *Virginia Journal of Social Policy & the Law*. 2(23), 23–41.

Ferber, A. L. (2007) The construction of black masculinity: White supremacy now and then. *Journal of Sport and Social Issues*. 1(31), 11–24.

Fuchs, C. and Sandoval, M. (2010) Towards a critical theory of alternative media. *Telematics and Informatics*. 27(2), 141–150.

Gabriel, J. (1998) *Whitewash: Racialised Politics and the Media*. London: Routledge.

Gerbner, G. (1972) Violence in television drama: Trends and symbolic functions, in G. A. Comstock and E. Rubinstein (eds) *Television and Social Behaviour, Vol. 1: Media Content and Control*. Washington, DC: US Government Printing Office.

Gregg, M. C. (2006) Posting with passion: Blogs and the politics of gender, in A. Bruns and J. Jacobs (eds) *Uses of Blogs*. Brisbane: Peter Lang, 151–160.

Hamilton, J. (2000) Alternative media: Conceptual difficulties, critical possibilities. *Journal of Communication Inquiry*. 24(4), 357–378.

Harp, D. and Tremayne, M. (2006) The gendered blogosphere: Examining inequality using network and feminist theory. *Journalism and Mass Communication Quarterly*. 83(2), 247–264.

Herring, S. C., Kouper, I., Scheidt, L. A. and Wright, E. L. (2004) Women and children last: The discursive construction of weblogs, in L. Gurak, S. Antonijevic, L. Johnson, C. Ratliff, and J. Reyman (eds) *Into the Blogosphere: Rhetoric, Community, and Culture of Weblogs*. Retrieved from: http://blog.lib.umn.edu/blogosphere/women_and_children.html

hooks, B. (2000) *Feminist Theory: From Margin to Center*. London: Pluto Press.

Hudson-Weems, C. (2004) Africana Womanism: An overview, in D. P. Aldridge and C. Young (eds) *Out of the Revolution: The Development of Africana Studies*. Maryland: Lexington Books, 205–217.

Hylton, K. (2012) Talk the talk, walk the walk: Defining critical race theory in research. *Race Ethnicity and Education*. 15(1), 23–41.

Institute for Public Policy Research (2010) Recession leaves almost half young black people unemployed, finds IPPR. Retrieved from: http://www.ippr.org/news-and-media/press-releases/recession-leaves-almost-half-young-black-people-unemployed-finds-ippr

Isokariari, M. (2013) How can the angry black woman stereotype be challenged? *The Voice*, 28 September. Retrieved from: http://www.voice-online.co.uk/article/how-can-angry-black-woman-stereotype-be-challenged?utm_source=dlvr.it&utm_medium=twitter

Kellner, D. (2000) Habermas, the public sphere, and democracy: A critical intervention. *Perspectives on Habermas*. 259–288. Retrieved from: http://knowledgepublic.pbworks.com/f/Habermas_Public_Sphere_Democracy.pdf

Kolb, D. A. (1984) *Experiential Learning: Experience as the Source of Learning and Development*. New Jersey: Prentice-Hall.

Liu, S. H., Liao, H. L. and Zeng, Y. T. (2007) Why people blog: An expectancy theory analysis. *Issues in Information Systems*. 8(2), 232–237.

Milner, H. R. (2007) Race, culture and researcher positionality: Working through dangers seen, unseen and unforeseen. *Educational Researcher*. 36(7), 388–400.

Mitra, A. and Watts, E. (2002) Theorizing cyberspace: The idea of voice applied to the internet discourse. *New Media and Society*. 4(4), 479–498.

Morley, D. (1992) *Television, Audiences and Cultural Studies*. London: Routledge.

Moyo, L. (2011) Blogging down a dictatorship: Human rights, citizen journalists and the right to communicate in Zimbabwe. *Journalism Theory Practice and Criticism*. 12(6), 745–760.

Nardi, B. A., Schiano, D. J., Gumbrecht, M. and Swartz, L. (2004) Why we blog. *Communications of the ACM*. 47(12), 41–46.

Page, N. and Czuba, C. E. (1999) Empowerment: What is it? *Journal of Extension*. 37(5), 1–5.

Papacharissi, Z. (2002) The virtual sphere: The internet as a public sphere. *New Media and Society*. 4(1), 9–27.

Papacharissi, Z. (2007) Audiences as media producers: Content analysis of 260 blogs, in M. Tremayne (ed) *Blogging, Citizenship, and the Future of Media*. London: Routledge, 3–20.

Pedersen, S. (2008) Now read this: Male and female bloggers' recommendations for further reading. *Participations* 5(2). Retrieved from: http://www.participations.org/Volume%205/Issue%202/5_02_pedersen.htm

Schradie, J. (2012) The trend of race class and ethnicity in social media inequality: Who still cannot afford to blog? *Information, Communication and Society*. 15(4), 555–571.

Sepp, M., Liljander, V. and Gummerus, J. (2007) Private bloggers' motivation to produce content: A gratifications theory perspective. *Journal of Marketing Management.* 27(13–14), 479–1503.

Shaw, F. (2011) (Dis)locating feminisms: Blog activism as crisis response. *Outskirts.* 24, 1–12.

Somolu, O. (2007) Telling our own stories: African women blogging for social change. *Gender and Development.* 15(3), 477–489.

Stavrositu, C. (2007) Technologies of psychological empowerment: The role of agency and community in blogging. Unpublished doctoral thesis, Pennsylvania State University, Pennsylvania.

Stavrositu, C. and Sundar, S. (2012) Does blogging empower women? Exploring the role of agency and community. *Journal of Computer-Mediated Communication.* 17(4), 369–386.

Steele, C. (2012) Blogging While Black: A Critical Analysis of Resistance Discourse by Black Female Bloggers. Selected Papers of Internet Research (12.0).

Tuchman, G. (1978) The symbolic annihilation of women by the mass media, in G. Tuchman, A. K. Daniel, and J. Benet (eds) *Hearth and Home: Images of Women in the Mass Media.* New York: Oxford University Press, 3–38.

# 2
## Unlocking the Gate? How NGOs Mediate the Voices of the Marginalised in a Social Media Context

*Glenda Cooper*

At the Live 8 concert in 2005, pop star Madonna provided one of the seminal images of the day: dressed all in white, she held hands with a young Ethiopian woman called Birhan Woldu (Carr-Brown et al., 2005). As a young child, Woldu had been the icon of the 1984–85 famine, with her emaciated form appeared in the BBC's news coverage of Ethiopia – and most famously at Live Aid 1985 to the soundtrack of The Cars' 'Drive'.

By 2005, Woldu was not only a symbol of hope but also, as the video was replayed, an uncomfortable reminder of the kind of imagery that had been used widely at the time by both journalists and aid agencies to shame the developed world into helping those affected by the famine (Bristow, 2005). The disquiet such images caused among NGOs sparked the *Images of Africa* report (van der Gaag and Nash, 1987) carried out by Oxfam that talked of 'truly pornographic' imagery of those affected by the famine, and which ultimately led to the Code of Conduct for International Red Cross and Red Crescent Movement and NGOs in Disaster Relief drawn up in 1992 and implemented two years later.[1] Along with the imagery, there were also few attempts to hear the marginalised voices of those most affected by such crises. Even the report by Michael Buerk, which alerted the wider world to the horrors taking place in Ethiopia, used only two voices: Buerk himself and a white Médecins Sans Frontières doctor (Cooper, 2009).

Today the conclusions of the Code of Conduct – that those caught up in disasters should be portrayed as dignified human beings and not 'hopeless objects' – may seem self-evident. Moreover, the crasser nature of some of the NGOs' fundraising and messaging in the 1970s and 1980s (Benthall, 1993) has been challenged, though Dogra (2012) makes a powerful case for the continuing decontextualisation of poverty in NGO imagery. Others have examined ongoing issues of difference and distance in how NGOs portray 'the marginalised' in their communications materials (Orgad and Seu, 2014). Indeed, many NGO media officers feel responsibility to ensure they do not perpetuate the idea of their organisations as 'speaking' for the marginalised.

While Orgad and Seu studied how NGOs attempt to facilitate a more equal portrayal of the marginalised via advertising/fundraising, this chapter instead focuses primarily on NGOs' media messaging – how they interact with journalists to ensure the marginalised are treated with dignity, and how they also attempt to give the marginalised a voice through the means of new technology. For some NGOs, this has meant taking imaginative new approaches: Oxfam GB's 'Twitter takeover' when it allowed a Syrian refugee to write unmediated tweets on its account; Save the Children's #hiddencrisis link-up with the social media news agency Storyful; and Plan UK's trip to Ethiopia accompanied by a blogger rather than a journalist. In such cases, the NGOs are going beyond their traditional roles of primary source (Anderson, 1991, 1997; Schlesinger, 1978; Schlesinger and Tumber, 1994) or gatekeeper (Beckett, 2009). Instead they become a mediator, using social media and inexpensive technology to afford a voice to the previously voiceless.

However, occupying such a new role is not an easy task. NGOs have found themselves caught up in a rapidly changing media age. Their media offices have had to adapt quickly to rapid-onset disasters, and political controversies in the so-called 1440-minute cycle (Bruni, 2011) that new technology has generated. Learning how to educate staff and beneficiaries in these new media environments has not proved straightforward.

## 'Communicating real voices'

This chapter draws on face-to-face semistructured interviews[2] with staff from media offices of the then 14 members of the Disasters Emergency Committee (DEC)[3] – the umbrella organisation that brings together aid agencies in times of large humanitarian crises. Not only are members of the DEC the leading aid agencies in the UK but they also represent a range of size, approach, background and capabilities. For example, at the time of the interviews carried out for this chapter, one agency had only two members in its press team, while another had a diverse media and

PR team and a separate 'global media unit' coordinated by the UK office with partner offices abroad. In the event of an emergency, response to the news story can be passed seamlessly from the UK, US and Australia, facilitating international 24-hour coverage.

In the interviews, participants were asked similar questions about their approach to media coverage, interaction with beneficiaries, and if and how that had changed in recent times. As part of their mission statements, evaluation policies and media work, DEC members emphasised the need to include marginalised voices. There was a commitment to hear 'real' voices – and even, as CARE International puts it, 'contrary opinions' (2013: 2). The past, where agencies spoke for survivors and beneficiaries of donations from such agencies and the public, was no longer seen as acceptable (Action Aid, for example, prefers to use the word 'rights holder' instead of beneficiary). Instead, aid agencies made clear their intention:

> [It's about] being rooted in the lives of real people, telling the true story, communicating real voices.
>
> (Christian Aid, 2009: 1)

> The voices and views of minority, disenfranchised and other groups with perhaps contrary opinions should also be heard and considered.
>
> (CARE International, 2013: 2)

While this was a laudable aim in theory, however, many of the agencies involved were grappling with how to do it in practice.

## New media – New opportunities?

One of the primary methods aimed at giving marginalised people an opportunity to speak was through the use of social media. Each of the agencies interviewed was clear that social media was now an integral part of its communications strategy. The most commonly cited trigger for this was the 2010 Haiti earthquake. This was dubbed the 'first Twitter disaster' since initially news about the quake broke via social networking sites (Brainard, 2010), and in the aftermath much of the fundraising came about via social media. According to Twitter-tracking service Sysomos, some 2.3 million tweets included the words 'Haiti' or 'Red Cross' between 12 and 14 January 2010. The Twitter account for the Red Cross, which had been adding 50–100 followers a day before the quake, suddenly added 10,000 new followers within three days. During that time, donations to the Red Cross exceeded $8 million (Evans, 2010). Twitter was not the only social media network to prove its effectiveness.

Oxfam America's Facebook fanbase jumped from 35,000 to 250,000 during the Haiti earthquake, helping to raise $1.5 million within 48 hours (Byrne, 2010).

The result of this surge in attention was what one agency dubbed a 'post-Haiti pressure' on all agencies to get involved. Those DEC agencies that were not on Twitter before Haiti, said that they have now all established a presence there. There has also been a division of approach between employing press officers to specifically tackle social media and incorporating it into general job descriptions. So, for example, Oxfam now insists that social media is integrated into all press officers' work, while the British Red Cross had two officers whose work was specifically to deal with social media. The main emphasis for media work in 2014 was Twitter – one agency described it as 'the professionals' network' (i.e. the best way to capture the attention of journalists) – while Facebook was 'the supporters' network'. Other social media explored by press offices of agencies included YouTube, Instagram, Audioboo and Google Plus (as of early 2014).

The integration of social media has had several effects on aid agencies. First, it has accelerated the change in work patterns: while the days of an NGO press office working nine to five had already long gone, most have reorganised on-call strategies and rotas since Haiti. One senior media officer had discovered (to their astonishment) that none of the digital team had out-of-hours working in their job description. Traditional ways of evaluating media hits had also changed, as agencies tried to judge whether social media or traditional media hits were more valuable.

> I do think that the whole Twitter generation has kind of thrown our old fashioned understanding of evaluation and reach, because it only takes one Stephen Fry to retweet what we've has said, and boom, you've got five million, you've reached five million people.
>
> (Interviewee A – digital press officer)

> If you get on the 10 O'Clock News, you get everything else as well... If we got a Huffington Post piece, plus a nice audio slideshow on the BBC website, we wouldn't turn that down, but it isn't going to get the reach that we require.
>
> (Interviewee B – senior press officer)

Most agencies went on to admit they had little sense of how effective their use of social media was, and that there were also sometimes unrealistic expectations of what could be achieved:

There will be times, like the Invisible Children campaign [KONY2012], there will be times when something will just take off and I don't think you can replicate that. Everybody wants that. 'Ooh, it'll go viral'. No, it won't bloody go viral. A sneezing panda goes viral.

(Interviewee B)

99 per cent of those conversations on Twitter are Agency A talking to Agency B talking to Agency C. Is that useful? I'd brutally say it's a waste of f***ing time.

(Interviewee C – press officer)

During the DEC Syria appeal, one of the tools the committee used was a live Twitter Q&A under the hashtag #decqs.[4] Stuart Fowkes, an Oxfam media officer seconded to the DEC press office,[5] sent out the following tweet, not entirely in jest: 'If anyone who doesn't work for an aid agency could ask us a question about Syria using #decqs in the next 2 hours I will love you forever' (https://twitter.com/stuartfowkes/status/315070173168144384).

Meanwhile the kinds of disaster that are privileged by the use of social media also tend to be the rapid-onset events: exactly the ones that commentators and NGOs have complained that journalists spend too much time on already (CARMA, 2006; Franks, 2006; Moeller, 2006). Twitter, Facebook, Instagram and Flickr lend themselves to the dramatic over the chronic; the 'success stories' of social media tend to be crises like Typhoon Haiyan and the Haitian earthquake rather than the East Africa famine.

The more forward-looking NGOs try to counter this by thinking creatively. For example, the Save the Children UK's 2012 campaign #*hiddencrisis* aimed to raise awareness for the West African hunger crisis. The stories of the victims had not had much traction in the media. This campaign was specifically planned as a Twitter event; the agency took Neal Mann, who was the then Sky News digital media editor and who has a huge Twitter following, out to Burkina Faso and linked up with Storyful, the self-proclaimed 'world's first social media news agency', to plot Mann and Save the Children's journey across the country. There was not a sufficiently strong 'news peg' to capture the attention of the mainstream media but it generated interest in social media because of the opportunity to follow it in real time.

This interest was not always necessarily positive, particularly when James Ball, a journalist at *The Guardian*, started a row on Twitter describing it as disaster or Twitter tourism and tasteless.[6] However, it does show aid agencies going beyond their conventional role as source or gatekeeper, and actively using new media tools to try to alter the conversation and interact with their audience.

## Different voices?

Instagram pictures with Hurricane Sandy, first person accounts of Haiti – the framing of stories through social media is unapologetically personal. Unlike the familiar arguments over objectivity in mainstream reporting, user-generated content has privileged the subjective (Allan, 2004; Allan and Thorsen, 2009; Thorsen and Allan, 2014; Wardle et al., 2014). Supporters of this kind of personalised approach claim it is a move away from what Chouliaraki (2006) has called the 'anaesthesia' of traditional disaster reporting. Focus groups consistently respond positively to UGC, seeing it as more authentic, real and emotional (Williams et al., 2011).

There has been effort by some NGOs to provide a platform for 'different' voices. For example, in March 2013, the Oxfam GB Twitter feed was handed over to Hasan, a Syrian refugee in the Zaatari camp in Jordan, for the day. His tweets, which included pictures of his newborn baby Leen, were retweeted by celebrities such as Stephen Fry and Damon Albarn, as Hasan talked about Leen and the joy of swapping a tent for a caravan – because when you live in a caravan you can lock it with a key and stand upright inside it. Those who saw it were impressed:

> What made it work really well, was it was clearly unmediated, his English was good, but you know, there was lots of mistakes, but that added to the sense of realness of it.
>
> (Interviewee B)

As well as Hasan's freedom to write what he wanted, there was the use of ordinary, everyday pictures displayed for a wider public – his children sitting in a tent, his newborn baby. On one level these should be 'private' pictures – taken by private individuals. But the division between private and public is increasingly being diluted (Becker, 2011; Wardle and Williams, 2008). As privacy theorist Helen Nissenbaum (2004: 119) points out, the fundamental problem here is a breakdown in what she calls 'contextual integrity'. Privacy means different things in different situations, and that privacy is violated when people do not respect two types of contextual norm – those of appropriateness (what information may be shared), and those of flow and distribution (whom the information is shared with). With sites such as Twitter and Facebook, this problem can easily arise. There are not the divisions in social relationships that there are in real life, or what Grimmelmann (2009) refers to as a 'flattening' of relationships. And when this flattening of relationships is taken further and pilfered by the media, then those contextual norms are transgressed.

There are also concerns from a security point of view about whether beneficiaries have full understanding of the implications of sharing information in this way. As Vincent Lusser of the International Committee of the Red Cross said, 'our colleagues in Kabul have to think that what happens in Afghanistan can affect our colleagues elsewhere in the world' (2006). This is equally true of survivors, who may be putting themselves in danger, as one agency press officer put it:

> Informed consent in this day and age includes making sure that the person giving it is aware that their identity could well be seen worldwide, and that their government might well become very quickly aware of what they've said. There's no getting away from the fact that in the internet age things like that are a lot, lot more important than they were perhaps 30 or 40 years ago, where the chances of a story even reaching a remote outpost in a war-torn hellhole were minute, these days the chances are very large that they will.
>
> (Interviewee D – head of media)

While many of the other agencies were positive about the Hasan Twitter takeover, or similarly said that encouraging beneficiaries to record their experiences either with phones or via cameras distributed by NGOs was to be commended, some were reluctant to encourage this. In the main they saw such endeavours as impractical and ineffective compared with the traditional method of aid agencies interviewing beneficiaries themselves and processing quotes for journalists.

> It's generally field staff and people who have been seconded [on our Twitter account], it's not necessarily press officers ... we haven't gone that far yet [with a Twitter takeover], but I think we should be.
>
> (Interviewee E – head of news)

> I think some of the material was lovely – but I wonder how much investment was made, what was used and the benefits really were for the kids involved.
>
> (Interviewee F – emergencies press officer)

Many saw the 140 character limit on Twitter as a problem because of the limited space for nuance. Most harshly it was dismissed as a 'novelty package'. Only one agency press officer admitted that they were nervous about what might actually be said: 'It's a risk – opposite to most of our work where it's about controlling the message' (Interview G – press officer).

## Another way?

One way NGOs have started to incorporate 'ordinary' or non-agency voices is with the use of bloggers. These voices are not NGO employees, are not survivors or beneficiaries, but are perceived as a step away from the mainstream media.

The impetus for this was the success of Save the Children UK's 2010 'blogladesh' campaign fronted by three 'mummy bloggers' (a popular term for mothers who blog about the minutiae of family life). Instead of taking journalists on a press trip, the charity took Josie George (who then wrote the blog sleepisfortheweak.org.uk), Sian To (mummytips.com) and Eva Keoghan (nixdminx.com) to Bangladesh to raise awareness of the upcoming Millennium Development Goals conference. While out there, the women blogged, tweeted and uploaded pictures to Flickr with the #blogladesh hashtag.

The innovative strategy appeared to have paid off for Save the Children. The powerful chat site Mumsnet invited Josie George to join a web chat with the deputy prime minister Nick Clegg, and the campaign was picked up by the BBC Radio 4 *Today* programme and the ITV lunchtime news. Such high-profile media targets had been reached for minimal outlay: Liz Scarff, organiser of the #blogladesh campaign, estimated that the whole event had cost around £5,000 – mainly on transport to get the women there (Cooper, 2011).

Unsurprisingly, the success of the #blogladesh campaign led to a spate of copycat trips – Save's *Pass It On* in 2011 which utilised YouTubers; Plan UK's 2011 Blog 4 Girls competition; World Vision's *ShareNiger* with mummy bloggers in 2012; and Tearfund's 2013 See For Yourself initiative. With #blogladesh, the normality of the women and their ability to relate to beneficiaries was emphasised. As Scarff put it, 'Who could be more powerful to tell stories about children than mothers who have their hopes and dreams for their own children?' (Cooper, 2011: 32).

Yet the bloggers were not so different from the journalists they were replacing. They tended to be – although not exclusively – white, middle class and privileged. For example, the #blogladesh mummy bloggers were all women who had previously worked in PR or had writing experience: To had a specialist parenting PR company, George ran a weekly writing workshop for other bloggers, and Keoghan, who had originally worked for the PR consultant Lynne Franks, now worked as a social media consultant. #ShareNiger used To again, while #PassItOn, organised by the same consultancy, Fieldcraft, used Christine Mosler, a freelance copywriter and photographer, who blogged under the name Thinly Spread; primary schoolteacher Lindsay Atkin, whose son was a prominent YouTuber; and political blogger Tracey Cheetham, who was also a local councillor and a director of Eclipse PR. Tearfund's bloggers all had to have a faith, as Tearfund is a faith-based agency, but one was a copywriter turned ordinand, another a cartoonist and the third an academic. Plan UK's blogging competition in association with *The Guardian* in 2011 was won by the blogger (and filmmaker) Waiki Harnais who had been brought up in the Democratic Republic of Congo (Ford, 2011).

Experienced as many of these writers were, most had not been trained as journalists, and did not therefore subscribe to journalistic norms of objectivity and distance. In the Tearfund trip to Uganda, Tearfund blogger Liz Clutterbuck wrote of her discomfort after a fellow blogger featured a photo of her with a local child: 'I felt like I was a throwback to the 19th century – a well-meaning white female missionary cuddling an African baby' (Clutterbuck, 2013). Well intentioned as this was, this 'personalisation' did not always have the desired effect of breaking down the 'us and them' dichotomies. When news stories traditionally involved 'ordinary' people in the years before social media, the result was often an opening-up of access to individuals rather than social groups or organisations. Such case studies were usually talking in a personal capacity about their own experience as opposed to a more analytic role (Manning, 2001). Cottle (2000) argued that while 'ordinary voices' were often routinely accessed into TV news items, they become what Beck calls 'the voices of the side effects' (cited in Cottle) – to symbolise the human face of a news story. While Cottle was talking about TV interviews, his argument could equally be applied to blogging and social networking:

> Television news positions ordinary people to symbolize or (literally) stand for ordinary feelings and responses to the consequences of environmental risks not to articulate a form of 'social rationality' much less discursively challenge 'scientific rationality'. With too few exceptions the discursive play of difference and contending rational accounts is preserved for other, non-ordinary voices.
>
> (Cottle, 2000: 31–32)

While #blogladesh blogger Josie George did get to meet Nick Clegg, much of the coverage was focused on the experiences of the women involved, and an attempt to make an emotional bridge between the mothers they met at Save the Children projects in Bangladesh and women back in the UK who read their parenting blogs. The blogs that the women sent back from Bangladesh often focused heavily on the bloggers' own thoughts and feelings. It became as much about their own ability/inability to deal with the powerful nature of the sights they were exposed to as the sights themselves:

> It is hard to find the words here. I didn't take pictures. Just staying upright and breathing in the space of so much ... so much horror, and horror it was, was the best I could manage.
>
> (Josie George, sleepisfortheweak, 2 September 2010)

> What does it take to be authentic and genuine? It's not just a matter of being yourself, sometimes things find you that resonate and make you reconsider not just who you are, but what you think and feel and say, and write. And of course what you do. Bangladesh is one of those rare experiences that makes you re-examine and question humanity and as you try and go to sleep, yourself. First on the agenda is the assimilation of this place, which is hot, busy and chaotic. How do I even begin to make sense of all this?
>
> (Eva Keoghan, Nixdminx, 1 September 2010)

Such blogposts started changing the emphasis from charity beneficiary to charity blogger. As a PR (and journalistic) approach, it produced some powerful writing that undoubtedly captured the media's attention, but it risked the marginalised fading into the background again. Chouliaraki has noted that we live in a society where

> our own private feelings are the measure against which we perceive and evaluate the world and others ... While news becomes part of this 'culture of intimacy' it implicitly allows us to focus on our own sufferings and disregard those 'others' outside our own horizon of care.
>
> (Chouliaraki, 2006: 13)

So while we may look at a Facebook page and click 'Like', or watch video tributes on YouTube and read tweets from refugees, this does not mean the distances between the marginalised and the developed world onlookers are being overcome.

## Conclusion

> The question is whether the international humanitarian community is willing to listen and put the voice of the survivors at the centre of their priorities and plans.
>
> (Gormley, 2014: 83)

Despite the investment that NGOs are increasingly making in new media, many remain unclear about what they are doing or trying to achieve – symbolised by the fact that many were still working on social media policies. While in their policy documents, NGOs reiterate that beneficiary voices have to be heard, there is still reluctance and nervousness about how best to achieve this most effectively. There have been some imaginative efforts, as outlined in this chapter, to harness the power of new media and ensure that it is used to overcome the distancing effect of traditional media, yet many still see traditional media as the most effective way to spread their message.

The current trend has been to embrace the use of bloggers as a 'safe alternative'. While the bloggers are not beneficiaries, they are not full-time journalists and thus – like other forms of non-mainstream media – are seen as more 'authentic'. For aid agencies, they are often chosen because they have a large number of guaranteed 'followers' – and are likely to blog and update on several occasions if not every day, instead of supplying just one final piece. The difficulties of a media trip with conventional journalists – at the mercy of a changing news agenda, and the essential need for news pegs or case studies – appear less intense with bloggers for whom much of the framing of the story is their own personal experience.

Added to that, these bloggers can be overawed at the opportunity that they are being given and tend to respond with gratitude to the aid agency for taking them, and frequently inform their audience of this, rather than taking the 'critical friend' approach of most journalists. Waiki Harnais, for example, summed up her trip to Ethiopia with Plan as follows:

> Overall, everywhere we went, we noticed Plan had quite a strong presence in these communities, from health centres to schools and youth projects, all built by Plan and most handed over to the community. Although it was clear that the people in these communities still needed more help and support, it was very inspiring to see the difference that Plan is making in their lives ... I am hoping that you will be touched by some of the things you have read in this post, and

will visit the Plan website to find out more about how you can help these communities.

(Harnais, 2011)

By utilising bloggers, the consequence can be that NGOs, wittingly or not, are effectively becoming more, not less, efficient gatekeepers in telling stories.

## Notes

1. In particular, article 10 of the code reads: 'In our information, publicity and advertising activities, we shall recognize disaster victims as dignified human beings, not hopeless objects'. See more at http://www.ifrc.org/en/publications-and-reports/code-of-conduct/#sthash.Zc43Lkvq.dpuf.
2. These interviews were conducted in 2012–2014 as part of a wider PhD project.
3. The DEC is an umbrella organisation that brings together agencies in times of large humanitarian crises. It currently consists of British Red Cross, Christian Aid, World Vision, Oxfam, Tearfund, Plan UK, Action Aid, CAFOD, Concern Worldwide, Islamic Relief, CARE, Age International and Save the Children UK. Merlin (a previous member) and Save the Children announced in July 2013 they were to merge.
4. The full Q&A can be read at https://twitter.com/search?f=realtime&q=%23decqs&src=hash.
5. During DEC appeals, member agencies send press officers from their own office to the central DEC office.
6. https://twitter.com/jamesrbuk/status/203873386030563328; https://twitter.com/jamesrbuk/status/203873518805454848.

## References

Allan, S. and Zelizer, B. (eds) (2004) *Reporting War: Journalism in Wartime.* London: Routledge.
Allan, S. and Thorsen, E. (eds) (2009) *Citizen Journalism: Global Perspectives.* New York: Peter Lang.
Anderson, A. (1991) Source strategies and environmental affairs. *Media Culture Society.* 13(4), 459–476.
Anderson, A. (1997) *Media, Culture and the Environment.* London: UCL Press.
Becker, K. (2011) Looking back: Ethics and aesthetics of non-professional photography, in K. Anden-Papadopoulos and M. Pantii (eds). *Amateur Images and Global News.* UK: Intellect Books, 23–41.
Beckett, C. (2009) *NGOS as Gatekeepers to 'Local Media': Networked News for Developing Countries.* London: LSE.
Benthall, J. (1993) *Disasters, Relief and the Media.* London: IB Tauris.
Brainard, C., 13 January 2010-last update, New media crucial in the aftermath of Haiti [homepage of Columbia Journalism Review], [online]. Available at: http://www.cjr.org/the_observatory/new_media_crucial_in_aftermath.php (accessed 16 May 2012).

Bristow, J., 7 July 2005-last update, Who saved Birhan Woldu's life. Available at: http://www.spiked-online.com/newsite/article/886#.vmamf0sozg0 (accessed 26 January 2015).

Bruni, N. (2011) *Tweet First, Verify Later*. Oxford: Reuters Institute for the Study of Journalism.

Byrne, K. 24 March 2010-last update, Social media plays growing role in aid world [homepage of Thomson Reuters Foundation], [online]. Available at: http://www.trust.org/item/?map=social-media-plays-growing-role-in-aid-world (accessed 4 July 2013).

Care International (2013) *Care International Evaluation Policy*. Available at: https://www.care.at/images/_care_2013/expert/pdf/programming%20principles/ci_evaluationpolicy.pdf (accessed 3 March 2015).

Carma. (2006) *The Carma Report on Western Media Coverage of Humanitarian Disasters* [homepage of Carma International], [online]. Available at: http://www.imaging-famine.org/images/pdfs/carma_%20report.pdf (accessed 24 April 2012).

Carr-Brown, J., Fielding, D. and Clifford, N. (2005) Embracing the face of famine.

Chouliaraki, L. (2006) *The Spectatorship of Suffering*. London: Sage.

Christian Aid (2009) *Listening and Responding to Our Stakeholders: Christian Aid's Accountability*. Available at: http://www.christianaid.org.uk/images/christian-aid-accountability-0510.pdf (accessed 3 March 2015).

Clutterbuck, L. 27 February 2013-last update, Fulfilling a stereotype [homepage of Liz Clutterbuck], [online]. Available at: http://www.lizclutterbuck.com/2013/02/fulfillingastereotype/ (accessed 29 January 2014).

Cooper, G. 21 December 2009-last update, When lines between NGOS and news organisations blur [homepage of Nieman Lab], [online]. Available at: http://www.niemanlab.org/2009/12/glenda-cooper-when-lines-between-ngo-and-news-organization-blur/ (accessed 29 January 2015).

Cooper, G. (2011) *From Their Own Correspondent? New Media and the Changes in Disaster Coverage: Lessons to Be Learned*. Oxford: Reuters Institute for the Study of Journalism.

Cottle, S. (2000) TV news, lay voices and the visualisation of environmental risks, in S. Allan, B. Adam, and C. Carter (eds) *Environmental Risks and the Media*. UK: Psychology Press, 29–44.

Dogra, N. (2012) *Representations of Global Poverty: Aid, Development and International NGOS*. London: IB Tauris.

Evans, M. 15 Jan 2010-last update, Haitian earthquake dominates Twitter [homepage of Sysomos], [online]. Available at: http://blog.sysomos.com/2010/01/15/haitian-earthquake-dominates-twitter/ (accessed 17 May 2012).

Ford, L. 20 August 2011-last update, Blog on lack of educational chances for girls in DRC wins plan UK competition *The Guardian* [online]. Available at: http://www.theguardian.com/global-development/poverty-matters/2011/aug/10/plan-uk-blog-competition-winner (accessed 2 November 2014).

Franks, S. (2006) The CARMA Report: Western media coverage of humanitarian disasters. *The Political Quarterly*. 77(2), 281–284.

George, J. 2 September 2010-last update, Beauty and horror: Two sides to Bangladesh, sleepisfortheweak.org.uk/2010/09/02/beauty-and-horror-two-sides-to-bangladesh. Available at: https://groups.yahoo.com/neo/groups/bdosint/conversations/topics/7124?var=1 (accessed 3 March 2015).

Gormley, B. (2014) The changing face of humanitarian reporting – putting the survivor centre stage, in G. Cooper (ed) *The Future of Humanitarian Reporting*. UK: City University, 81–85.

Grimmelmann, J. (2009) Saving Facebook NYLS legal studies research paper no. 08/09-7. *Iowa Law Review*. 94, 1137.

Harnais, W. 27 November 2011-last update, A very personal encounter with Ethiopia, [online]. Available at: http://waikiharnais.com/2011/11/27/a-very-personal-encounter-with-ethiopia/ (accessed 2 Nov 2014).

Keoghan, E. 1 September 2010-last update, Blogladesh: Our visit to children's wards, [online]. Available at: http://www.nixdminx.com/2010/09/01/blogladesh/ (accessed 3 March 2015).

Laird, S., 20 October 2012-last update, Instagram users share 10 Hurricane sandy photos per second [homepage of Mashable], [online]. Available at: http://mashable.com/2012/10/29/instagram-hurricane-sandy/ (accessed 29 January 2014).

Lusser, V., 13 Dec 2006. Speaking at Dispatches from Disaster Zones conference, 13 December 2006, London.

Manning, P. (2001) *News and News Sources: A Critical Introduction*. London: Sage.

Moeller, S. D. (2006) 'Regarding the pain of others': Media, bias and the coverage of international disasters. *Journal of International Affairs*. 59(2), 173–196.

Nissenbaum, H. (2004) Privacy as contextual integrity. *Washington Law Review*. 79, 119.

Orgad, S. and Seu, B. (2014) 'Intimacy at a distance' in humanitarian communication. *Media, Culture and Society*. 36(7), 916–934.

Schlesinger, P. (1978) *Putting Reality Together*. London: Constable.

Schlesinger, P. and Tumber, H. (1994) *Reporting Crime: The Media Politics of Criminal Justice*. Oxford: Clarendon Press.

Thorsen, E. and Allan, S. (eds) (2014) *Citizen Journalism Global Perspectives Vol. 2*. New York: Peter Lang.

Van Der Gaag, N. and Nash, C. (1987) *Images of Africa: The UK Report*. UK: Oxfam.

Wardle, C., Dubberley, S. and Brown, P. (2014) *Amateur Footage: A Global Study of User-Generated Content in TV and Online News Output*. New York: Tow Center for Digital Journalism.

Wardle, C. and Williams, A. (2008) *Ugc@BBC: Understanding its Impact on Contributors, Non-Contributors and BBC News*. Available at: http://www.bbc.co.uk/blogs/knowledgeexchange/cardiffone.pdf: BBC.

Williams, A., Wardle, C. and Wahl-Jorgensen, K. (2011) Have they got news for us? Audience revolution or business as usual at the BBC. *Journalism Practice*. 5(1), 85–99.

# 3
# 'I Wouldn't Be a Victim When It Comes to Being Heard': Citizen Journalism and Civic Inclusion

*Einar Thorsen, Daniel Jackson and Ann Luce*

For disabled people, the UK political landscape has in recent years provided a particularly harsh backdrop of austerity and ongoing cuts to welfare and disability benefits. In November 2014, for example, a 39-year-old woman who was unable to work due to chronic pain following two road traffic accidents took her own life. The Department of Work and Pensions (DWP) had sent several letters threatening to cut off her disability benefits and also demanding that she pay back £4,000 she had already received. During the inquest into her death in March 2015, the county coroner, Anne Pember, noted that she believed the 'upset caused by the potential withdrawal of her benefits had been the trigger for her to end her life' (cited in Jones, 2015). According to freedom of information requests by the Disability News Network, the DWP had investigated some 49 cases where benefit claimants had died from February 2012 to February 2015 – 40 of these followed suicide or apparent suicide by the claimant, and 33 contained recommendations for improvements (Pring, 2015).

Those claiming disability benefits in the UK have also found themselves under attack from sections of the press – peddling, for example, 'cartoonish' depictions of disabled people as 'workshy scroungers' (Briant et al., 2011; Garthwaite, 2011; Slater, 2012). Time and again, flawed or inaccurate reporting escape censure from an ineffective complaints and regulatory system. These media representations can be toxic for those on the receiving end, and compound the challenges posed by the dismantling of the welfare state. Audience research meanwhile has found many people believed that the level of disability benefit fraud in the UK to be as high as 70%, and expressed support for the government position that many claimants did so as a lifestyle choice (Briant et al., 2011: 5).

If we accept that representation and understanding of their lifeworld is central to disability, then voice and access to the media become of paramount concern because they hold the potential power to self-representation, which may challenge such mainstream narratives and political agendas. Here, marginalised groups have increasingly sought ways to engender new spaces – through, for example, citizen journalism – to articulate both their physical and their discursive struggles to break down societal barriers. This chapter provides an analysis of one such citizen journalism project, initiated by a charity representing older and disabled people in the south of England. Through interviews and participant observation with the citizen journalists, we examine whether and how citizen journalism acts as a facilitator of citizen empowerment and a catalyst of social change. We explore their motivations and also the contradictory nature of citizen empowerment that was aroused by the project. Many of those interviewed highlighted the fear of publicly criticising the government as a genuine barrier to public voice, and felt vulnerable in the face of the government 'assault' on welfare and benefits. We nevertheless identify three distinct areas of empowerment experienced by the citizen journalists: community cohesion, civic inclusion and accountability impact.

## Representations of disability

Disability can be considered as 'fundamentally a struggle over "representation"' (Williams, 1996: 194). Scholars have argued (e.g. Despouy, 1991; Swain and French, 2000) that the greatest barriers facing disabled people today are those of prejudice, discrimination and social isolation. Part of the reason for this has been attributed to the persistence of the discourse of the Medical Model of disability which emphasises impairment as a 'problem' that is 'expertly' diagnosed and legitimated, and focuses on ways of 'fixing', or 'repairing', physical limitation (Barnes et al., 1999), as well as dominant media representations which perpetuate the Personal Tragedy Model that regards those with non-normative abilities as unfortunate victims, thus depicting disabled people as 'vulnerable' and 'strange'. Such discourses of 'difference' produce a binary social relation of 'othering' – that is, 'us' and 'them' (Despouy, 1991). The Social Model,[1] and more recently the Affirmative Model, of disability (see Swain and French, 2000) were in part a response by disability activists to the dominant media narratives. The adoption of the Social Model as an 'organising principle' by disability groups has enabled a start to be made in transforming the social world in terms of the opportunities for disabled people to participate in everyday life (see Hodges et al., 2014). However, as many studies have shown (e.g. Barnes, 1992; Cumberbatch and Negrine, 1992; Shakespeare, 1999), mainstream media representations have historically lagged behind the more progressive models of understanding disability and exclusion.

The relative lack of visibility of disabled people within the media has been well documented. Dominant media representations of disability have been criticised for being too simplistic, crude and one-dimensional (e.g. Cumberbatch and Negrine, 1992; Shakespeare, 1999), reinforcing stereotypes of disabled people as weak (Ellis, 2008; Wardle et al., 2009), treating disability sports as little more than 'human interest' (Berger, 2008), and encouraging audiences to view athletes, actresses, TV personalities and so on through their impairment rather than as people, thus erecting barriers to empathy and reinforcing a perceived distance between the audience and the objectified disabled character. Recent evidence from the UK suggests that progress has been made in terms of the quality and quantity of disabled representations on TV. Paralympians, for example, have become celebrities who are newsworthy for both positive and negative reasons (Claydon et al., 2015), though such representations can be double edged when it comes to tackling certain societal prejudices (Molesworth et al., 2015; Peers, 2012).

In the context of established media, the absence of disabled people in newsrooms and production studios has invariably lead to unbalanced coverage of disability issues (Goggin, 2009; Wardle et al., 2009). Indeed it has been long established that ordinary citizens in general are only given limited access to and representation in media through (ideologically) constructed forms of 'public opinion' (see e.g. Lewis, 2001). This problem is further exacerbated when citizens are classed as marginalised by the dominant hegemony. Indeed, the presence in media discourses of marginalised groups is frequently defined by health issues, where they are, according to Campbell and Scott (2011), ' "spoken of" by health professionals and members of government rather than having the opportunities to speak for themselves'. This perpetuates their social exclusion and undermines our understanding of their lived realities. Given slow progress on redressing these constructs, marginalised groups have increasingly sought alternative means to challenge their exclusion through different forms of citizen media, often combining social mobilisation with innovative participatory communication practices.

## Citizen journalism as agent for social change

New and alternative media afford (at least in theory) different opportunities for marginalised groups to discuss, organise, self-represent and pursue political action. Citizen journalism literature, for example, has documented how hyperlocal initiatives often arise due to the 'public's dissatisfaction with legacy media' and as an 'attempt to fill the perceived gap in public affairs coverage' (Metzgar et al., 2011: 782). Examples abound where disadvantaged or marginalised groups have adopted different forms of citizen journalism in this way to challenge their own civic exclusion, be that feminist movements, repressed indigenous people or increasingly globalised social movements (Allan and Thorsen, 2009; Thorsen and Allan, 2014). In so doing they engender new spaces to articulate both their physical and their discursive struggles to break down societal barriers. Viewed in this way, citizen journalism facilitates participatory forms of communication aimed at transformative social change, while at the same time energising the social cohesion of those marginalised groupings. This, according to Campbell and Scott (2011: 270), is 'dialogue and action that facilitate the development of confident and empowered identities'. In their analysis of health communication, they found that:

> It [citizen journalism] also seeks to encourage members of excluded groups into dialogue about their health amongst themselves, as well as giving them a voice in public debates about how to tackle obstacles to their well-being, and involving them in efforts to challenge and renegotiate the way they are represented.
>
> (Campbell and Scott, 2011: 277)

However, as research on disability and new media has documented, there are many issues concerning access and accessibility (e.g. exclusionary web design and unaffordable connection costs) that mean that online technology has often reproduced some of the environmental barriers that traditionally exclude disabled people from several aspects of social life (see Goggin and Newell, 2003; Vicente and Lopez, 2010). But spurred on by the climate of 'emergency' created by the coalition government's controversial plans for a welfare overhaul, there is a deep renewal in the structure, action repertoire and leadership of UK disability rights groups, and new media are at the heart of this revival (Trevisan, 2013, 2015). Trevisan (2013) identifies the emergence of a new generation of technologically savvy disabled 'leaders' who are capitalising on their familiarity with new media to provide an alternative and unmediated voice regarding disability issues.

Such important work is beginning to address the dearth of empirical work on the relationship between new media and disability activism, but it is largely focused on 'digitised activists' (existing disability activists who appropriate new technologies in their activities) and 'digital action networks' (online-only initiatives created and maintained by disabled bloggers-turned-activists with no prior experience of disability rights campaigning) (Trevisan, 2013, 2015). We know less about how 'formal organisations' such as disability charities – whose primary function is often not about advocacy and activism but everyday needs – have adapted to the opportunities afforded by new technology. Moreover, we still know relatively little about the lived experiences of disabled activists in appropriating new technologies and online platforms, and the challenges and opportunities they face.

## Access Dorset TV

Our entry point into these debates is the regional charity Access Dorset, and its citizen journalism project Access Dorset TV (ADTV). Based in Dorset on the south coast of the UK, the organisation was formed in 2010 as a 'user-led organisation' run by disabled people, older people and carers. Through its own membership and informal partnerships with 20 other like-minded organisations, it currently incorporates over 4,000 people in the region. The charity was established to help remove the physical, attitudinal and community barriers faced in everyday life by its members. Central to this mission was the ability to participate in and influence public discourse on issues that affect them – a necessity that has only been intensified by the inimical political environment in the UK as Access Dorset's CEO, Jonathan Waddington-Jones, explained:

> With statutory services being cut and increasingly focused solely on those in most critical need, there are growing numbers of disabled people, older people and carers who are unable to access the support they need to live independently, healthily and with dignity. Many, whether in rural or urban areas, are isolated from peer support and lack opportunities for civic engagement.
>
> (interview with authors, 2014)

For Access Dorset, citizen journalism was seen as a potential solution to these issues of peer support, civic engagement and public voice.

ADTV was conceived in 2013 to overcome the challenges of exclusion by creating a participatory platform of marginalised voices that can communicate direct to a diverse array of networked publics. Produced by and for its user groups, ADTV (http://www.accessdorsetcentre.org) provides web-based peer support, information and lifestyle videos about their life experiences, events, social action projects and independent living.

The ADTV project consisted of an initial cohort of 12 citizen journalists. They were a mixture of disabled and older non-disabled people. The disabled people had a range of hereditary and acquired disabilities, and all brought different challenges they are experiencing, as well as different emphases as to what they wanted to pursue in terms of story ideas. The group contained a number of people (approximately half) whose work had taken them into public life, such as a local councillor, community worker and disabled activist. Approximately half of them had some media experience, but as the subject of a story or as a source, not as producer.

Citizen journalism offers (at least in theory) an inherently empowering narrative, which can give voice to the voiceless in society and connect marginalised citizens to people within their communities. However, we should not make assumptions about how members of a marginalised group experience it, nor should we overlook the many different forms in which citizen journalism is manifest. Our approach in this study was therefore to examine a citizen journalism initiative from the inside:

- what public issues they were concerned with, how they felt such issues are covered in the mainstream media, and their views of journalism;
- how they understand civic agency and empowerment, and how these are experienced through citizen journalism.

The findings presented here are based on approximately 20 hours of data collected from in-depth interviews with the 12 participants before and after a series of workshops we hosted. Each interview was audio-recorded and transcribed, then analysed by us. We also conducted more than 20 hours of participant observations of their experiences during the training, and detailed analysis of their subsequent outputs. Our work was grounded in theoretical thematic analysis (Braun and Clarke, 2006), meaning the analysis was influenced by the research questions (and indeed the literature review), but there was also an inductive element allowing for themes to evolve during the analysis process.

In the following discussion, participants' names have been replaced by pseudonyms.

## Frustrations and motivations

Participants in the ADTV project clearly represented different marginalised groups, as described above, and they also had a vivid sense of their own social exclusion. Many talked openly about the Social Model as a way of understanding and addressing social barriers, shifting the emphasis from their disability to barriers that they face, and, crucially, stressing that those barriers could be removed. As such, these were not pacified and subdued individuals at some forgotten fringe but rather a highly active and motivated group with a clear sense of purpose about challenging their marginalisation.

Through our initial work with the participants, we sought to explore the issues that were important to them and how they viewed the media reporting of these. All the participants described a sense of injustice about how government funding had been cut under the auspices of austerity or made inaccessible through new assessment methods. Even where such policies did not affect them directly, they absorbed the perceived prejudice and some even took it personally as an affront to marginalised groups more generally. This came to the fore even more when the participants reflected on media coverage of disability issues. Frustration and even anger surfaced when they described how much of UK media victimise and demonise people receiving benefits:

> Because as I say with all the austerity measures that have been going on at the moment, with all benefits, the view of disability has slipped dramatically back down again. We are scroungers, we want this, we want that, we want everything, we want it now. But actually no, *you* get off your backside and go and get a job. You ever tried to get a job with a disability? It's virtually impossible, the discrimination that's there is more profound now than ever before because you're up against so many in the job market.
>
> (Terry, interview)

They were exercised not just by outright inaccuracy of reporting but also sensationalism and lack of empathy. 'They want the drama, they really do want the drama,' Hannah said in reference to established media. 'They don't want the good stories to come out, which rubs off onto disabilities being a very negative lifestyle.' Clearly disability is not a lifestyle choice, and yet this is the subtext in much of the reporting on the lived realities of disabled people, including the need to claim benefits in various forms. The discursive reduction of their illness was experienced by several as particularly demeaning, as Participant Hannah noted:

> I don't see why we should be pushed and shoved, and this is because you do feel a very vulnerable person in society...When you're on a train and you're compared to a piece of luggage.
>
> (Hannah, interview)

Mary echoed a sentiment also expressed by others, arguing that 'media have a slanted view of disability', placing undue attention on those 'people who abuse the system':

> They make out that there are so many disabled people out there, making out that disabled people are getting all this money who shouldn't be.
>
> (Mary, interview)

While she did not question the existence of benefit fraud per se, it was the generalised demonisation of a marginalised group as a whole that was problematic. Indeed, the generalisation was a consequence not only of misguided or misleading terminology used in reporting but also the inadequate attention given to communicating the lifeworld of disabled peoples. 'I don't think the press is very good at showing what living with a disability is really like day to day,' she argued. This attention to expressing and communicating everyday lived realities of marginalised peoples was a major motivating factor in why they chose to pursue their own form of journalism through ADTV. In this way the participants were hoping to not only normalise their lifeworld but also educate audiences about the barriers disabled people experience on a daily basis. Polly, who was paralysed from the chest down following a road traffic accident, expressed this poignantly in terms of offering alternative perspectives to raise awareness:

> I think I would like to feel I am improving and enhancing people's lifestyles by offering not alternatives but perhaps a different thought pattern and changing perspective of those that haven't had to use a wheelchair or have got a disability. Just to sort of think outside of what their life is like for a second...I think for me because it happened so suddenly, I wouldn't want my today to be their

tomorrow. Motivations – for others to see how disabled people live. Education.

(Polly, interview)

For Access Dorset, addressing such issues of representation and participation was at the core of the ADTV project. Indeed, its ambition was stated by some of the participants as an overt challenge to the political establishment – both locally and nationally. However, not everyone involved shared the same desire for activism. Instead they viewed participation in the project as a form of confidence-building and a way of networking with other marginalised people. In this way the ADTV project was also positioned as a vehicle to foster enhanced community cohesion – that is, bringing together people representing different marginalised groups (thus cohesion among the project participants), and also rendering visible their voices in the community so they could feel part of public life.

## Empowering marginalised voices

From November 2013 to January 2014, we delivered a five-week intensive training course for these volunteers on the foundation principles of video journalism, aimed at affording them the skills and confidence to develop the ADTV project alongside their other advice and support functions as charity workers. Outputs from the ADTV project have at the time of writing all been video based, with the variety of stories reflecting the different interests and motivations of the participants. Videos produced can broadly be classified as (1) information and lifestyle; (2) campaign and advocacy; and (3) reportage on marginalised issues. The project participants have made videos about living with cancer, anorexia, emergency medical treatment for older people, inaccessible footpaths for disabled people, and overcoming attitudinal barriers to disability, to name a few.

ADTV has evidently had a positive impact on the participating citizen journalists and their ability to vocalise concerns, even within its first year of operation. Three distinct areas of empowerment of participating citizens emerged through interviews we conducted during the project: community cohesion, civic inclusion and accountability impact.

### Community cohesion of marginalised groups

The notion of any kind of disabled 'community' existing writ large has always been problematic (see e.g. Hodges et al., 2014), due not least to the challenges of public voice, media representation and social isolation. Access Dorset is an umbrella organisation for various local and regional charities. As it serves a wide geographical spread of users – often living at the margins of society – creating a sense of shared identity and community cohesion is often an acute challenge, yet it is a primary purpose of the charity. Community media – be they for diasporas (see Ogunyemi, Chapter 8 in this volume), ethnic groups (e.g. Tsagarousianou, 2001) or women's movements (e.g. Isaacs-Martin, 2008) – offer the opportunity to produce content relevant to the lives of marginalised people, challenge dominant semiotics and give a public voice through self-representation. In terms of enhancing community cohesion, we found that this worked on two levels, related to both the inputs and the outputs of the citizen journalism project.

At the input level, the journalism workshops brought together people with very different backgrounds, ages and disabilities. Of the 12 citizen journalists, three were full-time Access Dorset employees and the rest were volunteers of varying regularity. Therefore a number of them barely knew each other at the start of the training. By participating in the workshops they established new friendships and strengthened their sense of shared purpose in an otherwise diverse and disparate organisation. So the *process* of developing a shared purpose and identity was empowering (see also Campbell and Scott, 2011):

> The other thing about the training, I thought, we've always had a very strong team ethos. I think some of us were initially concerned should we really all of us be involved in this, will it be cramping the style of volunteers in terms of learning. I think it quickly proved to be the right thing to do because it strengthened that team ethos, where we are all learning together... And certainly, I suppose, following on from it and stuff, I am in awe of some of my colleagues and how quickly they've grasped some of the things.
>
> (Peter, interview)

Like many other charities, Access Dorset exists on a small budget and is reliant on a network of volunteers. These volunteers need to be motivated and committed, and feel like their work is valued. For our participants, taking part in the training had the effect of galvanising some of the volunteer members into becoming more engaged with the charity, thus increasing its capacity.

This galvanising effect on the organisations' members also came through the outputs of the project. As Peter explains, the charity has been able to strengthen its broader network and better represent its members through the project, with the use of video being crucial:

> I think one of the things that we have found with all of this, we have really kicked in as an organisation. You look at the disabled organisations in the country, they tend to be of older people. It can often be difficult to involve younger people, they have different experiences than older people of the struggles around disability. So it can be difficult sometimes to attract and involve younger people. And particularly for an organisation like ourselves, working with people with learning disabilities, it can be difficult. How do you integrate with them without dumbing down what you are doing? What we found with ADTV and the whole approach was that young people want to make films. This is brilliant, what a great way to communicate and so we've made a number of films with people with learning disabilities who want to get involved and want to do more. So I think that alone has empowered us and made us stronger and a lot more confident as well.
>
> (Peter, interview)

### Giving people a voice: Empowerment and civic inclusion

Of the 12 citizen journalists who undertook the training and pioneered the project, approximately half made it clear through the interviews that they did not consider themselves disempowered, voiceless victims. At least three had had a career in public life in one way or another and were used to speaking to those in power. As Polly explains:

> I've got a pretty big mouth. I'm pretty good there. I would either say something myself or to say something more strongly like in the case of the town hall, I'd go to these guys. I'm pretty good like that. I wouldn't be a victim when it comes to being heard.
>
> (Polly, interview)

However, for the rest of the group of citizen journalists, the project brought them into the public sphere for the first time. For them, this was a transformative and empowering experience. The first emergent theme was that gaining the technical competences of video journalism gave them new confidence, as Jennifer explains:

> It's a lovely feeling. It's one of those things where I suppose my main skillset has never been on the technical side of anything and you

watch the television, you look at a corporate film that someone's put together and you can't even imagine, I can't even imagine being involved in that or being able to do that. But it's a lovely feeling to know 'I know actually how you do it and I have a good understanding of how you did it and I could have a good go myself.' It is a very empowering feeling. And it has certainly boosted my confidence in realising that I have other competencies, rather than just the ones I know I've got. And if I had the time I feel pretty confident that I could learn more.

(Jennifer, interview)

Jennifer was not the only participant to allude to an increased media literacy gained through becoming a practising citizen journalist. Others too spoke of the way they now watch TV and film in a new light, critically 'reading' the technical aspects of media production, but also deconstructing its ideological biases – both useful competences for the rounded citizen (see Livingstone et al., 2005).

The seemingly inherent growth in individual confidence through the development of new skills was, we argue, closely linked to a greater sense of collective voice as a disabled or older person, as Mary explains:

It's made me feel more empowered and it's given me more confidence as a person, to go out and do some filming and be proud of what I've done... Whether I do it for someone else or on my own, I'm equally proud of it... But the whole thing has made Access Dorset more empowered to really take on the issues that affect all disabled people. Actually we're the best people to film them because we know about them.

(Mary, interview)

For the Access Dorset citizen journalists, it was not only about gaining access to the modes of production but also about making a difference by being different. Referring to professional journalists, Laura observed how 'their motivations are completely different'. As a self-identified citizen journalist, she valued her 'freedom', reporting on 'issues that are directly affecting you on a local level, on a personal level and from the perspective of a person living everyday life rather than from the perspective of media trying to sell it'. This is a significant point concerning how they conceived the importance of authentic (disabled) voices. As Mary explains, the broader hope is that inclusion means empowerment:

I think for the project its about...disabled people or older people within Access Dorset saying actually this is an issue we need to address and you are the best person to talk to. It's not right for us to come and do it for you if you can do it yourself or identify one of the team who are going to do it and it makes a difference. It puts it out there, makes people more aware of an issue or makes someone feel less isolated, you know, then that's successful. If people feel that they are in control of what they do themselves and have some control over it or some control to change it or put it out there than that's a good thing, it empowers people to do more for themselves.

(Mary, interview)

Through the course of our interviews and observations it was clear that many of the citizen journalists spoke of their new-found empowerment, internal political efficacy and a strong sense that what they were doing would be empowering for others like them. But most were also aware that there are many real-world barriers for disabled people that their ADTV project was yet to overcome, which speaks directly to the contradictory nature of citizen empowerment. For instance, of all the barriers to having their voice heard we explored with interviewees, physical and mental impairment were virtually absent; but the fear of publicly criticising the government was a genuine barrier for many, who felt vulnerable in the face of the government 'assault' on welfare and benefits. 'Historically in Dorset, disabled people have been very passive because they are frightened they are going to lose their care,' Terry commented, 'so they've always remained not expressing any desire to challenge anything.' Robert added: 'This is typical of everybody out there: people are terrified. We're consumers of these [public] services. It's very difficult to be using them and criticizing them at the same time. So that's the barrier, a huge barrier.' In working with such vulnerable and isolated people who have agreed to be filmed, the citizen journalists were acutely aware of treating their subjects with the necessary caution so as not to leave them exposed. Therefore an important tension in this project was the way that the citizen journalism of ADTV spoke to power, which we unpack further below.

## Holding power to account and accelerating impact

Many of our participants were, as noted earlier, active, confident citizens, and through their work with Access Dorset they had already campaigned on issues they care about. However, the citizen journalism they pursued through ADTV appears to have elevated (if not transformed) their visibility to those in power, and hence their effectiveness at achieving policy changes. Specifically, the *video* format, and the publicness (through the web and social media) of ADTV, were highlighted by several participants as appearing to have a more immediate impact than the traditional campaigns they had previously experienced. 'I think in the journalism and in the filmmaking we found a medium that people are more interested in listening to,' Jennifer commented. 'Before, when we're talking about engaging and making ourselves heard, it's an email, it's a letter, it's a phone call ... They [local government] get a lot of those. Making your point through a film and quite publicly has had impact multiple times.' In other words, video-based citizen journalism has enabled these marginalised groups to dramatically accelerate action on issues they campaign on.

One of the most high-profile reports has been in support of their campaign to make a local railway station accessible to disabled people. The video and campaign have made local headlines, gained the support of local politicians and even been discussed in parliament. This is an overtly political video, supported by an e-petition (underneath the video), and headed by one of the most politically empowered members of the ADTV team. However, it has a tone of voice which is characteristic of the type of relationship to power the organisation is trying to achieve, a point which was repeated several times among interviewees:

> somebody might say we've got an agenda but for example Poole and Bournemouth Council are not on the agenda, this is not what we're here for. It's not hitting the councils on the head with their mistakes. If you highlight a real issue and a good, positive way and you say: 'Are you aware of this? This is the problem it's causing. Are we going to be able to do something about it?' I think you're more likely to get something done.
>
> (Mary, interview)

The citizen journalists were thus acutely aware of not wanting to be a negative force, criticising the authorities from the sidelines and subsequently being ignored. A recurring theme of the journalism they produce, then, is to position themselves as an engaged, passionate advocacy group 'who don't pull any punches' (Peter, interview) in pointing out the failings of the authorities, but whom the authorities can also work with to make things better.

There is still an ongoing tension in this position, though. For example, Access Dorset is now being approached by the local council and other authorities to make films about accessibility on their behalf. This is obviously beneficial to accelerate impact and achieve the organisation's goals, but it also raises tensions over its role as a critical voice that is independent from the authorities, as Jennifer explains:

> It's scary because that's obviously not our roots and we're learning as we go as well but our unique selling point and what is attractive about us is that, obviously all the films that have been commissioned are from a user-led, disabled people angle, and that why we are different. All these people, BH Live and the council have used commercial companies before but they've decided they want to approach us because I think: 'Well, we've seen the films that they do, they are doing a good job but also on top of that they've got all the right contacts, they are selling it from the right angle' ... That's the power of us and that I suppose we need to take forward, our unique selling point.

As we know from studies of pressure group politics, becoming an insider group can have many benefits for voice and influence, but it can create tensions with the grassroots of an organisation who wish to remain at arm's length to the powerful (see Grant, 2000). Our participants were well aware of this tension. To be able to respond to such commercial requests that might conflict with the citizen journalism, Access Dorset is setting up a commercial filmmaking arm to try to create some distance between it and the ADTV project.

## Conclusion

It seems clear that the political establishment in the UK is failing to adequately address the needs of marginalised groups on a number of levels, as exemplified at the outset of this chapter. Many vulnerable people are afraid of speaking up against social injustice – some in our study, for example, citing people with concerns about having their support systems eroded as a consequence. When established media perpetuate this anxiety through inaccurate reporting and misleading generalisations, it is little wonder that those who are marginalised seek alternative means to break through these societal barriers. Ordinary people are making efforts to regain control over their own mediation and representation, often expressed through different forms of citizen journalism or community media – seeking, in other words, a sense of empowerment and civic agency through (self-)communication.

ADTV is just one of many online citizen journalism projects that has surfaced over the past two decades in response to a perceived lack in public affairs reporting and as a way of mobilising ordinary people around shared causes. We found that the ADTV project was an effective focal point for Access Dorset to mobilise a core group of volunteers. Including disabled and older people in the production of online video also empowered people who are otherwise marginalised from both the production of news and the representation of issues that concern them. Participants in the ADTV project were given responsibilities and opportunities many of them thought they would never have experienced. Moreover, they were able to command a public platform for their voices and draw attention to their campaigns in ways they had not been able to do before. In so doing, otherwise marginalised people were able to put themselves at the centre of public debate – in a way that *they* felt comfortable with. Indeed, the expression of their voices through a highly personalised, raw and often impressionistic video format was seen to accelerate attention from the authorities and thus their ability to affect change.

It is evident from our research that the citizen journalists involved with ADTV experienced empowerment on a number of different levels. While this is often a deeply personalised experience, their ability to enter and shape public debates should also have a tangible effect on the lived experiences of others, be that through videos about home adaptations, triggering change to dropped curbs or campaigns about public transport accessibility. What they do not, as yet, have a clear sense about is to what extent citizen journalism is empowering their broader constituency – that is, non-participating members or user groups. However, what they do have is at least a mediated representation emanating from their own group that is helping to redefine what is meant by 'the centre'. Indeed, as the famous saying from *Shakespeare's Coriolanus* goes, 'the people must have their voices'. ADTV shows how some disabled and elderly people have given themselves a public voice through citizen journalism – one that appears to be transforming them both as individuals and as a collective force.

## Note

1. The Social Model of disability advocates that disability is socially constructed and therefore a consequence of the way society is organised, rather than an individual's impairment or difference.

# References

Allan, S. and Thorsen, E. (2009) *Citizen Journalism: Global Perspectives*, Vol. 1. New York: Peter Lang.

Barnes, C. (1992) *Disabling Imagery: An Exploration of Media Portrayals of Disabled People*. Halifax: Ryburn/BCODP.

Barnes, C., Mercer, G. and Shakespeare, T. (1999) *Exploring Disability: A Sociological Introduction*. Cambridge: Polity Press.

Berger, R. (2008) Disability and the dedicated wheelchair athlete. *Journal of Contemporary Ethnography*. 37(6), 647–678.

Briant, E., Watson, N. and Philo, G. (2011) *Bad News for Disabled People: How the Newspapers Are Reporting Disability*. Glasgow, UK: Strathclyde Centre for Disability Research and Glasgow Media Unit, University of Glasgow.

Campbell, C. and Scott, K. (2011) Mediated health campaigns: From information to social change, in D. Hook, B. Franks, and M. W. Bauer (eds) *Social Psychology of Communication*. Basingstoke, UK: Palgrave Macmillan, 266–284.

Claydon, A., Gunter, B. and Reilly, P. (2015) Dis/Enablement?: An Analysis of the Representation of Disability on British Terrestrial Television Pre- and Post- the Paralympics, in D. Jackson, C. Hodges, R. Scullion, and M. Molesworth (eds) *Reframing Disability? Media, (dis)Empowerment and Voice in the 2012 Paralympics*. London: Routledge, 37–65.

Cumberbatch, B. and Negrine, R. (1992) *Images of Disability on Television*. London: Routledge.

Despouy, L. (1991) *Human Rights and Disability*. United Nations E/CN.4/Sub.2/1991/31

Ellis, K. (2008) Beyond the AWW factor: Human interest profiles of Paralympians and the media navigation of physical difference and social stigma. *Asia Pacific Media Educator*. 19, 23–35.

Garthwaite, K. (2011) 'The language of shirkers and scroungers?' Talking about illness, disability and coalition welfare reform. *Disability & Society*. 26(3), 369–372.

Goggin, G. and Newell, C. (2003) *Digital Disability: The Social Construction of Disability in New Media*. Lanham: Rowan & Littlefield.

Goggin, G. (2009) Disability, Media, and the Politics of Vulnerability. *Asia Pacific Media Educator*. 19, 2–1–2–13.

Grant, W. (2000) *Pressure Groups and British Politics*. Basingstoke: Palgrave Macmillan.

Hodges, C., Jackson, D., Scullion, R., Thompson, S. and Molesworth, M. (2014) *Tracking Changes in Everyday Experiences of Disability and Disability Sport within the Context of the 2012*. London Paralympics: CMC Publications, Bournemouth University. Available at: https://microsites.bournemouth.ac.uk/cmc/files/2014/10/BU-2012-London-Paralympics.pdf (accessed 11 February 2015).

Isaacs-Martin, W. (2008) (Re)creating gender identities in community media. *Agenda: Empowering Women For Gender Equity*. (77), 140.

Jones, C. (2015) Northampton woman, 39, took her own life after 'constant battle' to receive disability benefit. *Northampton Chronicle & Echo*, 5 March. Available at: http://www.northamptonchron.co.uk/news/northampton-woman-39-

took-her-own-life-after-constant-battle-to-receive-disability-benefit-1-6615017 (accessed 8 March 2015).

Lewis, J. (2001) *Constructing Public Opinion: How Political Elites Do What They Like and Why We Seem to Go Along with It.* Columbia University Press.

Livingstone, S., Van Couvering, E. and Thumin, N. (2005) *Adult Media Literacy: A Review of the Research Literature.* OfCOM. Available at: http://stakeholders. ofcom.org.uk/binaries/research/media-literacy/aml.pdf (accessed 20 February 2014).

Metzgar, E., Kurpius, D. and Rowley, K. (2011) Defining hyperlocal media: Proposing a framework for discussion. *New Media & Society.* 13(5), 772–787.

Molesworth, M., Jackson, D. and Scullion, R. (2015) Where agendas collide: Online talk and the Paralympics, in D. Jackson, C. Hodges, R. Scullion, and M. Molesworth (eds) *Reframing Disability? Media, (Dis)Empowerment and Voice in the 2012 Paralympics*, London: Routledge, 123–137.

Peers, D. (2012) Interrogating disability: The (de)composition of a recovering Paralympian. *Qualitative Research in Sport, Exercise and Health.* 4(2), 175–188. Available at: http://www.tandfonline.com/10.1080/2159676X.2012. 685101 (accessed 11 September 2014).

Pring, J. (2015) Secret DWP reviews called for improvements after benefit deaths. *Disability News Service*, 6 March. Available at: http://www.disabilitynewsservice. com/secret-dwp-reviews-called-for-improvements-after-benefit-deaths/ (accessed 8 March 2015).

Shakespeare, T. (1999) Art and lies? Representations of disability on film, in M. Corker and S. French (eds) *Disability Discourse.* Buckingham: Open University Press, 164–172.

Slater, J. (2012) Stepping outside normative neoliberal discourse: Youth and disability meet – the case of Jody McIntyre. *Disability & Society.* 27(5), 723–727.

Swain, J. and French, S. (2000) Towards an affirmative model of disability. *Disability and Society.* 15(4), 569–582.

Thorsen, E. and Allan, S. (2014) *Citizen Journalism: Global Perspectives*, Vol. 2. New York: Peter Lang.

Trevisan, F. (2013) Disabled People, Digital Campaigns, and Contentious Politics: Upload Successful or Connection Failed?, in R. Scullion, D. Lilleker, D. Jackson, and R. Gerodimos (eds) *The Media, Political Participation, and Empowerment.* London: Routledge, 175–191.

Trevisan, F. (2015) Contentious Disability Politics on the World Stage: Protest at the 2012 London Paralympics, in D. Jackson, M. Molesworth, and R. Scullion (eds) *Reframing Disability? Media, (Dis)Empowerment and Voice in the 2012 Paralympics.* London: Routledge, 154–171.

Tsagarousianou, R. (2001) Ethnic community media, community identity and citizenship in contemporary Britain, in N. Jankowski and O. Prehn (eds) *Community Media in the Information Age: Perspectives and Prospects.* Cresskill, NJ: Hampton Press, 209–230.

Vicente, M. and Lopez, A. (2010) A Multidimensional Analysis of the Disability Digital Divide: Some Evidence for Internet Use. *The Information Society.* 26(1), 48–64.

Wardle, C., Boyce, T. and Barron, J. (2009) Media coverage and audience reception of people with disfigurement or visible loss of function. *The*

*Healing Foundation.* Available at: http://www.cardiff.ac.uk/jomec/resources/ 09mediacoverageofdisfigurement.pdf (accessed 16 May 2013).

Williams, G. (1996) Representing disability: Some questions of phenomenology and politics, in C. Barnes and G. Mercer (eds) *Exploring the Divide.* Leeds: The Disability Press, 194–212.

# 4
# The Voices of Extremist Violence: What Can We Hear?

*Barry Richards*

This chapter is not about the recognition and empowerment of marginalised or voiceless groups but offers a complementary discussion of a different set of margins. It seeks to develop a psychologically based understanding of how and why violence gathers around the edges of the mediatised public sphere, and then erupts onto centre stage in the form of terrorist attacks.

The mental health factor in politics demands more attention than it normally gets. Its voices are not usually recognised, though they are particularly important in relation to extremist violence. It is necessary to take issue with the dominant tendency in research and writing about terrorism, which is to rule out individual psychological disturbance as a major driver of terrorism and other forms of extremist violence (e.g. Crenshaw, 2000; Horgan, 2014; Silke, 2014). From that viewpoint, if the terrorist cause is one we might have some sympathy with, we may explain the violence in terms of the realistic desperation of the terrorist, who can be understood as a rational actor who can see no other way of pursuing their cause. If the cause is one we are at odds with (let's say it might be the neo-Nazi defence of a purified nation), we may explain it with reference to various societal phenomena – traditions of unreconstructed racism, mobilised by demagoguery in times of austerity, and the general dynamics of 'othering'. This takes us closer to the mind of the individual concerned, and less academic versions of this approach may even use words such as 'sick' to describe the perpetrator, but typically we stop at the gates of a more probing psychological inquiry.

There are practical difficulties in enquiring further. Most students of this topic have access only to limited information about the individuals concerned, typically that which is put in the public domain by journalists, drawing on court proceedings, psychiatric reports, family and acquaintance testimonies, and sometimes investigative journalism into a perpetrator's history. But we may suspect that is not the reason for the lack of psychological curiosity: I will offer an alternative explanation later.

## Psychic problems meet ideological solutions in the online universe

My basic argument here is that in many examples of contemporary terrorism we are witnessing an intersection of two different forces. One is the broad and deep pool of psychic suffering which exists in any society, including large numbers of people out there whose psychic stability may be precarious, who may for all kinds of life history reasons be struggling with overwhelming feelings of, for example, anger, emptiness or fear. Some of these people will fall within the categories of psychiatric diagnosis, and some of these may be in receipt of some degree of support from mental health services. Others will not (or not yet) have come to any professional attention. Some may live in cultural milieux where thresholds for acknowledging psychological difficulties are set very high so that only those with grossly psychotic behaviour are seen as in need of help. And for still many others the emotional damage or difficulties from which they suffer do not produce any signs or symptoms which convey their inner condition, perhaps not even to themselves. This is an important point: psychological damage and disturbance does not necessarily issue in psychiatric illness. Some of the studies which have concluded that terrorists are 'normal' people do so because there is no evidence in cases they have reviewed of psychiatric illness. Even if that is the case, that does not mean that we can assume the people involved are psychologically 'normal', in the sense of having good enough mental health and emotional functioning. (I am using the term 'normal' here in a prescriptive, criterion-based sense; good mental health may or may not be a statistical 'norm'.) Poor mental health may take various forms other than frank psychiatric disability. There are, for example, what psychiatry calls 'personality disorders', forms of damage and dysfunctionality built into the individual's make-up as a person, and therefore not only less visible as 'pathologies' but also often more resistant to change than the conditions underlying episodic mental breakdown. While sometimes leading 'symptom'-free lives, people with personality disorders may behave in ways that are hurtful or destructive to others, or are self-sabotaging, or both. They have emotional needs which they cannot satisfy, and at some level their grasp of reality is lacking or insecure.

There is also the stage of emotional development loosely called 'adolescence', wherein we may find a lot of people who go on to grow into well-functioning individuals but who for a time operate with erratic behavioural controls and delusional worldviews. This very large group of 'adolescents', who can be well into the age of physical adulthood, includes an important constituency of emotional vulnerability to extremist propaganda.

There is, of course, a danger of dismissing views one doesn't like by 'pathologising' them – that is, by attributing them out of hand to some psychological disorder or to immaturity. But without examining the mental health factor we cannot fully understand the fears, rages, obsessions, blindspots and sometimes downright delusions that are major forces in politics. So we must proceed, cautiously, using robust concepts, clear criteria and good evidence.

There are two general points to note here: one is that we are talking about deep and hidden levels of the personality, which are likely to be unconscious, and the other is that in the psychological domain there is no sharp dividing line between health and ill health. There are traces of the neurotic and psychotic in all of us, and shades of disorder in all our personalities. What matters is the balance of forces, the overall organisation of someone's mind and personality, whether there is a clear predominance of pro-social emotion and contact with reality, or of destructive emotion and distorted perception.

So the first premise of my argument is the presence of a substantial amount of psychological disorder in the population at large. The second premise requires much less introduction for a politically informed readership. It is a disturbing and apparently global development of the last two decades: the growing prominence of extremist ideologies, characterised primarily by the rise of ethnonationalist and neo-Nazi movements in Europe, and the spread of violent jihadism.

Putting these two phenomena together, my contention is that extremist ideologies which advocate violence are now providing psychologically damaged people with new ways of trying to manage their inner turmoil. We are seeing a lengthening list of cases in which individuals have sought to conquer their emotional disturbances by taking up a cause and inflicting (or planning to inflict) injury or death on others in the name of that cause. They claim to speak in the voice of a cause, but that public voice obscures the inner voices to which they are giving expression. These are often hidden voices, likely to be despairing, chaotic, deluded and bizarre.

Why does this topic belong in a book about politics, media and marginalisation? It does so because the context within which this inter-section occurs, this malign fusion of psychological crisis and ideology, is primarily a media one. It has for some years been a truism of terror-ism studies that online media are now a primary recruiting ground for potential terrorists, certainly of the two types (jihadist and neo-Nazi) that we currently have most to be concerned about in the UK. Whether or not they have identifiable psychiatric problems, troubled people are now out there in cyberspace, trying like millions of other people to solve their problems online. At the user interfaces of extremist websites, ide-ology meets psychic need. The nature of that need varies: it can include a need for meaning and purpose in life, a need to cancel a deep inner sense of humiliation, and a need for permission to act out murderous aggression which the individual is struggling to control. The web brings all the world's remedies for despair within reach of any moderately lit-erate internet user. Some of those whose need is for therapeutic help of some sort may be refusing therapeutic ways of dealing with their states of mind and turning to other apparent remedies, which may include conversion to an extreme ideology.

This toxic intersection, and its product in the recruit to terrorism, is only one outcome among many possibilities. There are numerous other ways in which an individual might pursue relief from inner demons: along a pacific spiritual path, say, or through an ascetic commitment to sport. However, not many lifestyle alternatives would have given the same licence to aggression as violent extremism does, except perhaps a career in organised crime. So there are particular needs, associated with violence, which render some individuals more susceptible than others to 'radicalisation' – that is, conversion to an ideology of violent extrem-ism. But particular circumstances also need to be in place: the ideology must be easily found, and easy to understand, and it must offer some kind of salvation. For that, the roles it offers to the convert must be dra-matic and heroic ones (here the inevitable coverage of terrorist attacks in the mainstream media play a role), and there must be a possibility for the convert to feel that they are joining a community, and are gaining an identity and acceptance, or at least can know that somewhere there are people who will applaud their choice. In other words, the ideology must have a following, something which is conveyed to all of us through mainstream media, and to the potential recruit also in a positive way via propaganda websites. So it is not only the ideology itself which is medi-ated but also its credibility, a sense that it is possible and in some way desirable to adopt it, because others have embraced it, and indeed that it is heroic to do so. With these features of online propaganda, available to an audience hungry for ways of solving or managing its psychological problems, we have a high risk that some individuals in that audience will be drawn into a malign process of so-called 'self-radicalisation'.

In the rest of this chapter we will explore this psychological dimension to contemporary violent extremism through a comparison of terrorist attacks with non-ideological 'rampage' killings.

## Terrorism and rampage killings

A man walks into a building (a hotel, say, or a university building) with an automatic weapon. He wears military fatigues and a full balaclava over his head. He takes aim at people in the foyer indiscriminately. He then goes up the first flight of stairs and enters a room where a few people are trying to barricade themselves in, and he shoots them all. He continues his deadly rampage in the corridor, before barricading himself into a room and shooting at people in the street from the window. A little later he is fatally shot when armed police storm the room. Within the next hour, a video made by the gunman announcing what he was about to do, and a lengthy multimedia statement by him, are being viewed by thousands of people on the web.

This could be a description of a 'Mumbai-style' terrorist attack. It could also be describing the last half hour of a 'crazed gunman', a deranged individual who for no obvious reason has embarked on what media reports sometimes describe as a 'rampage killing'. This term is often applied to outbreaks of killing which typically leave several people dead, including the killer, within minutes or hours.

Let us explore the similarities and differences between these non-ideological killings and some deadly terrorist attacks, particularly suicide missions. This comparison may be of interest both to those seeking to understand the dynamics of terrorism and to those in the field of criminology. Some recent work in the US has begun to make such comparisons. Lankford and Hakim (2011) compared volunteer suicide bombers in the Middle East with 'rampage' shooters in the US. They describe some differences between the two: the community approval for, and sometimes financial reward to the family of, the suicide bomber, as well as the imagined reward of eternal bliss, the bomber's apparent lack of mental disorder and the absence of women among rampagers. However, they find the similarities to be stronger: troubled childhoods, low self-esteem, experience of their environments as oppressive, precipitating personal crisis, and desires for revenge, fame and glory. They conclude that the differences between the two types of killer are more at the cultural level, and that in the underlying psychology and motivation there is much in common between the two types. Lankford (2011, 2013) continues this approach to argue that suicide bombers are driven by suicidal motives rather than by the political rationales commonly advanced for their actions, such as foreign occupation of their nation (though we can note that military occupation might resonate powerfully with personal feelings of humiliation).

The category of rampage killers includes, in the UK, Michael Ryan in Hungerford in 1987, Thomas Hamilton in Dunblane in 1996 and, most recently, Derrick Byrd in Cumbria in 2010. In the US, major examples are the Columbine killers Eric Harris and Dylan Klebold in 1999, Cho Seung-Hui in the Virginia Tech College in 2007 and Elliot Rodger in California in 2014. Elsewhere – for example, in Finland – there has been Pekka-Eric Auvinen and Matti Saari in 2007 and 2008, respectively. Examples where the killer has not died (as in the cases of Jared Loughner in Arizona in January 2011 and James Holmes in Colorado in 2012) might also be included, because to go on a killing rampage puts the killer at risk of being killed. In any event it usually brings the end of that person's life as a free individual, so might arguably be seen as a parasuicidal or symbolically self-annihilating action.

The category of suicide terrorist attacks is a broader one. It includes 9/11 and 7/7, and many cases from Palestine, Iraq and Afghanistan, though, of course, there are important differences between the various historical and contemporary types of suicide mission. Individual terrorist attacks on the public that do not end in suicide (e.g. that by Timothy McVeigh in Oklahoma) could also be brought into the analysis, though that would extend the inquiry, so they will not be discussed here. The focus in this discussion is on violent jihadism, since terrorist attacks in the name of a neo-fascist or extreme ethnonationalist cause are rarely suicide missions, and are less frequently aimed at the general public, though they do share other key features with Islamist terrorism.

## Humiliation

In both groups it is common to leave a self-justifying video message for the public to consume. As well as occasional stylistic similarities in the accusatory tone and gestures of some of these videos, their verbal content often points towards a psychologically important similarity: the perpetrator's profound sense of humiliation, often masked by a degree of apparent 'normality' or by massive contempt for others. This humiliation is explicit in the messages of Cho Seung-Hui, and written large in the stories of others: Ryan was sexually rejected by a woman who consequently became his first victim, Hamilton was enraged by the authorities' rejection of his request to work with children, and Byrd felt belittled by his more successful brother and by his taxi-driver colleagues. In the statements of Islamist jihadis (e.g. the self-valedictory video of 7/7 leader Mohammad Sidique Khan) there is evidence that a profound sense of humiliation is a key theme in their identity and motivation. This is typically expressed in a focus on what is perceived to be the oppression and humiliation of Muslims globally. This theme has been explored in, for example, the work of the psychoanalyst Vamik Volkan (1998, 2004) on ethnic and nationalistic movements. The corollary of humiliation is the rage against the oppressor responsible for the humiliation, whether that is a specific government (and its people), or a vast and abstract enemy such as the West, or the kaffir world of unbelievers, or – for a rampage killer – an incoherently sensed 'system' or the 'world'.

The issue is not whether killers of either category were *actually* subject to humiliation by others but whether they came to be driven psychically by an internal feeling of humiliation, irrespective of the origins of that feeling.[1] The low self-esteem and the consequential desires for revenge and for glory, the burning sense that one's environment is intolerably oppressive (whatever the reality of it) – all these features identified by Lankford and Hakim as common to suicide terrorists and rampage killers can be seen as consequences of a deep inner sense of humiliation. So in both types of killing there is an explosive response to an intolerable inner state, which typically centres on feeling humiliated. And this response is at least in part directed towards the public. Both types of killing seem to embody very primitive attacks on the shared life represented by public spaces and those who occupy them. When the public, which for all of us is a symbol of human collectivity and of secure coexistence, becomes the target, the aim is to attack the very civilisation which it represents. This is, of course, explicitly the aim of some terrorists, and is also a plausible reading, I suggest, of the aim of the perpetrator of the eruptive killing burst, for whom life with others has become unbearable.

### Ideology and idealism

The most commonly observed difference between these two categories is the ideological rationale for terrorism which provides a moralised justification for its actions, and the absence of this in rampage killing. This is often seen as a fundamental difference, though is less clear-cut than it might first appear to be. Rampage killings are often also driven by primitive moral rage, by a sense of grievance and of the necessity to act upon it. On the other side, the idealism of the potential terrorist is actually also part of the problem, a part of the mindset which commits to murder. Viewed psychoanalytically, the idealism may be part of a defence against an underlying despair; it can be seen as an attempt to preserve some image of goodness amid the carnage which the terrorist is producing, in a world which they see as fundamentally dominated by evil. It is an *absolutist* idealism (see Figlio, 2006, on 'absolute' states of mind), and so is part of the soil in which commitment to a fundamentalist creed grows. It rationalises the wish for a radically different world, and so legitimates the destruction of the actually existing world. And once the individual is enmeshed in a worldview of fundamentalist antagonism, all pro-social tendencies are subordinated to the cause, whatever that might be. This is arguably a key factor in the psychology of terrorism, and perhaps of violent extremism more generally. If so, a key to the understanding of terrorism lies in the process by which the desire for belonging and community becomes subordinated to impulses towards destruction.

## Social embedding and the virtual 'host'

Another difference often assumed to exist between the two categories is that the suicide mission has been seen (Gambetta, 2006: 260) as invariably planned and executed with the support of a 'host organisation', however loose or distant it may be. Rampage killings are the work of unassisted individuals, though the pairing of the Columbine killers qualifies that proposition. Here then may lie a profound psychological difference between terrorists and non-ideological rampage killers – it may be not so much in the terrorist's commitment to an ideology per se but in their relationships with the charismatic figures and/or peers with whom they are in contact. The ideology serves the relationships, not the other way around; it is not a primary driver but an expression of the delusionally based bonds which hold the group together, and is an instrument for the shaping of behaviour by those guiding the aspiring terrorist. In many extremist groups the individual's experiences of group comrades are based on projections of idealised facets of the self – hence the proclivity of extremist organisations to endless splits and splintering, as members find each other unable in reality to embody the idealisations they need to merge themselves with.

In contrast with this importance of the external world in nurturing the suicide bomber, the rampage killer's mind has presumably been struggling for some time with itself, a process in which a murderous impulse or, to use Hyatt-Williams' (1998) term, a 'death constellation', gradually becomes the dominant force in the mind, until it reaches bursting point. While the terrorist has an ideological rationale, and sees themselves as part of a movement, the eruptive killer has a personal grievance and does not act on behalf of a group. The difference between group membership and aloneness is, on the face of it, the most fundamental.

In the pre-digital past, co-option into a violent cause depended on some direct contact, usually face to face, with people who were already activists for the cause, and through them with an organisation that could inspire belief in the creation of a new society. Without this capture of idealism, the individual's inhibitions against violence would be more resilient. The ideology of this organisation was the home for both the destructive and the idealistic tendencies in the mind of the individual recruit. Now, however, there is no absolute need for a 'host *organisation*' to support the transition into terrorism; the web is a vast universe of homes for all kinds of feeling and need. It is a 'host' both in the sense of providing supportive accommodation and also in the sense of generating an impression of an army of fellow soldiers, a military host, with its promise of incorporation into a glorious new future. In this context there are grounds for predicting that 'lone wolf' terrorism will continue to increase in frequency. The potentiation of violence requires its legitimation and rationalisation, and there are many stops on the 'information superhighway', as the internet was once called, where these are on offer, and where anger and yearning can be fused together in a terrorist project.

This substantive facilitation by the virtual host is not necessary to unleash the anger of the non-ideological killer. He (there are no instances yet of females in this category) is signing off from human society, not imagining himself to be transforming it. His superego is shattered by his first murder, and there is no possibility of, and certainly no plan for, reconstituting it around an ideology. Yet can the increasing frequency of rampage killings also be linked to the growth of communications in the digital age, and specifically to the ubiquity and omnivalence of the web and other new media? Mass murderers around the world can now be seen and read about, the terror they produce can be savoured, and their actions can be placed within thinkable repertoires of human responses to living. Does the 'virtual host' offer something seductive to the alienated and unintegrated individual: an exemplar, a script, the promise of a global stage and the central role in an apocalyptic drama of revenge?

### Political violence and personal rage

Some recent cases, mainly of 'sole actor' or relatively isolated terrorists, add to the blurring of the distinction between ideological terrorist and deranged loner. While the 'shoe bomber' Richard Reid can be classified as a terrorist in the sense that he had a history of involvement in extreme Islamism and had organisational backing for several years, in personality terms he was clearly not the best choice for Al Qaeda. An isolated, unstable individual who had committed mugging offences in the 1990s, he converted to Islam while in Feltham Young Offenders Institution. His co-conspirator Saajid Badat was another troubled young man, though apparently one with greater emotional resources which enabled him to cancel his mission to explode an aircraft (though not to alert the authorities to Reid's similar deadly plan). The Exeter Giraffe Café bomber, Nicky Reilly, is even more clearly someone of inadequate personality whose inner turmoil came to be aligned with a jihadist agenda. He claimed to have acted alone, guided only by internet sources. Police did not believe that, though they have been unable to identify those others who might have been involved. Andrew (Isa) Ibrahim, another disturbed young man with drug problems who planned an attack in his native Bristol, also seems to have been a self-radicalised loner. Another individual apprehended like Reid while trying to detonate explosives on an aircraft, Farouk Abdulmutallab, presents a somewhat different picture: his movement from piety to militancy was probably self-propelled, but he received training in Yemen and was in contact with leading jihadist Anwar al-Awlaki. He also appears to have been less obviously damaged psychologically, but his behaviour had disturbed his family, from whom he cut himself off, and there is evidence of an immature and defended personality (Abdulmutallab, 2008).

The most recent perpetrators of Islamist terror in Europe can also be cited here. The killers on a London street of a British soldier in 2013, Michael Adebolajo and Michael Adebowale, and the trio responsible for the Paris shootings in January 2015, all had biographies featuring emotional damage, in some cases with psychiatric and criminal histories.

Some other relatively recent cases of 'homegrown' terrorism in the US also point to a convergence of political violence and personal disorder. At one end of the spectrum, Jared Loughner is a lone individual with a psychotic disorder. Yet his selected target (a congresswoman meeting constituents) was a political, or quasipolitical, one, albeit not in response to Sarah Palin's notorious cross-hairs. Colleen LaRose's online radicalisation and acquired identity as Fatima LaRose (which became 'Jihad Jane' to sections of the media) were clearly an attempt to bring some order and purpose into a life of chaos and hopelessness, including failed relationships, petty crime, alcohol abuse and a suicide attempt (Halverson and Way, 2012). She did not actually get to plan a suicide mission but expressed the wish to be a martyr. LaRose was arrested as one of a group planning to kill the Swedish cartoonist Lars Vilks (creator of some of the 'Danish cartoons' of the prophet Mohammed), as was Jamie Paulin-Ramirez ('Jihad Jamie'), another female American convert with a similar history of an empty, angry life. Michael Finton could present to some people as a nice and normal guy, but he had a troubled childhood and a conviction for aggravated burglary before he converted to Islam and nurtured a dream of being a martyr, which he came close to realising by detonating a truckful of explosives outside a federal building. He is another whose main route to jihad was the superhighway of the web.

In these cases there is some merging of the categories. This is not to say that any of those individuals would have become rampage killers, or killers of any kind, without the seduction exercised or the opportunity provided by an ideology of violence, but the blurring shows how the recruitment of a suicide attacker can mesh with certain kinds of psychological damage, and that this is happening more frequently. It may be that such cases occur when the recruitment net is cast wider and Al Qaeda's 'standards' are lowered. Or it may be that as terrorism acquires a more established cultural presence and familiarity, so more people are inclined to consider it as a path for themselves, as a kind of container for deadly anger. This is not to blame the media for any particular presentation of it, but to acknowledge that when choices of any kind are increasingly seen in the public domain, they enter into the realms of possibility for more people. In this sense the likelihood of becoming a terrorist is at one level comparable with that of jogging through city streets or covering your body with tattoos. Both of these behaviours would a few decades ago in the UK have been unimaginable for all but a tiny handful of eccentrics, but they are now firmly established within the envelope of normality. This is not a flippant point but an illustration of the cultural determination of what most people take to be their available choices and possibilities. In Palestine, Iraq and Afghanistan, suicide martyrdom has acquired some normative currency, and is thus available as a way of responding to a range of different personal experiences.

## Conclusion

If there is any truth in the analysis advanced here, it will have implications for combating terrorism, particularly in relation to the production of counternarratives deigned to reduce its attractiveness to potential recruits. These must be sophisticated yet compelling ideas, arguments and images which can address the unconscious dimensions of fundamentalist appeals – including the needs for revenge on the humiliators and for a new self-experience as heroic saviour, praised and valued. If these powerful magnets in jihadi propaganda are not matched, they will continue to serve as effective recruitment tools. Moreover, given the importance of the web and of social media in the capture of destructive feelings and their deployment towards acting out in murderous ways, they are likely to be the key sites for propagating alternatives.

## Note

1. The theme of humiliation also emerged as central in a study I undertook of Norwegian terrorist Anders Breivik, a short summary of which has been published (Richards, 2014) and which will be reported more fully in further publications. I have also discussed the general provenance of humiliation in a previous paper (Richards, 2009).

## References

Abdulmutallab, U. F. (2008) Available at: http://msnbcmedia.msn.com/i/msnbc/ sections/tvnews/dateline%20nbc/autobiography.pdf (accessed 30 November 2012).

Crenshaw, M. (2000) The psychology of terrorism: An agenda for the 21st Century. *Political Psychology*. 21(2), 405–420.

Figlio, K. (2006) The absolute state of mind in society and the individual. *Psychoanalysis, Culture and Society*. 11(2), 119–143.

Gambetta, D. (2006) Can we make sense of suicide missions?, in G. Gambetta (ed) *Making Sense of Suicide Missions*. Oxford: Oxford University Press, 259–300.

Halverson, J. and Way, A. (2012) The curious case of Colleen LaRose: Social margins, new media and online radicalisation. *Media, War and Conflict*. 5(2), 139–154.

Horgan, J. (2014) *The Psychology of Terrorism (Political Violence)*. London: Routledge.

Hyatt Williams, A. (1998) *Cruelty, Violence and Murder*. London: Karnac.

Lankford, A. (2011) Could suicide terrorists actually be suicidal? *Studies in Conflict and Terrorism*. 34, 337–366.

Lankford, A. (2013) A comparative analysis of suicide terrorists and rampage, workplace, and school shooters in the United States from 1990 to 2010. *Homicide Studies*. 17(3), 255–274.

Lankford, A. and Hakim, N. (2011) From columbine to Palestine: A comparative analysis of rampage shooters in the United States and volunteer suicide bombers in the Middle East. *Aggression and Violent Behaviour*. 16, 98–107.

Richards, B. (2009) Explosive humiliation and news media, in S. D. Sclater, D. Jones, H. Price, and C. Yates (eds) *Emotion: New Psychosocial Perspectives*. Basingstoke: Palgrave Macmillan. 59–71.

Richards, B. (2014) What drove Anders Breivik? *Contexts*. 13(4), 42–47.

Silke, A. (2014) *Terrorism (All That matters)*. London: Hodder & Stoughton.

Volkan, V. (1998) *The Need to Have Enemies and Allies*. Northvale, NJ: Jason Aronson.

Volkan, V. (2004) *Blind Trust: Large Groups and Their Leaders in Times of Crisis and Terror*. Charlottesville, PA: Pitchstone Pub.

# Part II
# Mediating Margins

# 5
# European Media Policy: Why Margins Actually Matter

*Monika Metykova*

This chapter argues that media policy-making in European countries tends to be restricted to nation-centric frameworks, and it shows that pan-European agents are not empowered to work with transnational approaches to cultural diversity when it comes to media regulation. The nation-centric approach is particularly striking when we take into account the 'new' complexity of contemporary Europe, which is linked particularly to migration that has been a major factor in the social (as well as the cultural and demographic) transformation of contemporary societies. The underlying principles and approaches that characterise European media policy are largely ignorant of these developments on the ground in Europe and remain caught up in the 'national container' approach.

A conceptualisation of society as a bounded national container limits questions about 'why the boundaries of the container society are drawn as they are and what consequences follow from this methodological limitation of the analytical horizon – thus removing trans-border connections and processes from the picture' (Wimmer and Glick Schiller, 2002: 307). Such a conceptualisation impacts on policy-making and on understanding the role of media in contemporary European societies, resulting in an ignorance of the margins and those at the margins, including transnational migrants and non-indigenous minority populations. In this chapter I concentrate on how European/EU media policy-making addresses the margins, and I argue that there are some recent developments that suggest a new regulatory willingness in relation to diversity. However, these efforts are actually confined to the margins of policy-making.

Media form a particularly complicated area of policy-making as they are credited with a variety of roles – from economic all the way to cultural (see e.g. Bardoel and d'Haenens, 2004; Hesmondhalgh, 2013; Murdock, 1992). In Western European societies we find PSB that – in its various forms and under various national regulatory regimes (see e.g. Hardy, 2008; Kelly et al., 2004) – is tasked with serving the interests of the public as citizens rather than as consumers, and as such also has special responsibilities in representing the (very broadly defined) diverse populations living in contemporary societies. The Broadcasting Research Unit identified the principles of PSB as the following: universal accessibility (geographic); universal appeal (general tastes and interests); particular attention to minorities; contribution to a sense of national identity and community; distance from vested interests; direct funding and universality of payment; competition in good programming rather than for numbers; and guidelines that liberate rather than restrict programme-makers (as quoted in Raboy, 1996: 6, see also Scannell, 1992; van den Bulck, 2001).

It is, however, important to stress that PSB is a quintessentially European and national project, mainly promoting national culture (or, indeed, also some – often officially recognised – minority cultures) and a national public sphere. While it is not my aim here to closely analyse the role of PSB in promoting cultural diversity as such or to provide a detailed analysis of how various European PSB systems and regulations deal with the representation of minorities, I need to highlight criticisms of European public service broadcasters – and importantly the regulatory frameworks that they are subjected to – exactly in this respect. In the UK context, production practices as well as staff working at the British Broadcasting Corporation (BBC) have been analysed within a cultural/ethnic diversity framework (see e.g. Campion, 2006; Malik, 2001; for industry statistics, see e.g. Creative Skillset Employment Census of the Creative Industries) and so has the larger policy framework (see e.g. Goblot, 2013; Malik, 2013).

It is important to note that PSB may represent (employ) some at the margins but it does so within a national frame. There are no pan-European regulatory mechanisms that would address cultural diversity in PSB and that is because it remains in the jurisdiction of individual EU member states. This arrangement was reinforced in the Protocol on the System of Public Service Broadcasting in Member States (part of the Treaty of Amsterdam) which acknowledges that the PSB system is 'directly related to the democratic, social and cultural needs of each society and to the need to preserve media pluralism'.[1] Each member state is responsible for conferring, defining and organising the public service remit and securing funding for it. However, such funding should not 'affect trading conditions and competition in the Community to an extent which would be contrary to the common interest' (ibid.).[2]

In interviews with civil servants working in the EU's media and competition directorates, PSB proved to be an important topic. An interviewee characterised it as solving 'a particular problem in a particular market with a particular technology' (anonymous, personal communication, 27 May 2009). He went on to describe issues that increased competition in relation to PSB. With the establishment of commercial TV the task was to

> create some space to resolve how exactly you have some grounds for fair competition in relation to the commercial television interest which we let in partly for promoting pluralism in the 1980s...and now we have somehow to situate public service broadcasting in a broader and much more competitive context which is multi-sectoral and convergent with press and publishing as well.
>
> (anonymous, personal communication, 27 May 2009)

This interviewee suggests that the repositioning of PSB does not involve a broader encompassing of 'non-national' 'marginal' groups of people such as transnational migrants.

The *protocol* as well as the interviewee refer to pluralism, an important aspect of EU media policy, but one that is not necessarily linked to cultural or social objectives. Media pluralism has been on the agenda of individual member states since the establishment of private broadcasting and it has been largely understood as an issue of ownership and markets/competition. National measures (including those that support PSB) as well as EU-wide ones, such as EU competition law and measures already introduced in the Television without Frontiers Directive (1989), aimed to deal with pluralism, often addressing it in terms of ownership and concentration or non-monopolistic production (measures to support independent producers). The EU regulatory framework includes two types of intervention related to media pluralism: access remedies (which limit the market power of those who control access to networks or associated facilities) and safeguards to guarantee basic users' interests that would not be guaranteed by market forces (e.g. interoperability of consumer digital TV, frequencies granted in case of scarcity).

The key question regarding these interventions is whether their goal is to ensure the functioning of the internal market or whether there are other justifications (e.g. social and cultural ones) at stake. The competing economic and cultural justifications and goals of EU audiovisual regulation have been extensively discussed in the academic literature (see e.g. Collins, 1994; Humphreys et al., 2008; Hirsch and Petersen, 2007; Schlesinger, 1997; van Cuilenburg and McQuail, 2003), and while scholars vary in their assessment of the impact of economic or public interest interventions in audiovisual policy, there is a general consensus on the prevalence of economic goals. Humphreys (2008), for example, argues that social and cultural goals are taken seriously, though there is a bias towards economic benefits.

Cultural and social aspects of media policies represent a challenging regulatory area at the EU level because they are normally not transposed into the legislation of member states; media, similarly to culture, represent an area where the subsidiarity principle[3] applies. A civil servant working for the European Commission puts it succinctly: EU media policies are merely 'the tip of the iceberg' as media are 'not an area like competition or electronic communication where there is a fully harmonized European Commission law based on an article of a Treaty or a set of directives. It's not an area where European Commission competences are very strong' (anonymous, personal communication, 27 May 2009). It is thus understandable that efforts to introduce pan-European regulation on media pluralism – even understood purely in ownership/market terms – have thus far been unsuccessful. The 1992 green paper 'Pluralism and media concentration in the internal market: An assessment of the need for commission action' did not find a clear need for concerted European Commission action. A similar conclusion was reached in a consultation paper in 2005 – namely, that it is difficult to propose any harmonisation of rules between the member states, and also that the member states consider media pluralism and its safeguarding a task for themselves.

It has been argued that European audiovisual policy is restricted (if not completely misconceived) in its approach to pluralism.[4] La Porte et al. (2007), for example, point out that EU audiovisual policy addresses only external aspects of pluralism – advocating the premise that the non-monopolistic provision of content involving a multiplicity of channels and producers guarantees diversity. In contrast there is a need for measures that support internal pluralism which takes into account the content itself. A cultural approach to both forms of pluralism would potentially guarantee that different types of social sensitivity are addressed and accessed through media contents (La Porte et al., 2007). Some academics acknowledge the role of the European Parliament (and in rare cases also of the European Economic and Social Committee) in initiatives that aim to introduce harmonised interventions in support of media pluralism (and also in cases when pluralism is understood broader than media ownership, see e.g. Harcourt, 2005; Humphreys et al., 2008; Sarikakis, 2005).

The most important recent development in this respect unfolded in 2007 with the European Parliament inviting the European Commission to propose measures for media pluralism at the European level. In the process the EU commissioned an *'Independent Study on Indicators for Media Pluralism in the Member States – Towards a Risk-Based Approach* [that will] develop a monitoring tool for assessing the level of media pluralism in the EU Member States and identifying threats to such pluralism based on a set of indicators, covering pertinent legal, economic and socio-cultural considerations'.[5] The outcome of the project is the so-called Media Pluralism Monitor tool that was developed in 2009. This includes cultural pluralism as one area in need of assessment and lists ten indicators for it, including the representation of cultural and social groups in the media (as well as in the media workforce), and the state of minority and community media. The European Parliament earmarked €500,000 from the 2013 EU budget for a pilot implementation of this tool in nine EU member states, and the results were made public in the second half of 2014. Cultural pluralism, however, has not been identified as a risk area.[6] This conclusion was published a few months after Lenny Henry and other prominent UK actors of ethnic minority background launched a campaign for greater ethnic diversity in the UK media industry, and indeed after the BBC earmarked £2.1 million for a diversity creative talent fund.[7]

In October 2014, OFCOM – the UK's communications regulatory body – addressed stakeholders within a consultation on indicators for the measurement of media plurality. This is a step towards fulfilling the UK Government's commitment to commission a measurement framework for media plurality in the country. Documents that accompany the commissioning of the measurement framework make it clear that one of the measurement indicators should be media ownership, and importantly also that the type of content most relevant to media plurality is news and current affairs. While these are clearly linked to the information needs of citizens (and indeed to deliberation that is key for democracy), this approach clearly ignores the cultural dimension of media production and content.

While these efforts at preparing a measurement for media plurality are ongoing and it is premature to speculate about their results or impact, it is becoming clear that the 'old' policy framework is likely to continue – namely, that ethnic diversity (or more broadly understood cultural and social aspects of media diversity) will remain in the jurisdiction of individual member states and in the case of the UK are likely to continue to be linked mainly to the public service broadcaster, the BBC. This, however, means that those at the very margins of European societies will continue without having their needs addressed in media policies – at the national as well as the pan-European level. In the following I turn to one example of such a marginalised pan-European minority – Roma.

The Roma are the largest (transnational) ethnic minority group in the EU. There are an estimated 10–12 million Roma (I use this as an umbrella term for gypsies, Sinti, travellers, etc.) living in the member states with a large majority in new ones. They do not have a nation state as such, an issue that has very serious implications (not only) for media policy, as I show further. Various groups of Roma living in a single state may not share the same dialect, which proves particularly challenging in policy terms. Roma have long suffered from social exclusion as well as violations of human rights.[8] With the 'eastward enlargement' of the EU they became more visible on the policy agendas of 'old' member states. However, as Huub van Baar (2011) argues, they are represented as a 'European problem' rather than a European minority.[9] Van Baar also suggests that some new member states opted to shift the responsibility for the 'Roma issue' to the EU (see also Fekete, 2014).

Policies related to Roma at the level of individual nation states as well as at the pan-European level have concentrated on combating social exclusion, poverty and discrimination that they face in 'old' as well as 'new' EU member states, but their impact has been dubious. Policies aimed at Roma at the EU level are, however, concerned only with a few select areas. The most important initiative in this respect is the 2011 EU Framework for National Roma Integration Strategies up to 2020.[10] The framework covers socioeconomic rather than cultural issues, and at its heart is a demand to eradicate discrimination against Roma in four key areas: education, employment, healthcare and housing. The document sets out goals and monitoring systems that aim to make a difference in ten years' time. However, areas of cultural rights, language rights or indeed the media needs of Roma are completely missing from the framework.

The EU also organises two types of 'deliberative event' at which issues impacting Roma specifically are discussed: European Roma Summits which involve the highest decision-making levels of the EU, national and regional authorities and civil society actors (three such summits have been held thus far – in 2008, 2010 and 2014); and the European Platform for Roma Inclusion, which brings together national governments, representatives of the EU, international organisations and Roma civil society actors, and meets more frequently (between 2009 and 2014 there were eight platforms held). The main focus of both types of deliberative event are measures that would lead to the social inclusion of Roma. Having alerted readers to this overall focus on the social and economic aspects of Roma inclusion, it will not come as a surprise that the first ever EU-level legal instrument on Roma integration adopted in December 2013 refers to mediation, but media and culture are not mentioned at all.

This lack of attention paid to media reflects the fact that migration, increased mobility and the existence of transnational minorities (e.g. Roma) are outside the radar of audiovisual policy-makers. A European Commission civil servant acknowledged that

> some of these communities are very granular at the level of member states. If I look at the Roma community which is transnational, that's a much bigger case. If you are a transnational community then it's a deal breaker basically, if you are not based in a country. In general, I don't think that there is a vast amount of new thinking and I also don't think that the European Commission will accommodate whatever comes from the outside but it's not systematically being thought of, probably because nobody wants to change their lecture notes very much at national level.
>
> (anonymous, personal communication, 27 May 2009)

And it is an example of policies at the national level to which the following section turns. The Czech Republic joined the EU in May 2004 in the first wave of 'eastward enlargement'. Roma media and their regulation that exist in the Czech Republic illustrate some of the key issues at the national level (at least in the new EU member states). The EU Agency for Fundamental Rights carries out regular surveys among Roma living in 11 EU member states (Bulgaria, the Czech Republic, France, Greece, Hungary, Italy, Poland, Portugal, Romania, Slovakia and Spain) that focus on the four key areas (education, employment, healthcare and housing) identified in the framework. According to the most recent survey results available,[11] 46% of all Roma taking part in the survey had felt discriminated against in the past 12 months compared with 62% of Czech Roma.

In the Czech Republic, public service broadcasters have special responsibilities for the provision of programmes for ethnic minorities. The Czech public service radio station, Český rozhlas, has had a Roma editorial group since 1992, and at the time of writing it produces a weekly one-hour programme, *O Roma vakeren Romové hovoří* (Romani and Czech for Roma speak), broadcast mainly in the Czech language on Saturday evenings. The aim[12] is to promote positive representations of Roma (its features centre on successful Roma individuals, NGOs and their projects). Education and the promotion of mutual understanding between the majority Czechs and minority Roma are also central for Roma print media[13] published in the Czech Republic. Examples of such media include the biweekly *Romano Hangos/Romský hlas* (Romani and Czech for Roma voice; http://www.srnm.cz/index.php/nase-sluzby/kultura/romano-hangos) published by a Roma NGO with financial support from the Czech Ministry of Culture, and the monthly *Romano vod'i/Romská duše* (Roma soul; http://www.romea.cz/cz/archiv-rv) published by a different Roma NGO and also supported by the Czech Ministry of Culture and also mainly written in Czech. The monthly magazine aims to cover the lives of Roma from a variety of angles and 'to finally strengthen Roma's self-confidence with the help of "their own" periodical'.[14]

The scope of this chapter does not allow a detailed discussion of the state of Roma media in the Czech Republic, but the brief description above at least alerts readers to the vulnerability of such media and also to the restrictions that they face. If we consider funding mechanisms, it is clear that all the media are dependent on some form of financial assistance from the Czech Government – there is no for-profit Roma medium in the Czech Republic. While funding for PSB is relatively stable, it is still a political issue and, moreover, government funding is usually awarded for 'socially desirable' media coverage (hence the stress on education, positive representations and mutual understanding), while other aspects as well as formats which may arguably be equally attractive for readers/viewers are missing (particularly those linked to lifestyle, 'low' culture, etc.).

The examples above also highlight the limitations of policies that create 'safe havens' for the production of minority content with narrowly understood socially desirable aims. Roma journalists whom I interviewed in the Czech Republic either embraced their 'educational role' wholeheartedly or complained about how it restricted their work as journalists. It is not unusual for Czech Roma media to be founded and essentially run by a single person, which raises serious concerns about their long-term sustainability. There are other issues that the Czech Roma media are illustrative of. Roma living in the country speak a number of dialects and in addition the written and spoken versions of a dialect vary. This may be one reason – as already described above – why the media broadcast/are published mainly in Czech. Clearly this is also linked to a rather fuzzy notion of the target audience. The radio programme as well as the print media target both Roma and the Czech majority in their effort to provide positive representations (role models) and promote mutual understanding.

It can, of course, be argued that new media technologies in particular enable the creation of cheap and wide-ranging content for minorities. The empowering role of new media has, however, been challenged as research suggests that the digital divide continues to play a role (see e.g. Campos-Castillo, 2014). Moreover, at least in theory, establishing transnational Roma media should also be easier and cheaper, thanks to technological developments. One such attempt originated from the Czech Republic in the form of online transnational Roma radio, again as a civil society initiative rather than a commercial enterprise. Radio Rota gained its broadcast licence in the Czech Republic and intended to cover the Czech Republic, Hungary, Slovakia, Bulgaria, Romania and Spain. However, the licence was revoked in 2011 because the station did not begin broadcasting until 180 days after the licence was granted.

Although this discussion of Roma media in the Czech Republic is by no means exhaustive, it highlights some of the shortcomings of policies that operate within a 'national container'. From a media policy perspective, Roma are a marginalised group that is to be served by PSB targeting them (and possibly the majority Czech population) and promoting positive representations in a rather educational manner. Czech PSB as well as Roma print media exist in a narrowly conceived 'safe haven' and provide only a limited range of media content (as well as journalistic employment opportunities). This content (as well as analyses of performance, particularly of PSB) focus on representations of Roma in news and current affairs and ignore other 'less serious' genres.

Unfortunately the Czech case also suggests a lack of a new perspective on media and those in the margins – in line with the already mentioned observation of an EU civil servant. Migrants, non-nationals, transnationals, diasporas, Roma and their cultural heritage, languages, information needs and so on are only of secondary importance, even in policies that specifically target 'unity in diversity' as these operate primarily within the national container, the national cultures in member states (Sarikakis, 2007). This then leaves us with a rather disheartening conclusion regarding the possibilities of overcoming the national framework in European media policies as 'neither trans-state nor suprastate levels are generators of post-nationality, unless they too reproduce the logic of democratic openness favourable to people's empowerment beyond national constraints' (Carvalhais, 2007: 108).

## Notes

1. http://www.lisbon-treaty.org/wcm/the-lisbon-treaty/protocols-annexed-to-the-treaties/680-protocol-on-the-system-of-public-service-broadcasting-in-the-member-states.html.
2. For more on the regulation of state aid for PSB, see Communication from the commission on the application of state aid rules to public service broadcasting 2009/C 257/01. http://eur-lex.europa.eu/legal-content/EN/TXT/?uri=uriserv:OJ.C_.2009.257.01.0001.01.ENG.
3. The principle of subsidiarity is defined in Article 5 of the Treaty on the EU. It ensures that decisions are taken as close as possible to the citizen and that constant checks are made to verify that action at the EU level is justified in light of the possibilities available at the national, regional or local levels. Specifically, it is the principle whereby the EU does not take action (except in the areas that fall within its exclusive competence), unless it is more effective than action taken at the national, regional or local level. It is closely bound up with the principle of proportionality, which requires that any action by the EU should not go beyond what is necessary to achieve the objectives of the treaties.
4. It would be a mistake to argue that there are no discussions about the cultural/social and other aspects of pluralism in European institutions. See, for example, a working document on the globalisation of media and its impact on cultural diversity prepared for the Scientific and Technological Options Assessment Panel (La Porte Alfaro and Sabado, 2001).
5. http://ec.europa.eu/digital-agenda/en/independent-study-indicators-media-pluralism.
6. For more detail, see https://reutersinstitute.politics.ox.ac.uk/sites/default/files/Media%20Pluralism%20Monitor%20Pilot%20Test%20-%20Executive%20Summary%20UK%20Report.pdf.
7. At the time of writing, the UK Parliament's Media, Culture and Sport Committee has not concluded its inquiry into the future of the BBC. Written and oral submissions on ethnic diversity formed part of the evidence-gathering and can be accessed at http://www.parliament.uk/business/committees/committees-a-z/commons-select/culture-media-and-sport-committee/inquiries/parliament-2010/future-of-the-bbc/.
8. The European Roma Rights Centre – an international public interest law organisation that has consultative status with the Council of Europe, as well as with the Economic and Social Council of the United Nations – lists cases that it lodged against a number of European countries with the European Court of Human Rights. See http://www.errc.org/strategic-litigation-european-court-of-human-rights.
9. In October 2013, the Russian daily *Pravda* even managed to drag Roma (or rather the solution to the Roma problem) into the dispute between the EU and Russia over the status of Ukraine. An article entitled 'Europe ready to give all its Roma to Ukraine' suggests that Western Europe is unable to handle the legal immigration of Roma from Romania and

Bulgaria and hence 'the tolerant EU is thinking of deporting them. A proper destination has been found, and all Roma camps from the EU will be moved to Ukraine.' http://english.pravda.ru/society/stories/08-10-2013/125834-europe_roma_ukraine-0/.

10. The goals of the EU-led initiative are very similar to those of the Decade of Roma inclusion 2005–2015 which, however, involves a different set of actors and countries. See www.romadecade.org.
11. These are from 2011 and are available at http://fra.europa.eu/en/publications-and-resources/data-and-maps/survey-data-explorer-results-2011-roma-survey.
12. See http://www.rozhlas.cz/radiozurnal/porady/_porad/114.
13. For an overview of Roma media in the Czech Republic, see http://romove.radio.cz/en/clanek/18378.
14. https://en-gb.facebook.com/pages/Romano-vo%C4%8Fi/134600163277347?sk=info.

# References

Bardoel, J. and d'Haenens, L. (2004) Media meet the citizen: Beyond market mechanisms and government regulation. *European Journal of Communication.* 19(2), 165–194.

Campion, M. J. (2006) Diversity, or just colour by numbers? *British Journalism Review.* 17(1), 71–76.

Campos-Castillo, C. (2014) Revisiting the first-level digital divide in the United States: Gender and race/ethnicity patterns, 2007–2012. *Social Science Computer Review,* [online]. Available at: http://ssc.sagepub.com/content/early/2014/08/21/0894439314547617.full.pdf+html (accessed 8 November 2014).

Carvalhais, I. E. (2007) The cosmopolitan language of the state: Post-national citizenship and the integration of non-nationals. *European Journal of Social Theory.* 10(1), 99–111.

Collins, R. (1994) *Broadcasting and Audiovisual Policy in the European Single Market.* London: Routledge.

Creative Skillset (2012) *Employment Census of the Creative Industries.* [pdf] Available at: http://creativeskillset.org/assets/0000/5070/2012_Employment_Census_of_the_Creative_Media_Industries.pdf (accessed 6 November 2014).

Fekete, L. (2014) Europe against the Roma. *Race and Class.* 55(3), 60–70.

Goblot, V. (2013) BBC Four as 'a place to think': Issues of quality, cultural value and television archive in the digital, multiplatform age. Ph.D. Goldsmiths College.

Harcourt, A. (2005) *The European Union and the Regulation of Media Markets.* Manchester: Manchester University Press.

Hardy, J. (2008) *Western Media Systems.* London: Routledge.

Hesmondhalgh, D. (2013) *The Cultural Industries* (3rd edn). London: Sage.

Hirsch, M. and Petersen, V. G. (2007) Enlargement of the arena: European media policy, in W. A. Meier and J. Trappel (eds) *Power, Performance and Politics. Media Policy in Europe.* Baden-Baden: Nomos, 21–39.

Humphreys, Peter et al. (2008) *Globalization, Regulatory Competition and Audiovisual Regulation in Five Countries: Full Research Report ESRC End of Award Report, RES-000-23-0966.* Swindon: ESRC.

Kelly, M., Mazzoneli, G. and McQuail, D. (eds) (2004) *The Media in Europe: The Euromedia Handbook* (3rd edn). London: Sage.

La Porte Alfaro, M. T. and Sabada, T. (2001). *Globalisation of the Media Industry and Possible Threats to Cultural Diversity.* Working document for the 'Scientific and Technological Options Assessment Panel'. Brussels: Directorate General for Research of the European Parliament.

La Porte, T., Medina, M. and Sádaba, T. (2007) Globalization and pluralism: The function of public television in the European audiovisual market. *The International Communication Gazette.* 69(4), 377–399.

Malik, S. (2001) *Representing Black Britain: Black and Asian Images on Television.* London: Sage.

Malik, S. (2013) 'Creative diversity': UK public service broadcasting after multiculturalism. *Popular Communication: The International Journal of Media and Culture.* 11(3), 227–241.

Murdock, G. (1992) Citizens, consumers, and public culture, in M. Skovmand and K. C. Schrøder (eds) *Media Cultures: Reappraising Transnational Media.* London: Routledge. 34–48.

Raboy, M. (ed) (1996) *Public Broadcasting for the 21st Century.* Luton: University of Luton Press.

Sarikakis, K. (2005) Defending communicative spaces: The remits and limits of the European Parliament. *International Communication Gazette.* 67(2), 155–172.

Sarikakis, K. (2007) The place of media and cultural policy in the EU, in K. Sarikakis (ed) *Media and Cultural Policy in the European Union.* Amsterdam: Rodopi. 13–22.

Scannell, P. (1992) Public service broadcasting and modern public life, in P. Scannell, P. Schlesinger, and C. Sparks (eds) *Culture and Power.* London: Sage. 317–348.

Schlesinger, P. (1997) From cultural defence to political culture: Media, politics and collective identity in the European Union. *Media, Culture and Society.* 19(3), 369–391.

van Cuilenburg, J. and McQuail, D. (2003) Media policy paradigm shifts: Towards a new communications policy paradigm. *European Journal of Communication.* 18(2), 181–207.

van Baar, H., (2011) Commentary: Europe's Romaphobia: Problematization, securitization, nomadization. *Environment Planning D: Society and Space,* 29(2), 203–212.

van den Bulck, H. (2001) Public service broadcasting and national identity as a project of modernity. *Media, Culture and Society.* 23(1), 53–69.

Wimmer, A. and Glick Schiller, N. (2002) Methodological nationalism and beyond: Nation-state building, migration and the social sciences. *Global Networks.* 2(4), 301–334.

# 6
# The Rise of 'Creative Diversity' in Media Policy

*Sarita Malik*

This chapter addresses the theme of media and margins by analysing the ways in which PSB – a public sphere with a key role in national culture – has addressed the realities of a multicultural society. It argues that PSB in the UK has seen a series of discursive shifts marked by a flexible narrative of 'diversity'. This reflects a deep level of anxiety about the best way of managing an increasingly multicultural public at a time when state multiculturalism has ended.

Through a critical review of recent literature and policy concepts, this chapter puts together history and analysis to consider the relationship between 'race' and UK PSB. Building on earlier work that recognises a paradigmatic shift from 'multiculturalism' to 'cultural diversity', it identifies a third phase, 'creative diversity'. This provides a further incremental depoliticisation of 'race' in PSB contexts. Here, ideas of 'quality' and 'creativity' are foregrounded over (structural) questions of (in)equality or the positive recognition of social and cultural difference.

The chapter situates the rapid rise of 'creative diversity' alongside parallel developments in the 'crisis of multiculturalism', UK equality legislative frameworks and creative industries policy. It is argued that 'creative diversity' shifts the paradigm of the multicultural problem (in PSB), enables the 'marketisation' of TV and multiculture, and ultimately continues to safeguard the interests of PSB. Therefore the social and political basis of the diversity agenda has been diminished through the discourse of 'creative diversity'. This has serious implications for PSB because it is a cultural, not just a material, resource.

## PSB media and the margins

TV is a key site in which 'sociological outcomes' are imagined (Born, 2000: 420). How public service TV responds to various social identities, including race and ethnicity, tells us how they are culturally organised, produced and communicated to the nation and, increasingly, beyond. The importance of such cultural meanings is that they 'organise and regulate social practices, influence our conduct and consequently have real, practical effects' (Hall, 1997a: 3). The chapter examines how notions of race and ethnicity, broadly linked here to the UK's 'visible' ethnic minorities – namely, 'Black and Asian' (South Asian, African and Caribbean) Britons – are discursively formed, produced and circulated through cultural policy. Until now, these ethnic minority communities have experienced a unique relationship with UK PSB, a public sphere with a key role in national culture (Kumar, 1977). The relationship has been based around patterns of marginalisation and foregrounding, access and constraint, specialist programming and mainstreaming.

Policy (as an aspect of regulation) is situated as an important part of cultural practice in the circuit of culture (Du Gay et al., 1997). The discussion therefore points to the role of policy in cultural life and, in turn, the central place of culture in contemporary public communications and politics (Hall, 1997b). It examines how and where 'race' does and does not 'occur' within current PSB policy frames, what these frames are symptomatic of, and the implications for cultural practice and representation. The recent diversity policies of the UK's two public service broadcasters – the BBC (funded by a public licence fee) and Channel 4 (publicly owned, commercially funded) – will be used as case studies, enriched by an understanding of how each broadcaster has historically addressed issues of race, ethnic minorities and representation in their policy and programming approaches (Born, 2006; Saha, 2012). I want to suggest that the latest diversity plans of these two broadcasters are indicative of a discursive turn to 'creativity' in how race and racism are now officially handled and driven underground, after multiculturalism. Creative diversity thus turns 'bad', 'risky' diversity policy (multiculturalism, cultural diversity) into 'good' diversity policy (creative diversity), while also embracing the economic rationalism that underpins public facilities today.

UK PSB has positioned 'diversity' as a core pursuit and framework through which programme-makers and executives are apparently tasked to deliver public service. The chapter considers the specific political, social and market expediencies that the flexibility of the term 'diversity' opens up for public service broadcasters in salient contexts. I situate these concerns alongside PSB's own trajectory in the years following the UK 1990 Broadcasting Act since when the public service case for multiculturalism in broadcasting has been increasingly undermined by the emerging cultures of commercialism triggered by increasing competition, lighter touch regulation and technological developments. The current circumstances in which the traditional 'welfare consensus of liberal democracy' (Lunt, 2009: 136) criteria of public service is being challenged by an aggressively competitive media market in a global economy make it especially rich for such an analysis.

Running concurrently is the major sociopolitical context of the UK's sharply contested project of managing difference, marked by a critical shift against the ideological principles underpinning multiculturalism (Kundnani, 2007; Lentin, 2012). Since UK PSB has traditionally been tied to the ideal of national broadcasting, particular problems and solutions materialise when the idea of the national itself becomes complicated. I go on to suggest that the turn away from multiculturalism in broadcasting has been cosseted by a broader consensus of the perceived need for social cohesion rather than multiculturalism.

These dual industrial and sociopolitical backgrounds are mutually significant in helping us to map what can be identified as now three phases – 'multiculturalism', 'cultural diversity' and 'creative diversity' – each indicating an incremental depoliticisation of 'race' in PSB contexts. The rise of 'creative diversity' specifically relates to this because the term 'creativity' signifies a post-multiculturalist, falsely post-racial understanding. I argue that the particular nuance inscribed in '*creative diversity*' originates from an emergent post-racial discursive politics (not from post-racial times) and towards economic rationalism. The depoliticisation of difference in PSB coincides with the creative marketisation of TV and multiculture accommodated by a wider shift from state to market in public provision (Garnham, 2005). Thus media policy developments are directly linked and seen, in this analysis, to coincide with complex social issues, simultaneously altering the relationship of 'minority cultures to mainstream, national cultural traditions' (Hall, 1997b: 227).

The concern is with the critical shift in policy emphasis, tone and, it is argued, intention, where policy itself becomes a mechanism for a range of functions. The analytical aim of this discussion is to intervene in media policy studies and make a multifaceted argument about the varying, overlapping forces. These include the political economic, state responses to multiculturalism, neoliberalism and discourses of creativity and innovation that shape PSB's approach to the 'problem' of cultural difference.

The field of policy studies is helpful for how it links policy, discourse and motivation. The language games in policy discourse, framing and reframing can reveal to us a strong normative impulse, often strategically shifting the 'paradigm of a problem' (van Eeten, 2007: 255–256). Thus policy acts as a tool to publicly manage what might be commonly understood as problematic situations (such as multiculturalism) while also serving alternative agendas (e.g. social cohesion). Multiculturalism, in the public imagination, has been popularly conceived of as one such 'problematic situation' for politicians, policy-makers and indeed for diverse publics themselves. This is apparent in the widespread European claims that multiculturalism is a politics of recognition incompatible with collective citizenship (Lentin and Titley, 2011), a tension that is now seen to be resolved by a new social cohesion directive. The chapter draws on these dynamic contentions around policy functions, motivations and predicaments by putting the spotlight on *creative* diversity as a mechanism through which 'race' is now being publicly managed.

## Mediations of multiculture: Mapping the changes in PSB

If 'multiculture' describes the lived realities of a society's cultural heterogeneity, 'multicultural*ism*' refers to strategies designed to govern or manage 'the problems of diversity and multiplicity which multicultural societies throw up' (Hall, 2000: 210). While there are various interpretations of multiculturalism (or multicultural*isms*) (Hall, 2000), state-sponsored multiculturalism had itself publicly redirected the attention away from the evolving anti-racist movement of the 1970s and 1980s (Gilroy, 1987). Multiculturalist principles employed an overt group-based approach in which certain ethnic communities were targeted for inclusion and access. Although not without its own politics of limitation and ghettoisation (Cottle, 2000), this version of state multiculturalism should be noted for being written into media policy and commissioning structures, and for being grounded in a particular (albeit soft) version of anti-racism.

It is this version of multiculturalism that has, since the turn of the millennium, been actively undermined as a normative principle within wider political and public discourse. For Lentin and Titley (2011) this crisis of multiculturalism has become *the* contemporary articulation of racism, mediated and managed by the strategising and neoliberalising of 'good diversity' and citizenship (Horsti, 2009; Lentin and Titley, 2011).

State-led social cohesion provides a space in which more assimilation can be pressed for, in which a proliferation of social anxieties can converge (particularly acute with the global security agenda after the War on Terror) and where we can relegate racism to the past.

The expansive scholarly work on the crisis of multiculturalism has highlighted its connection with 'post-racial' discourse. The idea of post-race (Gallagher, 2008) is predicated on a theory of racelessness (Goldberg, 2006) rather than on support for a post-racial state in which racial equality has been achieved. We can relate these wider social trends (in which a new preferred assimilationist model of managing social and cultural difference exists) to the rise of creative diversity. The collective language of citizenship within a liberal polity has popular appeal because it values what we all value (flexibility, creativity and imagination), as does 'creative diversity'. We are all invited, and indeed expected, to be included in its broad 'diversity' frame. Like the discourse of 'meritocracy' which has been 'normalised as wholly beneficial' (Littler, 2013: 53), I suggest here that 'creative diversity' is further evidence of the ways in which difference, diversity and equality have been marketised under neoliberalism (Littler, 2013). Nicholas Garnham suggests that creative industries policy is centred on four key themes – 'access', 'excellence', 'education' and 'economic value' (Garnham, 2005) – and versions of these are apparent in the creative diversity vision. It is a policy frame that involves a pro-creative not pro-cultural vision in line with a broader 'creative industries turn' that led in UK broadcasting to 'the need to open British broadcasting to international competition, consolidation and inward investment in order to compete in the global programme market' (Garnham, 2005: 26).

The timing of the crisis of multiculturalism has also been noted for its significant impact on European PSB systems and representations (Horsti and Hultén, 2011; Horsti et al., 2014; Leurdijk, 2006). It has coincided with a contrasting PSB drive strategised as an institutionalised and redemptive (from the old order of multiculturalism) mainstreaming of diversity.

## Signs of 'creative diversity' in public communication

Before I go on to pinpoint instances where 'creative diversity' (as a discourse of public value) has become central to this public-service drive, I want to signal an important link with the broader equality legislative setting. The UK has recently seen a restructuring of the 'equality architecture' (Walby et al., 2012) during the formation of the Equality and Human Rights Commission and under New Labour in 2007. This was cemented by the 2010 Equality Act (Government Equalities Office, 2011a), which adopts a single legal framework (covering nine 'protected characteristics' of which race is one), thus merging together different areas of discrimination law including the Race Relations Act 1976. One aspect of the act is the Public Sector Equality Duty (PSED), making the public service broadcasters' current diversity strategies the mechanism for their response to the new duty (Government Equalities Office, 2011b). This legislative background is one against which we can start to understand the rise of 'creative diversity'.

The creative diversity agenda formulates ideas of 'quality' and 'creativity' over (structural) questions of (in)equality. In periodising the shift from 'multiculturalism' and 'cultural diversity' to 'creative diversity', we see how each incarnation becomes increasingly all-encompassing, including and containing all possible forms of diversity in society (van Ewijk, 2011) and claiming to broaden access 'to the widest possible range of cultural experiences' (Garnham, 2005: 27). In fact, each element of the newest policy paradigm suggests a departure from the welfare and structural concerns identifiable in earlier (multiculturalist) media policy and an orientation towards market and industrial priorities, dealt with by 'creativity'. On the question of why 'creative' (diversity) rather than 'cultural' (diversity), we can identify a parallel with arts and media policy debates about the terms 'creative industries' and 'cultural industries' linked to the competitive global economy (Garnham, 2005). The rise of creative industries policy becomes a key backdrop against which this shift from cultural to creative occurs and highlights how PSB is also implicated in the overarching shift towards neoliberal market models.

So where do we find discourses of 'creative diversity' in PSB and what are the connections with its antecedents: 'cultural diversity' and, prior to that, 'multiculturalism'?

Notable in identifying the shift from 'cultural' to 'creative' is the industry-wide Cultural Diversity Network (CDN) of which the BBC and Channel 4 are both members (and which the BBC currently chairs). The CDN was originally set up in 2000 to promote cultural diversity and was therefore an organisation founded specifically to deal with issues of diversity in the industry. In 2011 it merged with the Broadcasting and Creative Industries Disability Network, announcing 'a new name to reflect the network's remit' (CDN, 2011), the *Creative* Diversity Network. The significance of the literal replacing of 'Cultural' with

'Creative' in this instance is that the network's members include all the major UK public service and commercial broadcasters, demonstrating both the current expansiveness of 'creative diversity' and its triumph over cultural diversity within media policy. The rebranded CDN declares its priority 1 as 'Making the business case for diversity' (CDN, 2011). With regard to ethnicity within this broader schema, it seeks to 'put a greater focus on BAME [Black and Minority Ethnic]-led initiatives aimed at senior level recruitment' and collate data to help members understand 'diversity within diversity' (CDN, 2011).

Although it goes much wider, the new principles of 'creative diversity' are also evident within the BBC and Channel 4 – public service broadcasters that are more or less considered together in what follows because of their manifest derivative politics in how they attempt to 'out public service the other' in their responses to ethnic minorities.

Of specific note is the BBC's current diversity strategy, 'Everyone has a story: The BBC's diversity strategy 2011–15', unveiled in 2011 and approved by the BBC Trust, the governing body of the BBC. According to the BBC's head of diversity, Amanda Rice, the strategy is influenced by two things: 'our desire to connect with all audiences to ensure licence fee-payers' feedback helped shape the strategy, and the recently introduced Equality Act 2010' (Rice, 'Everyone has a story – the BBC's new diversity strategy', 24 May 2011). Diversity policy at the BBC is now organised into three main pillars: this new diversity strategy, the equality information report ('Telling our story', BBC, 2011) in line with the specific duties under the PSED and finally its divisional diversity action plans, required by each BBC division. Close analysis of these BBC documents reveals two key messages: first, the idea of an all-encompassing 'One BBC' (Rice, op. cit.) aligned with the new single equality legislative framework; and second, a business-oriented case for 'creative diversity'. The 'context for a new diversity strategy' is that 'the challenges of diversity in the UK offer a genuinely creative opportunity' (BBC, 2011). Thus the 'challenges' produced by cultural diversity can be resolved by creativity.

A major facet within these scripts is 'quality', led by the BBC's 'Delivering quality first' (DQF) (2012) editorial strategy that coincided with the approval of its new six-year licence-fee settlement. DQF for the BBC is about the '*best* journalism, *outstanding* children's content, *inspiring* knowledge, music and culture, *ambitious* UK drama and comedy...' (BBC, 2011; my emphasis). Also clear is the weight given to 'strategy', 'procurement' and 'people'. Therefore 'Equality analysis of non-content related activity will become increasingly important' (BBC performance return on the public sector equality duty: Quarter 1 2011–12). Specifically, equality concerns are configured around the diversity profile of the workforce – for example, in strategic and senior posts, employment policy, divisional restructuring, board procurement and 'Delivering quality first' (BBC, 2012). The shift in these guiding principles is not just towards questions of recruitment practice and human resources (talent, training, mentoring and development) but away from the more contested, messy, ideological terrain of cultural representation. Implicit is that more diverse recruitment and 'creative workers' (see Garnham, 2005) will make the difference for the equality agenda. This turn away from questions of representation and identity politics is the critical dimension of the story of the rise of creative industries policy (and the shift away from 'multiculturalism' and 'cultural industries' policy).

Over at Channel 4, 2010 saw the unveiling of a new 'fully converged content and commissioning structure' (Channel 4, 2010, http://www.channel4sales.com/news/print/148) in which the cultural diversity team now reports (along with indie relations, the disability executives and the paralympics (coverage) team) into a new position, the director of creative diversity (headed by Stuart Cosgrove). The primary concern of Channel 4's conceptualisation of creative diversity is based on diversity of supply and regional diversity, helping drive the commission of multiplatform content from newer companies through to the regions (Channel 4, 2010). The absorption of cultural diversity under the rubric of creative diversity is a significant development for this fascinating public service broadcaster and suggests a further attempt to remove race or outdated identity politics from 'diversity' matters. Indeed, Channel 4 in its diversity strategy for 2011 openly welcomes the new single Equality Act because it sees it as being 'entirely consistent with Channel 4's own objectives' (Channel 4, 2012). For Channel 4 now, 'Diversity is not about the colour of someone's skin; it goes way beyond that. Diversity is about being all-inclusive, regardless of culture ... race' and so on because 'Diversity of thought and opinion helps us to innovate, be distinctive and encourage people to think in different ways' (Channel 4, 2012: 1). Thus the openness of the term 'diversity' is utilised by Channel 4 here and overlaid with an emphasis on innovation and creativity, which draws parallels with how it tends to operate within creative industries policy at large. It is possible for cultural diversity to be subsumed into the rhetoric of creativity because of the wider creative industries turn that now guides arts and media policy-making.

## Meanings of 'creative diversity' after multiculturalism

I want to pull together these various sets of concerns to suggest that through 'creative diversity' the major contemporary dilemma of multiculturalism in social and cultural life is reconfigured as a 'post-racialised' modality of public service. Creative diversity policies are underpinned by market, regulatory and social motivations, meeting marketplace requirements, safeguarding PSB interests and ultimately shifting the paradigm of the multicultural problem (in PSB and beyond). Basically, by renaming and reframing cultural diversity as 'creative diversity', three major, overlapping market, regulatory and social predicaments are dealt with.

### Market: 'Creative diversity' and creative enterprise in the cultural industries

First, it attends to the *market* predicament by mobilising an innovation imperative for particular kinds of (ethnic) creativity or excellence (with an emphasis on popular formats and styles of programming; Lunt, 2009; Malik, 2013) rather than fixate on social concerns. Importantly, this serves the logic of the contemporary broadcasting marketplace very well and, in turn, a neoliberal register of cultural governance.

What these 'creative diversity' scripts start to tell us about updated principles of 'public service', branding and accountability is that 'quality' and 'creativity' are now foregrounded over (structural) questions of (in)equality. Human resources becomes more important than content, and a broad sense of diversity is promoted rather than the naming of specific (ethnic) communities. Furthermore, the ubiquitous creative diversity paradigm is shaped by a pro-creative agenda and openly *not* by a politics of recognition of social or cultural difference.

### Regulatory: Diversity policies, institutional requirements and PSB

Second, it settles *regulatory* and remit predicaments by both promoting itself as a source of 'diversity' (and hence public value) and enabling compliance with wider legislative and policy frameworks – namely, the PSED component of the single Equality Act 2010. In these ways, diversity – vis-à-vis creativity – becomes just another means for public organisations to promote themselves and allow the 'accumulation of organisational value' (Ahmed, 2012: 110).

Taken together, new diversity in media policy cements the value of public service when PSB is most in need of public justification. I attribute the role of social change, the single legislative settling and the state in rejecting principles of multiculturalism to the ways in which an environment has been provided for PSB to *be able to* transfer its priorities to an increasingly culturally unspecific trope of 'diversity' through a unifying diversity frame. While these operate in relation to the market, not from a politics of equality, it is also necessary to bring to light the particular (less market-focused) ethical (social, political and cultural) dilemmas involved in public communication (Born, 2006).

### Social: Policy and post-'crisis of multiculturalism' thinking

Finally, it deals with *social* predicaments by attaching itself to strategic 'creative' objectives that are already present in the cultural sector, such as innovation, quality and excellence (see McMaster, 2008). In so doing, a depoliticised, raceless 'diversity' consensus is achieved, taking the heat out of 'the multicultural problem', smoothing over difference, and deflecting claims of special treatment and rights because we are now *all* included in this intentionally culturally unspecific (and socially cohesive) 'creative' frame.

Current predicaments are seemingly resolved through 'creative diversity' 'speech acts', rendered so because while they pertain to public value and interest, they produce an ambivalent response to a thriving lived multiculture. A politics of racelessness, which forms part of the critique presented here, is retrenched by blurring the moral, social and economic case for diversity. The conventional metaphors of community, access and inclusion are implied, but it is the arguments of the market state (that have traditionally worked against such ideas) which are declared through the new economy of 'creativity'.

## Conclusion

This analysis has identified the emergence of 'creative diversity' and set this within parallel 'crisis of multiculturalism' contexts in order to contribute to debates about PSB, multiculturalism and citizenship – all highly significant in wider discussions around the media and the margins. I have discussed the implications and currency of 'diversity' in these evolving policy settings, what it really represents and how it is *acted out*. I have explicated the 'racelessness' of creative diversity rhetoric, through its lack of engagement with inequalities and racisms. The crux of my argument is that quality/creativity have been foregrounded over structural inequality in recent policy developments and that 'creative diversity' is essentially founded upon the denial of social and cultural difference. Creative diversity demonstrates the depoliticisation of race in PSB contexts.

The issue remains of whether future PSB will be a likely vehicle for diversity issues except insofar as ensuring 'creative content' unlikely to be provided by other parts of the market. The fallout is that PSB as a truly unifying space continues to be undermined, in spite of its potential as one of 'the primary "theatres" for contemporary pluralism' (Born, 2006: 114) or, indeed, as a progressive multicultural public sphere.

## References

Ahmed, S. (2012) *On Being Included: Racism and Diversity in Institutional Life.* Durham, NC: Duke University Press.

BBC. (2011). 'Everyone has a story: The BBC's diversity strategy 2011–15'. Retrieved from: http://www.bbc.co.uk/diversity/strategy/documents.html

BBC. (2012). Delivering quality first. Retrieved from: http://www.bbc.co.uk/bbctrust/our_work/strategy/delivering_quality_first.html

Born, G. (2000) Inside television: Television studies and the sociology of culture. *Screen.* 41(4), 404–424.

Born, G. (2006) Digitising democracy, in J. Lloyd. and J. Seaton (eds) *What Can Be Done? Making the Media and Politics Better.* Oxford: Blackwell, Special book issue of *Political Quarterly*, 102–123.

Channel 4. (2012) Equality objectives. Retrieved from: http://www.channel4.com/media/documents/corporate/C4_Equality_Objectives_2012.pdf

Cottle, S. (2000) *Ethnic Minorities and the Media: Changing Cultural Boundaries.* Open University Press.

Creative Diversity Network (CDN) (2011) Retrieved from: http://www.creativediversitynetwork.org/index.php

Du Gay, P., Hall, S., Negus, K., Mackay, H. and Janes, L. (1997) *Doing Cultural Studies: The Story of the Sony Walkman:* London and New Delhi: Sage (Culture, Media and Identities Series).

Gallagher, C. A. (2008) *Racism in Post-Race America: New Theories, New Directions.* Chapel Hill, NC: Social Forces Publishing.

Garnham, N. (2005) From cultural to creative industries: An analysis of the implications of the creative industries' approach to arts and media policy making in the United Kingdom. *International Journal of Cultural Policy.* 11(1), 15–29.

Gilroy, P. (1987) *There Ain't No Black in the Union Jack. The Cultural Politics of Race and Nation.* London: Unwin Hyman.

Goldberg, D. T. (2006) Racial Europeanization. *Ethnic and Racial Studies.* 29(2), 331–364.

Government Equalities Office [GEO] (2011a) *Equality Act 2010.* Retrieved from: http://www.equalities.gov.uk/equality_bill.aspx

Government Equalities Office [GEO] (2011b) *Equality Act 2010.* Public Sector Equality Duty. Retrieved from: http://www.homeoffice.gov.uk/equalities/equality-act/equality-duty/

Hall, S. (1997a) *Representation: Cultural Representations and Signifying Practices.* London, Thousand Oaks, New Delhi: Sage Publications in association with the Open University.

Hall, S. (1997b) The centrality of culture: notes on the cultural revolutions of our time, in Kenneth Thompson (ed) *Media and Cultural Regulation.* London: Thousand Oaks, Sage, 207–238.

Hall, S. (2000) Conclusion: The multi-cultural question, in B. Hesse (ed) *Un/Settled Multiculturalisms: Diasporas, Entanglements, Transruptions.* London, New York: Zed Books.

Horsti, K. (2009) Antiracist and multicultural discourses in European public service broadcasting: Celebrating consumable differences in the Prix Europa Iris Media Prize. *Communication, Culture & Critique.* 2(3), 339–360.

Horsti, K. and Hultén, G. (2011) Directing diversity: Managing cultural diversity media policies in Finnish and Swedish public service broadcasting. *Journal of Cultural Studies.* 14(2), 209–227.

Horsti, K., Hultén, G. and Titley, G. (2014) *National Conversations: Public Service Media and Cultural Diversity in Europe.* Bristol and Chicago: Intellect.

Kumar, K. (1977) Holding the middle ground: The BBC, the public and the professional broadcaster, in J. Curran, M. Gurevitch, and J. Woollacott (eds) *Mass Communication and Society.* London: Edward Arnold (Publishers) Ltd, 231–248.

Kundnani, A. (2007) *The End of Tolerance: Racism in Twenty-First Century Britain.* London: Pluto Press.

Lentin, A. (2012) Post-race, post politics: The paradoxical rise of culture after multiculturalism. *Ethnic and Racial Studies.* 1–19, iFirst Chapter.

Lentin, A. and Titley, G. (2011) *The Crises of Multiculturalism: Racism in a Neoliberal Age.* London and New York: Zed Books.

Leurdijk, A. (2006) In search of common ground: Strategies of multicultural producers in Europe. *European Journal of Cultural Studies.* 9(1), 25–46.

Littler, J. (2013) Meritocracy as plutocracy: The marketising of 'equality' within neoliberalism. *New Formations: A Journal of Culture/theory/Politics.* 80–81, 52–72.

Lunt, P. (2009) Television, public participation and public service: From value consensus to the politics of identity. *The ANNALS of the American Academy of Political and Social Science.* 625, 128–138.

McMaster, B. (2008) *Supporting excellence in the arts: From measurement to judgement.* Department of Culture, Media and Sport. Retrieved from: http://www.artscouncil.org.uk/publication_archive/mcmaster-review-supporting-excellence-in-the-arts-from measurement-to-judgement/

Malik, S. (2013) The Indian family on UK reality television: Convivial culture in salient contexts. *Television and New Media.* 14(6), 510–528.

Rice, A. (2011). Everyone has a story–the BBC's new diversity strategy. *BBC.* Retrieved from: http://www.bbc.co.uk/blogs/aboutthebbc/posts/everyone_has_a_story_the_bbcs_new_diversity_strategy

Saha, A. (2012) 'Beard, scarves, halal meat, terrorists, forced marriage': Television industries and the production of 'race'. *Media, Culture and Society.* 34(4), 424–438.

van Eeten, M. J. G. (2007) Narrative policy analysis, in F. Fischer, G. Miller, and M. S. Sidney (eds) *Handbook of Public Policy Analysis: Theory, Politics, and Methods.* Boca Raton: CRC/Taylor and Francis, 251–269.

van Ewijk, A. R. (2011) Diversity and diversity policy: Diving into fundamental differences. *Journal of Organizational Change Management.* 24(5), 680–694.

Walby, S., Armstrong, J. and Strid, S. (2012) Intersectionality and the quality of the gender equality architecture. *Social Politics.* 19(4): 446–481 (first published online 31 October 2012).

# 7

# Victims at the Margins? A Comparative Analysis of the Use of Primary Sources in Reporting Personal Tragedy in Norway and the UK

*Jackie Newton and Lene Brennodden*

While stories of death and disaster dominate the headlines, it is concerns about intrusion into grief that have understandably shaped ethical thinking about the journalistic reporting of such tragedies. Journalism is intrusive by nature (Newton and Duncan, 2012), and violent death always comes with its own 'intimate story of loss, grief, betrayal and violation' (Fullerton and Patterson, 2006: 305). For the journalist covering such stories, the demands are formidable and the ethical dilemmas intense, so it is little wonder that contact with bereaved families is seen as intrusive and avoidance of such contact the more ethical option, despite the families identifying themselves as the primary sources in the stories of their loss. Of course, not all deaths are recorded in the media, and many are reported only briefly, without personal factors such as photographs, obituaries or comment from their family or friends (Greer, 2007). For those left behind, their loved one becomes 'a man; a woman; a nurse; a construction worker' whose death is recorded factually without acknowledgement of their life.

Whatever the level of contact and amount of coverage, the mode of reporting and the representation of the victim have an effect on the families of those reported on (Newton, 2011). This chapter investigates the reporting of murder, manslaughter and deaths in road collisions in both the UK and in Norway, the latter seen as offering a model of journalistic self-regulation (Kirchner, 2012), in an attempt to assess the role given to families in stories of their bereavement. First, specific literature related to the coverage of death in the media and the relationship between the bereaved and reporters is considered. The respective regulatory and ethical environments in the UK and Norway are described, and the differences in perception of ethical standards are discussed. The following analysis of the coverage of fatal tragedy in a sample of newspapers from both countries is two-fold: a content analysis of the sources used in stories of death followed by an analysis of the imagery accompanying the stories.

## Intrusion or inclusion?

According to Coté and Simpson, the willingness of suffering people to talk to the news media does not give reporters a licence to interview them. They argue that journalists should not hesitate to decide that it is a bad time to interview a victim or a bereaved family, saying: 'the ethical burden is not on the interview subject but on the reporter' (2006: 101). It is an understandable assertion, bearing in mind that those in grief are perceived as needing a greater degree of privacy than others (Kieran et al., 2000). Yet while this would appear to be a reasonable position, it is one with which Newton (2011) takes issue, as it seemingly takes away the choice and therefore the control from the person at the heart of the story:

> Arguably no human being would want to trample over a bereaved person's right to mourn in private, and journalists have been shown to be no exceptions to this. However when we 'walk away' (Cote and Simpson, 2006) or 'phone in to the office with an excuse (Keeble, 2000; Castle, 1999) are we denying the family the right to involvement in a story that is essentially theirs, not ours?
>
> (2011: 2)

The argument here is that ethical concerns about death reporting tend to focus on the protection of the grieving and not on their inclusion. The study found that bereaved families define themselves as primary sources in such reporting and are distressed by the neglect of their viewpoint. It also found that some families felt excluded by the news, despite a willingness to cooperate with journalists (2011: 1). These findings are supported by the US National Centre for Victims of Crime and the National Organisation for Victim Assistance which both agree that 'families of crime victims deserve the right to participate in news coverage of their dead family member', and that interviews can be 'therapeutic' and a way to 'give a face and voice to the victims' (Rentschler, 2007: 227). The UK-based Disaster Action organisation recognises that approaches to the bereaved are often based on 'a desire to understand the first-hand experience of a disaster' and that such interviews can acknowledge the importance of the life and death of a victim and the consequences of such loss. The public acknowledgement of grief through communications such as obituaries, tributes and commemorative journalism is well documented (Duncan and Newton, 2010; Griffith, 2004; Roberts, 2006). Sensitive death stories have prompted public action and reaction, and have been acknowledged as memorials to the deceased (Griffith, 2004; Linklater, 1996). Again, in terms of public interest, some studies suggest the media helps a community understand tragedy and come to terms with loss (Griffith, 2004; Kitch and Hulme, 2008; Riegert and Olsson, 2007; Thomas, 2005). It is also posited that speaking about death and the experience of loss can be cathartic for interviewees, and that victims can gain 'mastery' over feelings of shock and helplessness by 'giving testimony' (Griffith, 2004; Raphael, 1986; Tait, 1996). This need to communicate with the wider community occurs through the web and social media even when journalists show little or no interest in the story, with relatives and friends using memorial sites and tribute pages on social media to express their grief (Duncan and Newton, 2010; Gibson, 2001).

Despite this evidence detailing the more positive aspects of the sensitive coverage of tragedy, the debate about the ethics of death reporting tends to focus on the paradox between the public's right to know and the right of the bereaved to privacy in their grieving. These are important and often contradictory concepts in such ethical consideration but they are by no means the only concerns. The picture becomes more complex when we consider the rights of the bereaved to be included in their own story versus the journalists' unwillingness to intrude on grief. When researching attitudes to the 'death knock' – the practice of contacting and interviewing bereaved relatives or close friends immediately after a tragic death – Duncan and Newton (2010) found that of the three groups of people consulted, journalists, journalism educators and bereaved families, it was the journalists who were the most negative about the practice, and the families who were most likely to be understanding of why that intrusion takes place. This finding is worrying in that there may well be families who want to speak to the media but are being marginalised in the coverage by the self-censorship of journalists who are unsure about the ethics of the practice.

## Press ethics and death reporting in Norway and the UK

The UK's National Union of Journalists, the BBC the UK's new newspaper self-regulatory body the Independent Press Standards Organisation (IPSO) and Norsk presseforbund (the Norwegian press association, NPA) all have codes of conduct addressing the issue of harm and offence, and intrusion into grief. IPSO notes in section 5 of its code of practice: 'In cases involving personal grief or shock, enquiries and approaches must be made with sympathy and discretion and publication handled sensitively.' The NPA writes in its code of conduct: 'Always consider how reports on accidents and crime may affect the victims and next-of-kin. Show consideration towards people in grief or at times of shock' (Norsk presseforbund, 2007). Intrusion into grief and causing someone harm are both contentious issues within ethical reporting, and, as Frost says, 'as with many moral judgements, one person's idea of what constitutes intrusion is another person's polite enquiry' (2011: 107).

The ethics of the UK press and its future regulation have been under scrutiny since the phone-hacking scandal, the subsequent Leveson Inquiry in 2011/12, the closure of the *News of the World* in 2011 and the jailing of former editor Andy Coulson in 2014. The fallout has set journalist against journalist, and resulted in police resources being diverted from major crime and terrorism to track down national newspaper reporters and their celebrity victims. At the centre of this perhaps unprecedented concern about media ethics was the hacking of a young murder victim's phone – the so-called 'Dowler effect' (Duncan and Newton, 2012). Stories had been emerging for some time about the hacking of celebrities' and Royals' phones, but it took this criminal act against a young murder victim to put the phone-hacking scandal at the top of the public and political agenda.

Phone-hacking is the latest in a series of concerns about the ethics of UK newspapers, which usually focus on the 'red top' tabloids and have evolved over a number of years to encompass news-gathering techniques as well as material published (Frost, 2011). Jempson and Powell (2012) suggest that complaints and controversies similar to those highlighted in the phone-hacking scandal have existed in some form for many decades, dating from the first Royal Commission on the Press in 1947, which looked into the commercial pressures on news values following the lifting of wartime censorship and shortages of newsprint, and continuing through the 'Calcutt years' of the late 1980s and 1990s when Sir David Calcutt QC led two reviews of press conduct, prompted in part by the 'stalking' of Princess Diana. The newspapers were told they were 'drinking in the last chance saloon' by Tory politician David Mellor in 1991, but decades later the UK press is still self-regulating in its chosen way, ignoring the findings of Leveson (Greenslade, 2014):

> There have been periodic outbreaks of concern about press intrusion and sensationalism and demands for statutory controls, none of which have had much impact in terms of curtailing press excesses.
>
> (Jempson and Powell, 2012)

As a contrast to the woes of the UK press, Scandinavian countries are often seen as beacons of good practice and restraint. They are consistently ranked highest in the world for both freedom of the press and participatory democracy (*Columbia Journalism Review*, 2012), and Norway's press council itself has been described as a case of 'self-regulation done right'. 'By all accounts the Scandinavian press council model is healthy, effective, and held in high regard' (Kirchner, 2012). The Norwegian 'one-stop shop ethics regime' has been put forward as a model for the reform of Australia's system into a more user-friendly process. There are 'lessons to be learned' from Norway, according to Lidberg (2011). This perception that Norway's press has higher ethical standards exists domestically, too. Bruras (2011) sees it as a good thing that Norwegian journalists 'keep a distance' from survivors and next of kin:

> The Norwegian press has a reputation for maintaining quite high ethical standards compared to that of many other countries. The news media are reluctant when it comes to calling on, interviewing and taking photos of human beings stricken by accidents or crimes. They normally keep a distance to survivors and next of kin who do not want to step forward, and news media do not publish photographs of dead or seriously injured people at the scene of an accident or a crime.
>
> (Bruras, 2011)

However the Norwegian press is not without its critics. Some members of the public who complained to Norsk pressforbund after the Utøya massacre thought journalists were more concerned with sensational headlines and pictures than with the impact such coverage would have on the victims, and their family and friends. One survivor of the attacks objected to the frequency with which a daily tabloid, *Dagbladet*, featured Breivik's photograph on its front page in the following weeks. Three other survivors, who escaped from Utøya by swimming away as Breivik shot at them, said they were retraumatised by a series of *Verdens Gang* photographs of Breivik's reconstruction of his crimes for the Oslo police.

Bearing in mind the reputation of Norway's press council worldwide, it is interesting to look at the results of these complaints about the coverage of the Utøya massacre. According to Kirchner, the council found that *Dagbladet* 'had not breached the journalistic code of ethics with its frequent coverage of Anders Behring Breivik on its front page, as the universal news value of the story merited that frequency'. *Verdens Gang* was also judged not to have breached the code with its graphic coverage of Breivik's re-enactment of his crimes, but rather that the paper had showed 'sensitivity' to survivors by only running the most disturbing photos on its inside pages rather than on its front cover. It appears from these judgements that news values trump retraumatising victims as their complaints were ultimately rejected, raising questions about why the regulatory system is deemed to be such a robust model. Arguably it is the bureaucratic efficiency and the early acknowledgement of such complaints that commentators find particularly effective rather than the outcomes for the complainants (Table 7.1).

## Analysing the sources

This study tested the perceived high ethical standards of two Norwegian newspapers along with two UK newspapers in terms of the representation of the victims of personal tragedies. The focus here was on inclusion of those 'primary sources' rather than intrusion into grief, and the journalistic product was analysed rather than the interviewing process. The conclusions of Newton (2011) were adapted as a content analysis tool on the basis that the study would assess whether the victims of tragedy

*Table 7.1* UK versus Norwegian newspapers

|  | Total no. of stories | Total no. of words | Words about the victim | Words about the perpetrator | Words from the family |
|---|---|---|---|---|---|
| UK newspapers | 77 | 38,030 | 6,397 (16.8%) | 6,869 (18.1%) | 5,975 (15.7%) |
| Norwegian newspapers | 82 | 40,114 | 2,571 (6.4%) | 8,262 (20.9) | 1,999 (5%) |

have a voice in the stories of their personal tragedies or risk being marginalised in the coverage. A detailed content analysis of *Dagbladet*, *Verdens Gang*, *The Independent* and *The Mirror* was undertaken with the primary aim of identifying sources and recording the percentage of coverage given to victims, alleged perpetrators and families. The project was carried out in two stages: *Dagbladet* and *The Independent* were analysed in November, December and January 2011, and *The Mirror* and *Verdens Gang* in April, May and June 2013. (Timing was convenience sampling based on the availability of researchers.) The choice of the papers was dependent on a number of factors but because the whole editions needed to be analysed, access to the full electronic editions was a limitation. For instance, the original aim was to look at *The Sun* rather than *The Mirror*, but there was no electronic archive available. The two Norwegian newspapers analysed were chosen partly because of the public complaints made against them after the Utøya massacre and partly because they are reasonably comparable to the UK papers in terms of audience demographic, although it is difficult to find true comparisons because the Norwegian media do not have the UK's tabloid/broadsheet divide (Eide, 1997; Sparks, 2000). To make the findings of Newton (2011) as relevant as possible, cases of murder, manslaughter and deaths in road accidents were examined (Table 7.2).

Norway's official population is much smaller than the UK's – some 5.1 million (Central Bureau of Statistics) vs. 64.1 million (Office for National Statistics), and the countries' respective murder rates also differ, with Norway's averaging 0.6 per 100,000 in the ten years between 2002 and 2012 (excluding the anomalous year of the Utøya massacre) and the

*Table 7.2*   Source frequency by newspaper

| | Total no. of stories | Total no. of words | Words about the victim | Words about the accused/ offender | Words from the family |
|---|---|---|---|---|---|
| *The Independent* | 24 | 9,638 | 1,658 (17.2%) | 1,059 (11%) | 697 (7.2%) |
| *Dagbladet* | 44 | 17,310 | 1,365 (7.9%) | 3,227 (18.6%) | 327 (1.9%) |
| *The Mirror* | 53 | 28,392 | 4,739 (16.7%) | 5,810 (20.5%) | 5,278 (18.6%) |
| *Verdens Gang* | 38 | 22,804 | 1,206 (5.3%) | 5,035 (22%) | 1,672 (7.3%) |

UK's averaging 1.2 per 100,000 during the same period, although this is a declining figure (United Nations Office on Drugs and Crime). It is clear, then, that personal tragedy plays a larger part in the news agenda of the Norwegian press than it does in the UK (see Table 7.2). Despite this, it was found that families of the deceased played a much more marginal part in the Norwegian press stories of murder, manslaughter and death by alleged driver negligence or error (5% of coverage compared with 15.7% in the UK sample), and that the emphasis was on details of the crime or on the alleged offender. The two UK newspapers studied were more likely to include details and quotes gained directly from the families than their Norwegian counterparts, and one of the effects of this treatment was that stories were more likely to centre on their response and the emotion of the loss. This was a consistent finding across the newspapers compared and in both time periods studied, but the scale of difference was unexpected. Both *Dagbladet* and *Verdens Gang* focused more heavily on the perpetrator, with *Dagbladet* giving roughly double the number of words to the accused/offender than to the victim (3,227 as opposed to 1,365) and *Verdens Gang* giving almost four times as much coverage (5,035 as opposed to 1,026 for the victim). By contrast, *The Independent* (see Table 7.2) gave 17.2% of its coverage to the victim and 11% to the perpetrator, while *The Mirror* gave fewer words to the victim than the perpetrator (4,739 and 5,810). However, again this looks reasonably balanced when compared with *Verdens Gang*'s proportions, which were 5.3% about the victim and 22% about the perpetrator. *The Mirror* also had the largest number of words from the family at 18.6% of coverage.

Only 5 out of 44 articles in *Dagbladet* included comments from the victim's family, while *The Independent* featured quotations from the family in 9 out of 24 articles. It was also found that *Dagbladet* relied more on comments from friends rather than family, while it was the opposite in *The Independent*. When the articles were broken down to word counts, it was found that only 1.9% of the words within the Norwegian sample came from the family, while it was 7.2% for *The Independent*.

It should also be noted that the 'popular' papers in the two countries were more likely to take an ethical stance from the families' point of view than were the more 'serious' papers. Perhaps one argument from political economy is that the popular press shields its audience from such harsh realities of death, while the 'broadsheet' press is more likely to confront them with more 'truthful' graphic images and descriptions. This can certainly be argued in wartime, and with the War on Terror the boundaries of such conflict are more fluid, but in the case of domestic personal tragedy it must be less of a consideration. One explanation could be that the closeness of the popular press to its audience means its journalists are more likely to empathise with the grieving.

## Use of imagery

The media can make things much worse for victims and their families through the way that crime stories are presented – for instance, through photographs of bodies and body bags, the crime or the crime scene (Marsh and Melville, 2009: 110). According to Hanusch, written or spoken accounts can provide graphic details, but seeing blood and gore for oneself is a lot more persuasive: 'We trust photographs simply because 'seeing is believing' (2010: 55). Veteran American journalist Gene Foreman agrees that images or video of graphic violence or perceived intrusions on privacy are more potent than words in potentially disturbing the audience. Images, he says, affect people 'more viscerally' (Foreman, 2010).

The ethical challenges of providing a true representation of death and tragedy have been widely discussed (Hanusch, 2010; Morse, 2013; Zelizer, 2002) and, in the case of graphic imagery as in text, tend to fall into the dichotomy between maintaining the privacy and dignity of the victim and the public's right to know what has happened. However, much of the discussion concerns mass media events such as war, acts of terrorism and natural disasters causing mass casualties, rather than personal tragedies, which are more likely to attract regional rather than international coverage. Sometimes the editorial stance is heavily dependent on the editor's opinion, as Hanusch (2008a) reports after studying the contrasting policies of *The Australian* and *The Sydney Morning Herald*. Foreman's two-step process, which involves first recognising the words and content likely to cause offence and then weighing these against the news value of the story, is useful in that it encourages journalists to identify the elements of the dilemma, but perhaps amplifies the variables in an area without clear-cut guidelines. The different choices made by photo-editors worldwide over displaying a picture of the Madrid bombing which included a severed limb show the complexity of such choices (Irby, 2004).

Political concerns also intrude into the arena of photographing and displaying death. Morse (2013) describes a conflict between the Israeli Government and editors over the slaughter of a family. The government was keen to exploit the explicit shots of the deaths to demonstrate

Palestinian violence but the Israeli media thought the photographs too graphic and intrusive for publication. Bowen (2014) believes broadcasters go too far in censoring death, particularly in warzones, though Foreman believes the audience are unconvinced by the idea of the public's right to know and believe the media sensationalises death for its own commercial purpose.

While the quantitative element of this study allowed conclusions to be drawn about the sources involved and the choices reporters made, a qualitative analysis of the photographs accompanying these stories, based on Newton's conclusions and taking into account the work of Hanusch and Morse, identified interesting patterns which support the findings and add to the debate. In keeping with the textual content analysis, the stories were analysed to judge the main emphasis of the images – whether the focus was on the victim as they lived (e.g. pictures gained from families) or on the perpetrator. The 'taste' was also considered here, and images judged to be graphic or intrusive were analysed using Hanusch's implied death to contorted death frame and Morse's variables on the display of corpses (2013).

*Verdens Gang* featured victims as the main photographic focus in eight stories and the perpetrator in six. *The Mirror* featured victims as the main focus 29 times and the perpetrator 5 times. Whether by conscious decision or not, *The Mirror* had a preponderance of stories featuring a large picture of the victim as they were before the tragedy, and a smaller picture of the scene of crime/tragedy and/or the perpetrator. By contrast, pictures of the victims in *Verdens Gang* were generally smaller, with pictures of the scene or the perpetrator centre stage. There was no obvious 'display of corpses' (Morse, 2013) but there were numerous examples of bodies being taken from the scene on stretchers and in caskets, which arguably falls into his 'body in coffin' category and was identified by the UK's Press Complaints Commission as a source of upset for families. The size of such photographs was another variable. At least two of the shots which included a casket or body bag being removed from the clearly identifiable victim's home were almost double-page spreads on their own, making the depiction overly graphic and arguably sensational. A huge rock which fell on a car and crushed a young woman to death was given a half-page picture to itself. The type laid over the rock said: 'This rock took the life of \*\*\*\*.'

The analysis found that *The Independent* published just one photograph which can be described as graphic containing a car crash, but without blood or body bags. *Dagbladet* on the other hand had 15 articles with images that could be considered graphic. One image in particular was used in several of the articles – a photograph which showed a big glass window with blood running down it and the word 'God' written in the victim's blood. This image was placed with several rather sensational headlines, making the articles about this particular victim potentially extremely upsetting for the family to see. The Norwegian papers could be seen to be doing an about-turn on their ethical stance here, as although they do not impinge on the privacy of the victim's family physically they arguably do it graphically.

## Conclusions

In the area of sympathetic treatment of the bereaved there appears to be an ambiguity between the perceived ethical standards of the Norwegian media and the inclusion of family viewpoints. By contrast, the UK newspapers were more likely to comply with the wishes of the bereaved relatives interviewed by Newton (2011) and less likely to marginalise the victims' voices.

If Duncan and Newton's model of ethical cooperation between media and bereaved or traumatised interviewee was applied here, consisting of consent, control and context, it would appear that the Norwegian newspapers should be urged to reconsider their relationship with the victims and families in their stories. The unwillingness of reporters to intrude on privacy and grief is understandable and even commendable if the story is then dropped. However, if it goes ahead anyway, without a warning to the family or any approach that could be construed as gaining consent or offering them any element of control in how their loved one is represented, then the coverage could add to their suffering rather than avoid it. Therefore the 'distance' seen as a virtue by the Norwegian media could be a problem for the families in the initial coverage and could have a further detrimental effect in the long term.

In terms of context, reporters need to bear in mind that the incident has widespread repercussions, and the way they report it is likely to have an impact on the family's grieving. As interviewing has such a central role in news production (Adams, 2009), and the products of the interview often dictate the storyline (Steele, 2003), it would appear vital that those most affected by the tragedy are part of the coverage, whether through the dreaded 'death knock' or through a system of intermediaries.

Furthermore, the documented tendency of the Norwegian journalists to choose and publish graphic images of personal tragedy is at odds with the perception of the Norwegian media as highly ethical (Bruras, 2011) and their system of regulation as 'healthy and effective' (Lidberg, 2011). Although, as Bruras rightly says, the news media do not publish photographs of dead or seriously injured people, there were no examples of the UK newspapers adopting this practice either. However, the Norwegian newspapers do have a tendency to use 'body in coffin' photographs (Morse, 2013) and pictures from the scene of death with graphic elements such as blood, which suggest an approach favouring sensationalism over sensitivity. This was not a practice observed in the UK newspapers.

These findings pose challenging questions about the comparative ethics of death reporting and whether Norwegian journalists' well-intentioned desire to avoid intruding on grief can have the less desirable effect of excluding families from stories of their loved ones' death.

## References

Adams, S. (2009) *Interviewing for Journalists* (2nd edn). London: Routledge.

Bowen, J. (2014) We live in more violent times, no question about it. *Independent*, 9 March.

Bruras, S. (2011) Media Coverage of the Breivik Attacks. Magasinet Message. Retrieved from: http://svein-b.blogspot.co.uk/p/media-ethics-in-coverage-of-breivik.html (accessed 4 January, 2014).

Castle, P. (1999) Journalism and trauma: Proposals for change. *Asia Pacific Media Educator*. (7), 143–150.

Cote, W. and Simpson, R. (2006) *Covering Violence: A Guide to Ethical Reporting about Victims and Trauma* (2nd edn). New York: Columbia University Press.

Duncan, S. and Newton, J. (2010) How do you feel? Preparing novice reporters for the death knock, an exploration of attitudes and approaches. *Journalism Practice*. 4(4), 439–453.

Eide, M. (1997) A new kind of newspaper? Understanding a popularization process. *Media Culture Society*. 19(2), 173–182.

Foreman, G. (2010) *The Ethical Journalist: Making Responsible Decisions in the Pursuit of News*. Chichester: John Wiley and Sons.

Frost, C. (2011) *Journalism Ethics and Regulation* (3rd edn). Harlow: Longman.

Fullerton, R. S. and Patterson, M. (2006) Murder in our midst: Expanding coverage to include care and responsibility. *Journal of Mass Media Ethics*. 21(4), 304–321.

Gibson, M. (2001) Death and mourning in technologically mediated culture. *Health Sociology Review*. 15(5), 415–424.

Greenslade, R. (2014) IPSO, the new Press Regulator, is just the PCC with extra bells and whistles. *Guardian*, 8 June.

Greer, C. (2007) News media, victims and crime, in P. Davies, P. Francis, and C. Greer (eds) *Victims, Crime and Society*. London: Sage, 20–48.

Griffith, J. (2004) Private grief, public kindness. *Insight Magazine*, Winter 2004, 37.

Hanusch, F. (2008) Mapping Australian journalism culture: Results from a survey of journalists' role perceptions. *Australian Journalism Review*. 30(2), 97–109.

Hanusch, F. (2010) *Representing Death in the Media: Journalism, Media and Mortality*. Basingstoke: Palgrave Macmillan.

Irby, Kenneth (2004) Beyond taste: Editing truth. *Poynter.org*. Retrieved from: http://www.poynter.org/uncategorized/21742/beyond-taste-editing-truth/ (accessed February 2014).

Jempson, M. and Powell, W. (2012) Blame not the mobile phone, 'twas ever thus, in Richard Keeble and John Mair (eds) *The Phone Hacking Scandal: Journalism on Trial*. Bury St Edmonds: Abramis, 48–59.

Keeble, R. (2009) *Ethics for Journalists* (2nd edn). London: Routledge.

Kieran, M., Morrison, D. E. and Svennevig, M. (2000) Privacy, the public and journalism: Towards an analytic framework. *Journalism*. 1(2), 145–169.

Kirchner, L. (2012) Self-regulation done right, how Scandinavia's press councils keep the media accountable. *Columbia Journalism Review*, April 2012. Available at: http://www.cjr.org/the_news_frontier/self-regulation_done_right.php?page=all (accessed 17 Jan 2014).

Kitch, C. and Hume, J. (2008) *Journalism in a Culture of Grief*. New York: Routledge.

Lidberg, J. (2011) A one-stop shop for grievances: Norway's self-regulation model as a way to rebuild trust in Australian journalism. *Australian Journalism Review*. 1–33(2), 129–143.

Linklater, M. (1996) Why Dunblane was different. *British Journalism Review*. 7 (2), 15–19.

Marsh, I. and Gaynor, M. (2009) *Crime, Justice and the Media*. Oxford: Routledge.

Morse, T. (2013) Covering the dead. *Journalism Studies*. 15(1), 98–113.

Newton, J. (2011) The knock at the door: considering bereaved families' varying responses to news media intrusion. *Ethical Space: The International Journal of Communication Ethics*. 8(3–4), 7–13.

Newton, J. and Duncan, S. (2012) Hacking into tragedy: Exploring the ethics of death reporting in the social media age, in J. Mair and R. L. Keeble (eds) *The Phone Hacking Scandal: Journalism on Trial*. Bury St Edmonds: Abramis, 208–219.

Raphael, B. (1986) *When Disaster Strikes: How Individuals and Communities Cope with Catastrophe*. New York: Basic Books.

Rentschler, C. A. (2007) Victims' rights and the struggle over crime in the media. *Canadian Journal of Communication*. 32(2), 219–239.

Riegert, K. and Olsson, E. K. (2007) The importance of ritual in crisis journalism. *Journalism Practice*. 1(2), 143–158.

Roberts, P. (2006) From my space to our space: The functions of web memorial in bereavement. *The Forum*. 32(4), 1–4.

Sparks, C. (2000) The panic over tabloid news, in C. Sparks and J. Tulloch (eds) *Global Debates over Media Standards*. Lanham, MD: Rowman and Littlefield, 1–40.

Steele, B. (2003) Interviewing: The ignored skill. *Poynter.org*. Available at: http://www.poynter.org/latest-news/everyday-ethics/talk-about-ethics/12413/interviewing-the-ignored-skill/ (accessed 11 March 2014).

Tait, R. (1996) In *Dunblane: Reflecting Tragedy*. A report by the British Executive International Press Institute. London: British Executive International Press Institute, 31–33.

Thomas, M. (2005) *Every Mother's Nightmare: The Killing of James Bulger* (2nd edn). London: Pan.

Zelizer, B. (2002) Photography, journalism and trauma, in B. Zelizer and S. Allan (eds) *Journalism after September 11*. London: Routledge, 55–74.

# 8
# Public Service from the Margins: A Case Study of Diasporic Media in the UK

*Olatunji Ogunyemi*

The public service media aim to empower citizens irrespective of race, creed, ethnicity, gender or sexual orientation. However, the literature consistently concludes that the public service media fall short of satisfying the information and entertainment needs of diverse audiences in their programming (see Burns and Brugger, 2012; Cottle, 2000; Matsaganis et al., 2011; Ogunyemi, 2012; Ojo, 2006; Ross and Palydon, 2001). Such marginalisation perpetuates stereotypical representation of minority groups, portrays them as objects rather than subjects of stories, excludes them from expert sources, overlooks their contributions to the cultural and economic fabrics of the host society, and disempowers them as citizens.

To redress these challenges, all the five main established minorities in the UK – those of Indian, Pakistani, Bangladeshi, Black Caribbean and Black African background – and other smaller groups, such as Jews, Turkish and Chinese, established their own media to 'deal with issues that are of specific interest for the members of diasporic communities' (Bozdag et al., 2012: 97). But while these media contribute 'to the ethnic diversity of a multi-ethnic public sphere' (Husband, 2000: 206), they are heterogeneous in terms of institutional structure, role perceptions, content and audience appeal.

However, we have little understanding of whether diasporic media exhibit the attributes of public service media in their attempt to fill the hiatus in the provision of public service because the literature has predominantly focused on their marginality or factors that differentiate them from the mainstream media (see Karim, 2003; Matsaganis, 2011; Ogunyemi, 2012; Ojo, 2006; Rigoni and Saitta, 2012; Skjerdal, 2011).

But examining diasporic media from the prism of public service is a pertinent research inquiry because 'the political rationality of public service broadcasting (to educate, inform, and entertain) has been displaced by a new political rationality in which the paternalistic state has no role' (Jacka, 2003: 178). And it is pertinent because mainstream and diasporic journalists share a similar narrative in talking 'about having a sense of "doing it for the public"', of working as some kind of representative watchdog of the status quo in the name of the people, who "vote with their wallets" for their services (by buying a newspaper, watching or listening to a newscast, visiting and returning to a news site)' (Deuze, 2005: 447).

Such research inquiry should go beyond mere comparison of the institutional roles and should encompass a closer scrutiny of the impact of the public service ethos on role perceptions and content. Hence this chapter examines the literature on diasporic media for the attributes of the public service ethos and conducts an analysis of role perceptions and content through a case study of a diasporic press because previous 'research suggests that when it comes to role perceptions, which can be seen as expressions of different journalistic cultures, the national political context exceeds the influence of the organisational level and individual level' (Skovsgaard et al., 2012; van Dalen et al., 2010; Zhu et al., 1997).

## Attributes of public service in diasporic media

Scholars of PSB (see Burns and Brugger, 2012; Nguyen and Garcia, 2012; Ogunyemi, 2013; Powers, 2012) hardly include diasporic media in their empirical study because of the perception that they are not public service media, unlike BBC One, BBC Two, ITV, Channel 4, Channel 5, the BBC digital channels and S4C. While the diasporic media are not subject to performance monitoring by the regulatory body, the Office of Communication, a review of the literature reveals they exhibit semantic elements related to public service as they 'represent an alternative to traditional media outlets in terms of both content and purpose' (Skjerdal, 2011: 730) as presented in Table 8.1.

Mixed funding models are evident in both types of media as they balance public service and commercial imperatives. The diasporic media inform, educate and entertain by producing 'culturally relevant and locally vital information to immigrants in the host society' (Lin and Song, 2006: 362) and by playing 'important roles in educating their communities about voting rights' (Matsaganis et al., 2011: 62). They

*Table 8.1*   Semantic elements related to public service in diasporic media

| The public service ethos in public service media | Semantic elements related to public service in diasporic media |
| --- | --- |
| Relative freedom from commercial concerns. | Mixed funding models (grants, sales, advertising). |
| Provide entertainment, education and information for a mass audience. | Provide entertainment, education and information for a niche audience. |
| Serve their communities and contribute to nation-building. | Perform orientation role by helping audience negotiate what it means to be a citizen of a country. |
| Universal accessibility. | Appropriation of multimedia platforms including web portals, satellite, social media. |
| Universal appeal (general tastes and interests). | Appeal to the tastes and preferences of a niche audience. |
| Stimulating creativity and cultural excellence among diverse groups. | Stimulating creativity and cultural excellence among diasporic groups. |
| Represent the UK and bring it to the world and the world to it. | Perform connective role by providing sociocultural and politicoeconomic information about the homeland. |

serve communities by providing 'vital information that will help them understand what is going on around them and to make informed decisions about their lives' (Matsaganis, 2011: 15). And they are accessible by appropriating new technology, including on-demand audio and video, satellite and internet in order to act as 'a communal voice on issues of utmost importance to their audience or readership' (Ojo, 2006: 344).

The diasporic media appeal to audiences by deploying 'productions in new forms and with new kinds of content that reflect the needs and tastes of youth growing up in an increasingly globalized world' (Matsaganis et al., 2011: 261). And they stimulate creativity and cultural excellence by providing 'news coverage of local events, cultural festivals and community meetings' (Matsaganis et al., 2011: 58) and by helping their audience 'connect with other residents and become integrated into their new communities' (ibid.). Finally, they represent the host country by providing content and images which 'can reinforce familiarity with Britain's culture and history, making assimilating seem less difficult to potential migrants' (Matsaganis, 2011: 60). This appropriation of the public service ethos was made possible because of its ability to adapt to the changing media environment and of affordability of new technology to reach fragmented and niche audiences.

The implication is that the public service ethos shapes the construction and articulation of the diasporic journalists professional role perceptions and the selection and treatment of stories. Such orientation is not unusual because previous studies note similar trends with the appropriation of democratic ideals. For example, Relly et al.'s (2014) study found evidence of the impact of democratic ideals on the professional role perceptions among Iraqi Kurdish journalists. And Skovsgaard et al.'s (2012) study found that objectivity impacts on the role perceptions among journalists when performing an information role in noting that 'objectivity is more important with the role perceptions that emphasize a representative conception of democracy in which journalists inform about society, whereas it is less important when they emphasize the inclusion of citizens in a public, democratic debate" (ibid). From these perspectives it is pertinent to examine the impact of the public service ethos on role perceptions among diasporic journalists and how this is reflected in story selection and treatment.

## Methods

The researcher examined role perceptions through an in-depth interview with the managing editor, Jon Hughes, using the values that define professional journalism as a guide: 'public service (journalists provide a public service, as watchdogs or "news hounds", active collectors and disseminators of information); autonomy (journalists must be autonomous, free and independent in their work); and immediacy (journalists have a sense of immediacy, actuality and speed, inherent in the concept of "news")' (Deuze, 2005: 447). The telephone interview lasted 40 minutes and was recorded on 7 March 2013 in the studio of Siren FM, a community radio station based at the University of Lincoln, UK.

The researcher categorised the genres in the editions of *Nigerian Watch* newspaper published in September, October and November 2013 into public service and commercial content. Public service content is defined as content which delivers 'an experience that serves one or more of the public purposes defined by Ofcom . . . This content may take the form of information of value to the UK citizen, such as news and commentary, or content that delivers cultural or educational value' (Ofcom, 2008: 6). Then the researcher adopted framing analysis to identify the frame package in the public service genres – that is, news/politics (19 stories); education (8 stories); arts/culture/community (151 stories); legal issues

(6 stories); health issue (12 stories); and religious issue (3 stories), as noted in Table 8.2. The opinion (9 stories) and entertainment pages (56 stories) were not coded.

The literature notes that a frame package integrates the core frame, framing devices and reasoning devices (van Gorp and Vercruysse, 2012: 1275):

> The core frame is the implicit cultural phenomenon that defines the package as a whole, for instance, a value or archetype. The framing devices are manifest elements in a message that function as demonstrable indicators of the frame, such as vocabulary, catchphrases, and depictions. Reasoning devices form a route of causal reasoning that may be evoked when the ... [topic] is associated with a particular culturally embedded frame.'
>
> (ibid.)

These enabled the researcher to overcome the challenges noted by van Gorp (2010) that 'frame analysts must take account that their own mental construct may interfere with the identification of a frame' (ibid.).

## The impact of the public service ethos on the role perceptions

*Nigerian Watch* is a monthly newspaper launched in April 2012 in Edgware, London, and owned by Green World Media. According to the managing editor, 'it appeals predominantly to the Nigerian diaspora and friends of Nigeria from different social economic backgrounds living primarily in London and the South East' (J. Hughes, interview, 7 March 2013). The newspaper is printed on the last Friday of every month, and distributed freely across London and surrounding areas. The editor notes that 'the certified print has increased from 25,000 to 50,000 monthly due to demand and we are looking to increase again' (ibid.). Notably, the newspaper's rationale to 'inspire, inform and entertain' (*Nigerian Watch*) exhibits semantic elements related to public service, especially when you 'consider the forms in which the concept has been expressed – whether in writing and speech or as tacit knowledge in actions' (Brugger, 2012: 93).

Previous studies note that most diasporic journalists appropriate the journalistic practices of their host country. Hence Skjerdal (2011) argued that 'journalists who used to live in an oppressive media environment but now benefit from a free atmosphere with new media opportunities transform not only their working methods but their ideological approach to journalism altogether' (ibid.: 729). The data reveal evidence of a tendency to balance public service and commercial imperatives when the editor notes that 'we are a public service trying to exist on a private income' (J. Hughes, interview, 7 March 2013). However, the semantic elements related to the public service ethos were evident when he said 'our general criteria are to make something that will appeal to a great number of people, that will inform, engage and entertain' (ibid.).

There were semantic elements related to appealing to the tastes and interests of specific groups when the editor noted their focus on 'Nigerians primarily and Africans in general about issues affecting their community. In that sense we are different because we come from a different perspective' (J. Hughes, interview, 7 March 2013). This role perception is consistent with the finding that diasporic media 'operate counter-hegemonically to the mainstream media and...provide the missing social, cultural, historically, and political contexts necessary for understanding complex social realities that White Anglo journalists and editors are unlikely to understand' (Henry and Tator, 2002: 238).

The analysis found semantic elements related to serving the communities in the articulation of the newspaper's purpose – that is,

> to strengthen the community by having it more engaged and taken more seriously by others who read the paper. We do know that others do. For example, the newspaper is taken by government departments, Think Tanks such as Chatham House and that is incredibly important. The attitude of the community, the opinion and analysis of the community is understood by those people because they are in a position to influence further afield.'
>
> (J. Hughes, interview, 7 March 2013)

The data revealed semantic elements related to creativity and cultural excellence when the editor noted that

> 80 percent of Nigerian children in the UK obtain 5 O'Level and go on to A'Level and a good proportion goes on to higher Education. That attachment to aspiration and academic achievements is something we want to reflect and speak to. We are increasingly aware that we are talking to the second generation diaspora Nigerians.
>
> (J. Hughes, interview, 7 March 2013)

This role perception is consistent with the claim that 'one may find evidence of such a value by specifically examining journalists' images of their audience, and by looking at their views on what they do and how their work may affect (intended) publics – as citizens or consumers' (Deuze, 2005: 447).

There were semantic elements related to the representation of the world when the editor cautioned about the Nigerian General Election in 2015 that 'if the diaspora doesn't get the vote, there is a danger that they could drift away from the country. Nigeria should not lose the relationship with her diaspora' (J. Hughes, interview, 7 March 2013). However, there was little evidence of the appropriation of new media at a personal level when the editor noted that 'social media is one of my great failings, I do not understand and I do not really use it' (J. Hughes, interview, 7 March 2013). However, the data revealed semantic elements related to the appropriation of new media at an institutional level when the editor added that the newspaper runs 'a website which is essentially an information site which keeps readers up to date with news from Nigeria' (ibid.). This assertion is consistent with the claim that 'journalists have a sense of immediacy, actuality and speed, inherent in the concept of "news"' (Deuze, 2005: 447).

The preponderance of public service content at 55.23% compared with commercial content at 44.77% in Table 8.2 suggests the appropriation of the public service ethos in the selection of content despite the commercial imperative noted in the editor's statement that the newspaper's revenue 'is 100% from advertising. We live or die by what we turn over in our advertising revenue' (J. Hughes, interview, 7 March 2013). He explained that the newspaper derives revenue from four categories of: 'travel advertising from African businesses, diaspora who return home regularly; civil advertising from organisations like the police, local authority and charities; services from western union; and cultural advertising from African promoters or featuring African performers' (ibid.). This economic model is consistent with the claim that diasporic media provide a mixture of public and non-public service contents about 'issues such as employment, cultural identity, investment, parenting and social service, politics, business entrepreneurship and immigration affairs' (Ojo, 2006: 355). However, there was evidence to suggest that the public service ethos shapes the construction and articulation of role perception regarding editorial autonomy when the editor said that 'the advertisers have not asked me to compromise' (J. Hughes, interview, 7 March 2013).

*Table 8.2* Public service and commercial contents of *Nigerian Watch*

| Public service content | Total | Commercial content | Total |
|---|---|---|---|
| News/politics – voting, parliament | 19 (3.98%) | Personal finance, mortgages | 10 (2.09%) |
| Education | 8 (1.67%) | Travel | 2 (0.42%) |
| Arts/Theatre/culture/ community issues (parenting, events, birthdays, obituary) | 151 (31.59%) | Advertising (classified, half and full pages) | 197 (41.21%) |
| Legal issues – crime, immigration affairs | 6 (1.25%) | Real estate | 3 (0.63%) |
| Health issues | 12 (2.51%) | Travel | 2 (0.42%) |
| Religious issues | 3 (0.63%) | | |
| Opinion page – columns, letters to the editor | 9 (1.88%) | | |
| Entertainment, including film, music and sport | 56 (11.72%) | | |
| Grand total | 264 (55.23%) | | 214 (44.77%) |

## Frame package in public service genres

The data reveal a common frame package in six genres: news/politics; education; arts/culture/community; legal issues; health issues; and religious issues. These frame packages indicate how journalists 'connect a topic to notions that are part of this common ground: within a given culture, such as values, archetypes and shared narratives' (Clarke, 2006). Significantly, the analysis found that each frame package embeds semantic elements related to the public service ethos, as noted in Table 8.3. For example, the 'citizenship' and 'political participation' frame packages are most common in news/political genres as they inform and address the voting apathy among Black, Asian and minority ethnic (BAME) individuals. The editor defended this frame package by arguing that 'what we are trying to do is give the community confidence to have a voice' (J. Hughes, interview, 7 March 2013).

The 'social mobility' frame package is most common in the education genre as it addresses the challenges of educational underachievement

*Table 8.3* Frame packages in *Nigerian Watch*

| Frame packages | Definition of the issues | Causes | Consequences | Moral values involved | Possible solutions/actions | Metaphors, choice of vocabulary |
|---|---|---|---|---|---|---|
| Citizenship | Nigerians within the UK diaspora form part of a history of migration. | Migration waves began after the Second World War, followed by the Empire Windrush, which brought over 400 Caribbeans to help rebuild the UK, and by decades of migration from across the Commonwealth. | Lack of platform to address topics relevant to diasporans across the UK. | Be proud to celebrate Black history as a collective. | It is now time for diasporans to debate what the future holds. | Celebration, independence.[1] |
| Political participation | The report entitled the article quoted a report commissioned by the Operation Black Vote which reveals that 18% of all BAME citizens were not registered to vote at the last election, compared with 7% of the White population. | Many individuals feel powerless, particularly in the face of rising racial tension and the apparent inability of political parties to acknowledge persistent race inequalities, much less have a plan to deal with it. | BAME voters hold the balance of power in 241 constituencies, including 168 that are tightly contested 'marginals' – defined as being seats where the sitting MP has a majority of less than 6,000. | Political parties must wake up and realise that without the BAME vote they could lose, and devise policies to tackle persistent race inequalities. | The theory is that if the BAME community was organised and voted en masse for the party that best reflected its needs and aspirations, the BAME vote could swing the election. | We can swing 2015; it is a game changer.[2] |

| | | | | | | |
|---|---|---|---|---|---|---|
| Cultural value | A lot of the newer generations cannot relate to, or identify, their traditional rulers. | The monarchy structure has remained relevant in the political landscape of the country. | The monarchs have held no constitutional role since the monarchy system was abolished in 1963 in Nigeria. | Developing a sense of identity. | In this time of sectarian and insecurity crisis, that people generally see the diverse nature among its various people as a strength and not weakness or divide. | Like a tree without roots.[3] |
| Social responsibility | There is a need for discipline but we need to understand the difference between this and abuse. | We don't want to talk about domestic violence but in our homes there are wars with all sorts of weapons, be they knives, sticks or words. | We need to consider the impact of the economic recession because of loss of employment and the stresses that brings; and the welfare of our young people, who are experiencing gang warfare on the streets of London. | Most African parents get it wrong. | It's about trying to take ownership of our problems. So it's about time we started to talk about these issues so we can devise solutions to them, so our children can grow up in peace and prosperity. | Discipline, abuse, parenting.[4] |
| Life philosophy | Many do not pray because of unbelief. | For us to neglect the place of prayers is a sure sign that we don't believe that God can do what he says he will do when we pray to him. | Prayer is one of the greatest privileges of Christianity. | Unbelief has always been, and still is, the greatest hindrance to entering into God's provisions and engaging in a lifestyle of prayers. | Deal with the evil of unbelief and go on to enjoy the privileges of prayers. | Unbelief.[5] |

*Table 8.3* (Continued)

| Frame packages | Definition of the issues | Causes | Consequences | Moral values involved | Possible solutions/actions | Metaphors, choice of vocabulary |
|---|---|---|---|---|---|---|
| Social mobility | Though from an economically disadvantaged background, Emenike says he believes that there is no limit to what one can achieve with determination. | As a young boy growing up with my parents in the overly populated city of Lagos, I thought nothing of it each time we embarked on a journey and my father continued his old habit of giving out money to the police on duty at checkpoints. | Emenike says his interest in corruption developed from his realisation that it can be the root cause of many challenges that youth face globally, including unemployment. | I shared my beliefs with my parents and made them understand my stance regarding our value system. | The youth should reject any appearance of corruption. Most importantly, they should keep true to their words, acting upon what they profess; and one can imagine what the world would become. | Agent of change.[6] |
| Health awareness | Sickle cell anaemia (SCA) is a condition unique to people of colour, with no cure, and it is one of the world's most lethal genetic diseases. | SCA is caused by a genetic defect producing an abnormal type of haemoglobin called haemoglobin-S, which changes the shape of red blood cells, especially in conditions where oxygen levels are low, causing the cells to become crescent- or sickle-shaped. | The condition causes chronic pain and fatigue. It affects about 2% of Black people of African origin, plus people of Mediterranean and Middle Eastern descent to a lesser extent. | Inform your friends about your condition. | Treatment consists of antibiotics, oxygen therapy, blood transfusions and painkillers. Folic acid is given as a precaution against deficiency. However, even with improved treatment, life expectancy is still only just over 50 years for sufferers in the UK. | Taking control.[7] |

among Black youths. The editor defended this frame package by arguing that the newspaper aims 'to show the community that people from the community are being successful' (ibid.). The 'cultural value' frame package is most common in the arts/culture/community genres as it highlights cultural events and fosters a sense of identity among diaspora youths. Meanwhile the 'social responsibility' frame package is most common in the legal genre as it informs and addresses the grey area between the law and culturally acceptable discipline. The 'life philosophy' frame package is most common in the religious genre as it reinforces the belief system. Finally the 'health awareness' frame package is most common in the health genre as it informs about managing hereditary diseases properly and enjoying healthy living. These frame packages demonstrate that the newspaper appropriates and interprets the public service ethos to reflect both African cultural values and the shared narratives in the host country.

## Conclusion

This study shows that the diasporic press are capable of providing a public service from the margins, even if it is not explicitly expressed in their rationale. This was possible by focusing on the impact of the public service ethos on the construction and articulation of role perceptions on the one hand and on its reflection in the selection and treatment of content on the other. Significantly, the findings have implications for the role of diasporic media in the public sphere and for policy-makers in the way they engage with them. They suggest that the diasporic press complements the existing public service media and that it is worthy of recognition by policy-makers, not just as a conduit for reaching the diasporic groups but also as a vehicle for reducing social exclusion and enhancing political participation among BAME communities. However, we should not generalise the outcome of the findings because, as an exploratory study, it does not reflect how role perceptions vary among diasporic journalists working across media platforms in the UK. Therefore this subfield requires more robust empirical study to be able to conduct a cross-analysis of the diasporic media from the prism of the public service ethos.

## Acknowledgement

I thank Jon Hughes, managing editor of *Nigerian Watch*, for his support in collating the data for this study.

## Notes

1. 'It's time for a great debate' (2013) *Nigerian Watch*, October, p. 10. Available at: http://www.nigerianwatch.com/publication/ipad/Oct_2013.pdf (accessed 7 December 2013).
2. 'We can swing 2015' (2013) *Nigerian Watch*, September, p. 4. Available at: http://www.nigerianwatch.com/publication/ipad/Sept_2013.pdf (accessed 7 December 2013).
3. 'The king and I…' (2013) *Nigerian Watch*, October, p. 18. Available at: http://www.nigerianwatch.com/publication/ipad/Oct_2013.pdf (accessed 7 December 2013).
4. 'Diaspora fights back' (2013) *Nigerian Watch*, November, p. 15. Available at: http://www.nigerianwatch.com/publication/ipad/NOV_2013.pdf (accessed 7 December 2013).
5. 'Privilege of prayers – Part 2' (2013) *Nigerian Watch*, October, p. 39. Available at: http://www.nigerianwatch.com/publication/ipad/Oct_2013.pdf (accessed 7 December 2013).
6. 'Courageous story of our times wins transparency award' (2013) *Nigerian Watch*, September, p. 21. Available at: http://www.nigerianwatch.com/publication/ipad/Sept_2013.pdf (accessed 7 December 2013).
7. Living with sickle cell anaemia' (2013) *Nigerian Watch*, October, p. 30. Available at: http://www.nigerianwatch.com/publication/ipad/Oct_2013.pdf (accessed 7 December 2013).

## References

Bozdag, C., Hepp, A. and Suna, L. (2012) Diasporic media as the 'focus' of communicative networking among migrants, in R. Isabelle and S. Eugenie (eds) *Mediating Cultural Diversity in a Globalized Public Space*. London: Palgrave Macmillan, 96–115.

Brugger, N. (2012) The idea of public service in the early history of DR online, in M. Burns and N. Brugger (eds) *Histories of Public Service Broadcasters on the Web*. New York: Peter Lang, 91–104.

Burns, M. and Brugger, N. (eds) (2012) *Histories of Public Service Broadcasters on the Web*. New York: Peter Lang.

Clarke, J. N. (2006) The case of the missing person: Alzheimer's disease in mass print magazines 1991–2001. *Health Communication*. 19(3), 269 –276.

Cottle, S. (ed) (2000) *Ethnic Minorities and the Media*. Buckingham: Open University Press.

Deuze, M. (2005) What is journalism? Professional identity and ideology of journalists reconsidered. *Journalism*. 6(4), 442–464.

Henry, F. and Tator, C. (2002) Racial Profiling in Toronto: Discourses of Domination, Mediation and Opposition. Paper submitted to the Canadian Race Relations Foundation.

Hughes, J. (2013) Interview. Managing Editor of the *Nigerian Watch*, conducted on 7 March.

Husband, C. (2000) Media and the public sphere in multi-ethnic societies, in S. Cottle (ed) *Ethnic Minorities and the Media*. Buckingham: Open University Press, 199–214.

Jacka, E. (2003) Democracy as defeat: The impotence of arguments for public service broadcasting. *Television & New Media.* 4(2), 177–191.

Karim H. K. (2003) Mapping the diasporic mediascape, in H. K. Karim (ed) *The Media of Diaspora.* London: Routledge, 1–18.

Lin, W-Y. and Song, H. (2006) Geo-ethnic storytelling: An examination of ethnic media content in contemporary immigrant communities. *Journalism.* 7(3), 362–388.

Matsaganis, M. D., Katz, V. S. and Ball-Rokeach, S. J. (2011) *Understanding Ethnic Media. Producers, Consumers and Societies.* London: Sage.

*Nigerian Watch* (2013) About. Retrieved from: http://www.nigerianwatch.com/about-us (accessed 7 December).

Nguyen, A. and Garcia, A. (2012) When public service is the name of the game, in B. Maureen and B. Niels (eds) *Histories of Public Service Broadcasters on the Web.* New York: Peter Lang, 3–16.

Ofcom (2008) *Estimating the Value of Public Service Content Online.* Retrieved from: http://stakeholders.ofcom.org.uk/binaries/consultations/psb2_1/annexes/annex9.pdf (accessed 24 May 2012).

Ogunyemi, O. (2012) *What Newspapers, Film, and Television Do Africans Living in Britain See and Read? The Media of the African Diaspora.* Lewiston: The Edwin Mellen Press.

Ogunyemi, O. (2013) Challenges and prospects of delivering a diversity of public service content online: A case study of Channel 4 News Online. (2013) *Central European Journal of Communication.* 6(2–11), 234–248.

Ojo, T. (2006) Ethnic print media in the multicultural nation of Canada: A case study of the black newspaper in Montreal. *Journalism.* 7(3), 343–361.

Powers, S. (2012) From broadcast to networked journalism. The case of Al-Jazeera English, in B. Maureen and B. Niels (eds) *Histories of Public Service Broadcasters on the Web.* New York: Peter Lang, 207–219.

Relly, J. E., Zanger, M. and Fahmy, S. (2014) Professional role perceptions among Iraqi Kurdish journalists from a 'state within a state'. *Journalism.* 1–22. Online First. DOI:10.1177/1464884914550973.

Rigoni, I. and Saitta, E. (eds) (2012) *Mediating Cultural Diversity in a Globalized Public Space.* London: Palgrave Macmillan.

Ross, K. and Palydon, P. (eds) (2001) *Black Marks: Minority Ethnic Audiences and Media.* Aldershot: Ashgate.

Skjerdal, T. S. (2011) Journalists or activists? Self-identity in the Ethiopian diaspora online community. *Journalism.* 12(6), 727–744.

Skovsgaard, M., Albaek, E., Bro, P. and De Vreese, C. (2012) A reality check: How journalists' role perceptions impact their implementation of the objectivity norm. *Journalism.* 1–12. Online First. DOI:10.1177/146488492442286.

van Gorp, B. (2007) The constructionist approach to framing: Bringing culture back in. *Journal of Communication.* 57, 60–78.

van Dalen, A., De Vreese, C. and Albaek, E. (2010) Studying journalistic role conceptions and content cross-nationally. How wide is the gap between theory and practice? Paper presented at the 3rd European Communication Conference in Hamburg, 12–15 October.

van Gorp, B. (2010) Strategies to take subjectivity out of framing analysis, in P. D'Angelo, and J. Kuyper (eds) *Doing News Framing Analysis: Empirical and Theoretical Perspectives.* New York: Routledge, 84–109.

van Gorp, B. and Vercruysse, T. (2012) Frames and counter-frames giving meaning to dementia: A framing analysis of media content. *Social Science & Medicine.* 74, 1274–1281.

Zhu, J. H., Weaver, D., Lo, V. H., Chen, C. and Wu, W. (1997) Individual, organizational, and societal influences on media role perceptions: A comparative study of journalists in China. Hong Kong and the United States. *Journalism & Mass Communication Quarterly.* 74(1), 84–96.

# 9
## Space and the Migrant Camps of Calais: Space-Making at the Margins

*Anita Howarth and Yasmin Ibrahim*

In 2007, UK online national newspapers began to report on a handful of tents on scrubland near the French port of Calais occupied by migrants hoping to cross the UK border. By early 2009 this makeshift space, labelled 'the jungle' by migrants and the newspapers, had more than 800 occupants (Rawstorne, 2009). In September 2009, the French riot police demolished the camp and dispersed its occupants (Garnham, 2009) in the expectation of deterring new migrants from heading to Calais. In spite of this militant action by the French authorities, mini-camps sprung up all along the French coastline. The newspapers were concerned that these shelters could grow into 'mini jungles' (Allen, 2009c), and within a year a 'new jungle' had emerged in a small village near Dunkirk, only to be similarly demolished by the authorities (Finan and Allen, 2010).

This chapter examines how the online versions of the UK's two mid-market newspapers[1] framed the migrant camps or 'jungle' in the French town of Calais as interstitial spaces. The notion of marginality occupies a central premise in the discourse of the jungle; the migrants who congregate in these camps (while waiting to cross to the UK) are illegal bodies and hence marginal entities, the spaces they occupy are marginal lands within the town, and Calais' itself is in a marginal zone on the edge of the Schengen area of free movement and on the sea border between continental Europe and the UK. It is also a major transport hub en route to the UK and so the focal point of continuing media debates and cross-border tensions about illegal entry there, all of which combine to shape the politics of the margins – a politics of contestation over territory as well as meaning (Howarth and Ibrahim, 2012; Ibrahim, 2011).

We argue that the jungle as a physical entity is drawn into material and immaterial or discursive space construction in a multitude of ways which are complex and intertwined. The phenomenon of human migration highlights how border spaces become continually contested, redefined and reconstructed through the interaction of the corporeal body with the physical environment, policy discourses, and cross-border patrols with their attendant surveillance and combative practices. The jungle as a spatial metaphor has multiple readings, including the degradation of White civility through the migrant occupation. Equally the material and immaterial (i.e. discursive) construction and destruction have consequences for shaping human empathy, hence the politics of attachment in immigration debates.

## Making space, social imaginary and the media

The sociological imagination of space and the politics of space construction through a multitude of practices have implications for our sense of belonging, security and identity. Space is continually created in a multitude of activities connected with refugees, human resettlement and immigration. Space-making through discursive paradigms, media frames, the movement of corporeal bodies, policy discourses or the assertion of borders inscribe space as an intimate element of the human psyche in gaining both intimacy and distance to sensitive issues such as immigration. The complex ways in which spaces are created, destroyed, denied or deemed marginal reveal the enmeshing of power relations and the vulnerability of the human condition. Spaces can be socially, materially and discursively constructed (Harvey, 1973; Massey, 1991; May, 1996; Shields, 1999). Shields conceptualises the notion of spatialisation as a 'social imaginary' where spatial divisions and distinctions provide the means to ground hegemonic ideologies and social practices (1999). In these 'social imaginaries', issues of belonging, boundaries, marginality and 'othering' can reflect discursive and material practices of 'us' and 'them', inclusion and exclusion, as well as proximity and distance.

More recently, studies have developed the notion of social imaginary further, highlighting how landscapes and dominant features within them 'become spatially bounded scenes that visually communicate what belongs and what does not' (Trudeau, 2006: 421). Space and our social imagination of it become critical to the construction of a 'territorialized politics of belonging' in which the discourses and practices that maintain boundaries 'correspond to the imagined geographies of a polity and to the spaces that normatively embody the polity' (Trudeau, 2006: 421).

A central theme in this Western imaginary is marginality, where being on the margins has 'implied exclusion' (Shields, 2013: 216) in the sense of the geographically isolated, the site of 'illicit or socially disdained activities' and/or the 'other' in relation to the cultural centre (Shields, 2013: 13).

Margins, 'while a position of exclusion', can also facilitate critique because they 'expose the relativity of the entrenched, universalizing values of the centre and expose the relativism of the cultural identities which imply their shadow figures of every characteristic they have denied, rendered "anomalous" or excluded' (Shields, 2013: 217).

Benedict Anderson's (1991) concept of a nation as an imagined community enables people to imagine the boundaries of a nation or cultural centre even when these boundaries may not physically exist (1991: 6). He argues that one of the significant historical developments that facilitated the evolution of a national consciousness or imagination was the emergence of a profitable, mass-circulation press as it enabled national conversations about or with the unknown other. Such conversations allow people to be aware of each other's existence, experience and belonging to a community. Thus, media play a role in creating a national consciousness and a bond between individuals. Tangentially, space construction and media are intrinsically entwined.

Newspapers are inextricably implicated in space construction through their discursive and visual practices. They construct space through a multitude of techniques, including the use of images, imagery, narratives, metaphors, distance-framing and robust agenda-setting where notions of belonging to a defined discursive space can elicit both cerebral and visceral responses. As Durkheim observes (1915), time and space as social constructs are often subjected to ideological struggles over meaning. David Harvey's (1990) materialist construction of space as a product of social relations and ideological struggles imbues a Marxist perspective to space production, equally implicating media as a capitalist and ideological enterprise within this frame. Hence media's production of space in sustaining the social imaginary of the nation state is not divorced from the political context, power or ideological struggles. As David Harvey (1990: 419) observes, 'the very act of naming geographical entities implies a power over them, most particularly the way in which places, inhabitants and social functions are represented'.

The framing of space in the media while renewing the social imaginary of an imagined community is political. It is within this premise we analyse media and space construction where the concept of spatialisation as a social imaginary (Shields, 1999) emerges through the politics of territoriality centred on discursive and material practices of media in relating to border issues, immigration policy and the construction of the UK identity through the 'other'. It is also necessary to contextualise the jungle in Calais through the regional entity of the EU. The EU, and in particular France, is perceived as a space where large numbers of illegal migrants congregate at or near the French ports and where the French Government adopted a de facto policy of closing, banning or demolishing migrant shelters between 2002 and 2011. The media hence employ distinct spatialisation techniques to construct the violation of a bounded space in the discourses of the jungle. David Sibley (1995: 5) similarly asserts that the emergence of boundaries and stereotypical representations of others can reflect social practices of exclusion and inclusion. Theorists from different ontological perspectives, including post-structuralists and post-colonialists have mapped the connections between identity and space construction (see Bhaba, 1990; Shields, 1991) where distinctions such as centre and periphery can reinforce dominant ideologies and practices while polarising and dichotomising different spaces. In tandem, social identities emerge through the imagination and creation of space through both material and discursive practices.

The jungle as a case study provides a context to understand the complexity of space-making in a refugee settlement, or the border as both a marginalised space and one of tension and conflict due to its porous and juridical nature. The discursive and physical spatial constructions work to create both distance and proximity. The proximity-distance framing provides a duality of subduing the suffering of the 'other' while heightening the fear about the dissipation of order by casting the threat of physical violation as imminent in your backyard.

## The context of the jungle

We locate media constructions of the migrant spaces of Calais, in particular the 'jungle' camps, within the wider context of 'unregulated, unaccounted population shifts' across Europe resulting from the breakup of states, wars and revolutions (Geddes, 2003). EU states have struggled to deal with these shifts, a task further complicated by the infiltration of population movements by global networks of terrorists and people-traffickers (Bosworth, 2012). The EU has responded by reconstructing migration as a security threat to their spaces, so warranting the construction of 'Fortress Europe' (Millner, 2011), a 'security-judicial apparatus' with increasingly militarised external borders intended to keep out unwanted migrants and tougher laws criminalising those who do enter (Aas, 2011). However, militarisation has failed to deter new migrants from entering the EU or the re-entry of those deported. Instead it has pushed illegal migrants into marginal spaces in and around the French border ports, such as Calais (Thomas, 2013).

The French sea border is a marginal migration zone of transit and congregation of migrants looking for opportunities to cross the English Channel. Britain is the preferred destination for many of them because of language, family, historic ties and the perception that the country has (relatively) well-organised systems for processing asylum applications (Millner, 2011). However, the English Channel represents a major physical and security obstacle. Not only do migrants have to cross a sea barrier but they also have to bypass border controls to reach their preferred destination. In 1995, France opted into and the UK opted out of the Schengen Agreement on the undocumented movement of people between signatory states. The result was the alignment of a Schengen border (emerging from the agreement) with the French sea border, which meant the retention of border controls at the ports (Thomas, 2013), rendering the coastline as a marginal migration zone shaped by the politics of moving bodies and marking these spaces as transient.

The politics of the margin focuses on towns such as Calais where the French authorities struggle to manage congregating illegal migrants whose movement is obstructed by passport checks and further compounded by the social, environmental and humanitarian challenges posed by overcrowding of the marginal spaces they occupy (Rigby and Schlembach, 2013). On the other hand, immigration has moved up the political and policy agenda in the UK. Immigration and cross-border patrols have invariably become election issues, with successive governments tightening immigration policies and illegal migration across the English Channel. Within the UK, immigration has become a politically sensitised issue (Boswell, 2012) and externally the politics have given rise to a mix of cross-border collaboration and conflict. French-UK collaboration while seeking to tighten border security has nevertheless descended into a sustained blame game with each party holding the other responsible for the perceived policy failure and actions in arresting the number of immigrants who congregate at the borders. British politicians criticise their French counterparts for inadequate controls, labelling the border a 'sieve' that allows migrants to cross the English Channel illegally (Millner, 2011). Conversely, the French point the finger at the British counterparts for their benefit system, which is deemed to attract migrants. The UK has also been condemned for refusing to allow entry to former colonial subjects and opting out of the Schengen

Agreement, thus creating a bottleneck of moving illegal bodies that France has to deal with (Thomas, 2013).

The UK's national newspapers have played a critical role in shaping the public debate about and consciousness of the politics of the margins played out in Calais. The challenge for the media is that illegal migration is often invisible and hence difficult to cover. However, the earlier furore over Sangatte Red Cross shelter near Calais and its closure in 2002 highlighted how migrant shelters can provide visible and material manifestations of migration with the congregation of corporeal bodies in makeshift shelters, and of the English Channel as a major conduit for the movement of illegal migrants into the UK (Boswell, 2012).

## Approach to media-framing

This chapter examines how the online versions of two UK mid-market newspapers, the *MailOnline* and *Express*,[2] framed these migrant camps between 2007 and 2012. These newspapers are politically significant in that they have shaped the political agenda and public debate regarding a number of issues, including immigration (see Boswell, 2012; Davies 2009: 32; Migration Observatory, 2013; Park et al., 2014). Coverage is driven not only by competition between the two newspapers (Greenslade, 2004: 629) but also by their ideological opposition to immigration. NGOs have repeatedly criticised newspaper coverage of immigration as routinely 'discriminatory, sensational and unbalanced' reporting (Commission for Racial Equality, 2007: 98).

However, the editors of both newspapers contend that the UK is facing the biggest demographic change since the Norman invasion of 1066 (Esser, 2007). This means large numbers of illegal bodies are moving unchecked into the country and reconfiguring the spaces of the UK. What they cover and how they frame illegal migration is therefore, in the view of the editors, not only in the 'public interest' but also of major concern to the public (Esser, 2007). Illegal migration, however, is notoriously difficult for journalists to cover as much of it is furtive and largely invisible. The furore in 2002 over the Sangatte Red Cross centre gave the newspapers some entry into the clandestine world of migration. It drew newspaper attention to the English Channel as a major conduit for cross-border migration and the migrant camps in Calais as spatially visible manifestations of an otherwise invisible problem (Boswell, 2012). After the closure of Sangatte, the French authorities banned shelters so that migrants had to construct their own on unused, marginal spaces they could find in and around Calais. The jungle(s) of

Calais and Dunkirk were the most high-profile examples of these camps between 2007 and 2012 and they have been the focus of attention in both newspapers.

For the purpose of the analysis in this chapter, we did a key term search on *Mail Online* and *Express* online between 2007 and 2012 using 'Calais + immigration', 'Calais + migrant camp' and 'Calais + jungle', which elicited 121 articles. From a close reading of the texts we detected three dominant themes on the construction of marginal spaces: through the movement of the corporeal body and its interaction with the environment; policy discourses and practices; and cross-border tensions enacted through physical or material practices as well as through articulations. We then analysed these recurring frames. Framing refers to more than what is on the news agenda; it includes how media think about issues and shape public discussions. The power of frames lies in the ways in which they serve to make sense of events in the news; set the parameters of the debate; and persist in the selection, emphasis and inclusion or exclusion of certain discourses (Gitlin, 1980, cited in Semetko and Valkenburg, 2000: 94).

What emerged from our analyses of themes were a broad consensus and little divergence between the two online newspapers about the significant frames. Both of the media converged on presenting the Calais migrant as overcrowding the border town and denigrating the environment. The policies adopted to deal with this threat of the migrant were framed as failed initiatives and hence providing the resounding justification for the destruction of these illegal spaces. The failure resulted in a blame game, which saw manifest cross-border tensions and contestation with the French authorities around the problem of migration. The discourses used by *Mail Online* and *Express* in constructing these strands of narrative often unleashed a fear over imminence and magnitude of the problem, and equally the insurmountable social and physical costs to the British taxpayer. Within these discourses, these two media distanced the migrant in the reader's social imaginary and sought to depersonalise and delegitimise them through their occupation of the borderland. This then upheld the violent obliteration of the spaces and the combatant stance of the authorities.

## The corporeal body, the physical environment and (the absence) of empathy

The dominant discourse in both newspapers was of the constant, relentless movement of illegal corporeal bodies into border spaces near the ports. This was evident in descriptions such as 'flood' of migrants (see Allen and Dawar, 2012; Brown, 2011; Sparks, 2010). Such narrations beyond marginalising and depersonalising the migrant equally subsumed them in an amorphous mass of moving bodies (Reid, 2007). The tightening of border controls, however, constrained the onward movement of migrants. Too dangerous to go back to their home countries and blocked from moving on, the migrants found themselves occupying a liminal space on marginal sites and in a state of limbo. The camps along the French coastline were reconstituted as 'waiting room[s]' (Fagge, 2009a, 2009c) for migrants 'waiting for a chance' to climb onto a vehicle headed for the UK (Reid, 2007) or playing a 'waiting game' that goes on for months marking the capricious and futile predicament of the migrants (Sparks, 2012). Discourses also sought to criminalise the jungle as 'launch pads' for illegal bids to reach the UK (Allen, 2008a). Descriptions of the migrant's movements shifted from the benign 'leap' to the furtive 'sneak' and the criminalised 'smuggle' onto vehicles headed across the English Channel (Reid, 2007; Reynolds 2009; Sparks, 2009c). Narratives of the migrant movement also drew attention to the immense personal risks and their marginal existence between life and death. The act of leaping onto or hiding in vehicles portrayed the migrants as reckless and endangering their own lives. The newspapers carried reports of migrants falling between the wheels of fast-moving traffic, suffocating in airtight compartments (Reid, 2009) or being poisoned by toxic chemicals in the cargo of trucks (Allen, 2011; Reynolds, 2009). They were framed as perilous not just to the environment but to themselves. In the process of depicting the migrants as casualties or fatalities, the media thwarted emotional engagement and proximity to the migrant.

In line with this, the newspapers presented the willingness of migrants to risk their lives as foolhardy by reducing their aspirations for survival or a new life to visions of an 'El Dorado' (Allen and Murray, 2009; Bracchi, 2009; Fernandes, 2009; Reid, 2007) – a fantasy of illusory wealth and the pursuit of which could lead to the squandering of life. They constructed the migrant as ruthless and irresponsible in perpetuating their own unstable existence in the periphery, thus distancing their struggle to reach the UK. This frame of migrants' search for wealth provided newspapers with a useful tool to alienate them as an opportunistic and illegal corporeal body not worthy of a better life. Instead the migrants needed to be dealt with through either violence or juridical enactments in the form of detention and deportation from the EU. With reports of growing numbers of migrants, the newspapers conjoined discourses of their illegal movement with criminalisation, degradation and threat. This was evident in their association of the jungle with lawlessness and peril, characterised by gang wars over territory and a 'hiding place' where violent criminals could evade the police (Allen, 2008; Reynolds, 2009). This danger was seen as contaminating law and order spilling out from the periphery onto the streets of the town itself or into nearby villages (Allen, 2009c). As a result, local residents felt threatened and businesses were disrupted (Rawstorne, 2009). Barbarism in the form of the 'law of the jungle reigned' (Bracchi, 2009) as the police failed to check the violence of the migrants and the jungle into 'inhumane squalor' (Allen, 2009d) over which the putrefied 'stench' of rotting waste hung (Bracchi, 2009). The visualisation of the camp through sensory allusions and narratives of squalor again sought to distance the migrant from their audiences.

Thus the newspapers constructed the movement of corporeal bodies simultaneously as transient and illegitimate, leading to a disruption and denigration of the physical environment through its decomposition and degradation. Migration was constructed as a problem 'out of control' (see Rawstorne, 2009) that warranted the destruction of the jungle as a humane and rational response to the squalor, uninhabitable conditions, and the threat posed to its immediate environment and White civility.

The newspapers forestalled any empathy for the jungle inhabitants facing the destruction of their dwellings by dehumanising them. Not only did they, as already discussed, demean migrants' aspirations for a new life but also they displaced their suffering to the distant locale of their 'wartorn' or 'war-ravaged' countries of origin where threats to their lives and those of their families had forced them to flee their homes (Allen, 2008a, 2009a). Any empathy towards the migrants was negated not only by constructing them as reckless and responsible for their precarious existence but also by associating them with the people-traffickers who moved them across Europe (Fernandes, 2009), hid in their camps, contributed to the squalor and were often behind the violence that frequently broke out (Bracchi, 2009). The jungle inhabitants were not presented as subjects of trauma or suffering and hence were not seen as deserving of human empathy. Both newspapers supported the French ban on any semi-permanent shelters, opposed any attempts by charities to erect new ones (see Fagge, 2009d) and supported moves to demolish the jungle unequivocally. The destruction of the camp pushed the migrants into covert shelters described by the newspapers as 'hide-aways', 'hideouts' and 'hidden culverts' to avoid detection by the police (Giannangeli, 2009). Newspapers framed the destruction of the jungle as a rational response to all the social ills that had been presented to Fortress Europe and particularly the UK.

## Policy discourses and practices

Arguably the most de-humanising element of the coverage was the subsuming of the predicament of the migrant and their experiences of trauma within an overarching discourse of policy failure. The newspapers presented the growing number of migrants and the squalor presented by these camps as evidence of ineffectual policies that had failed to address a problem that had 'plagued' the coastline for a decade (Slack and Allen, 2009). The visibility of the jungle and its association with organised criminal activities became material manifestations of the inadequacies of French governance of the borders (Garnham, 2009). Due to failed policies, the papers claimed that an estimated 200 migrants a week were crossing the English Channel, although no one knew the 'true' numbers (Fagge, 2009c). The illusiveness of figures in representing the scale of the problem meant that the imminent threat of the jungle could be heightened by underscoring the ineffectual policy initiatives.

As the scale of the problems associated with the camp escalated, the newspapers resorted to a blame game. The UK Government was seen as culpable for allowing a 'black' economy to develop in which illegal migrants could find work (Reid, 2007), offering 'generous' benefits, housing and medical care (Young, 2009), and providing legal aid to fund asylum applications (Allen, 2009a). Conversely, the French were initially accused of 'ignoring' the problems of the jungle (Tristem, 2007), but after a series of raids on the camp the newspapers claimed that 'at long last' the French were getting 'tough' on the criminals sheltering in it (*Daily Mail*, 2009b; Slack and Allen, 2009). However, within days those arrested had been freed, shelters rebuilt and the 'problem' of illegal migration was left unaddressed (see Bracchi, 2009). The newspapers viewed this as evidence of a lack of political will to address the criminal encroachment and occupation of Calais. A new 'tough-talking' immigration minister, Eric Besson, set out to demonstrate state 'determination' to stop the 'rule' of people-traffickers in Calais (Slack and Allen, 2009). He announced that the camp would be demolished, the 'law of the jungle' would be stamped out, order restored (Bracchi, 2009) and the border made 'watertight' against people-smugglers and migrants (Fagge, 2009a; Slack and Allen, 2009). His British counterpart added that such decisive action would remove a 'magnet' for migrants and deter new ones from coming to Calais (Allen, 2009b).

These ongoing newspaper discourses legitimised the violent action. In a dawn raid in September 2009, French riot police bulldozed the shelters, chain-sawed any remaining vegetation and obliterated any reminders that the physical space had once housed hundreds of migrants (Allen, 2009c). Police arrested or detained many of those occupants of the camp who had not already fled. The act of physical destruction symbolised the reclaiming of space from the illegal corporeal bodies and the reasserting of law and order.

However, within hours of the police action, new camps had 'popped up' (Allen, 2009d) and over the next few weeks derelict properties, including Hovercraft buildings and wartime blockhouses, had been turned into 'secret homes' for migrants (Allen, 2009e; Fagge, 2009d; Reynolds, 2009). The demolition of the jungle did not persuade existing migrants to return to their country of origin or to stem the 'flood' of new ones into the town. Local charities dismissed the destructive act as a 'publicity stunt' intended to appease the British public (Sparks, 2010). Newspapers once again lapsed into the discourse that the governments had failed to 'seal off' the area to migrants, and instead the annihilation of the jungle had merely displaced the problem to ports all along the coastline (Giannangeli, 2009; Sparks 2009a). Within a year, a 'new jungle' had grown up in a village near Dunkirk, which too had been 'over-run' and 'invaded' by migrants and people-traffickers (Finan and Allen, 2010; Sparks 2010a). The parallels drawn with the earlier Calais jungle served to legitimise and rationalise the same action (i.e. the demolition of shelters and the obliteration of any reminders that this had once been a migrant shelter). However, this pattern of the construction, destruction and re-emergence reflected the making, unmaking and reconfiguring of space, conveying the struggle between illegal bodies and authorities of governance to reclaim space from the hands of those they deemed as illegal and unwanted in civilised Europe.

## Cross-border conflict and cooperation

Cross-border interactions also shape the territorial politics of space, and accounts of the failure of immigration policy threw into sharp relief areas of cooperation and conflict between the two governments. Not only did they concur on the need to demolish the jungle but they also collaborated on the militarisation and tightening of border controls intended to keep the unwanted other out of the nation state. Measures included the investment of millions of pounds in surveillance technology that included night vision, X-ray and heat-detection machines, and devices able to pick up heartbeats and carbon dioxide emissions in vehicles (Fernandes, 2009; Reid, 2009). The increased use of powerfully invasive technologies and the newspapers' uncritical coverage highlight the relative powerlessness of the migrants, particularly when juxtaposed with the hyperbolic discourse of ministers. The investment was hailed as part of the 'biggest shake-up' of immigration systems and security 'for a generation', intended to create 'one of the toughest border crossings' in the world at Calais and the epitome of Anglo-French collaboration (Allen and Slack, 2008). However, it failed to 'seal' the borders and policies of detention and deportation became areas of conflict between the two states.

The newspapers presented detection, detention and deportation in cases of failed asylum applications as a linear and, ideally, an inexorable process but undermined by French inefficiency and ineffectualness. After the demolition of the jungle, the authorities had moved migrants arrested during the raid into detention centres across France, but some escaped and 'were believed to be heading back to Calais', and the remainder were released after a court found 'procedural irregularities' in their detention (Fagge, 2009b; Sparks 2009b). The judge ruled that the 'collective arrests' that followed the destruction of the jungle infringed the 'fundamental freedom' and individual right of migrants to claim asylum where they chose (Fagge, 2009c). A furious *Mail Online* claimed the court action would leave migrants 'free to flood' the UK and exposed the French Government's promise to tighten up immigration control and security 'as a farce' (Mail Foreign Service, 2009).

At the same time, French private security firms and airline pilots refused to participate in forced deportations because such actions were seen as contrary to the humanitarianism at the root of what it meant to be French, so the UK had to provide the flights and guards, and the British taxpayer 'had to pick up the bill' (Allen and Slack, 2008). While ministers continued to claim that the two governments were 'joining forces to deliver joint returns', critics labelled it 'ridiculous' that the UK was having to solve its immigration problems and those of France (Allen and Slack, 2008). The newspapers were further incensed when, in 2009, joint French-British plans to repatriate migrants to their countries of origin faltered after a legal challenge in the French courts on humanitarian grounds (Reid, 2009).

Thus key elements of the security apparatus put in place to expel those who had eluded the border patrols were challenged by judicial safeguards on the rights of those within its borders irrespective of their nationality. The UK newspapers, though, viewed the humanitarian inclination of the courts as undermining the ability of the nation state to police its borders. In France, as opposition against detention and deportations grew, politicians increasingly presented illegal migration as 'fundamentally a British problem' as most of the migrants had come from its former colonies, shared a common history, spoke English, had family in the UK and were heading there (Allen, 2009). That is, by implication they belonged elsewhere and therefore the French politicians sought to devolve responsibility for deportations to their British counterparts. The Franco-British tensions over how to deal with migrants that had evaded border patrols exposed the primacy of the boundaries of the nation state and the fragility of cooperation over common borders.

## Conclusion

This chapter explores how the online versions of the UK's mid-market newspapers constructed a social imaginary around illegal migration in the marginal spaces of migrant camps on the French sea border dubbed the 'jungle'. In the process it demonstrates how spaces are socially imagined and constructed in the cultural and material artefact of the media. Our examination of the media's ability to present margins and borders as liminal spaces where norms can be suspended provides a lens to interrogate how space construction in the media can mediate both the social imaginary of national borders and our conceptions of the 'other', particularly in immigration policy and cross-border security discourses. It is in this context of the politics of territoriality and marginalisation that the jungle metaphor came to ascribe a broader process of space construction beyond the functional reference to migrant shelters, to embody the complex interweaving of discourses, which constructed the camps not only as symbolic spaces of degradation and barbarism but also as juridical sites where annihilation can be rationalised. The jungle also reveals the media's power to both build and diminish our sense of place and belonging.

## Notes

1. Our focus here is on the online coverage by two mid-market newspapers, *Mail Online* and *Express*, of the migrant camps known as the 'jungle'. The term 'newspapers' is used here to refer to these versions. We do not imply that coverage by the online and print versions is the same, and this chapter does not attempt to compare the two.
2. Although the newspaper is commonly known as *The Daily Express*, it changed its name to *Express* a number of years ago, and this is the name that appears on the website.

# References

Aas, K. F. (2011) 'Crimmigrant' bodies and bona fide travelers: Surveillance, citizenship and global governance. *Theoretical Criminology*. 15(3), 331–346. Available at: http://tcr.sagepub.com/cgi/doi/10.1177/1362480610396643 (accessed December 20, 2013).

Allen, P. (2008a) French U-turn as new Calais shelter for UK-bound immigrants opens after temperatures plunge. *Daily Mail*. 6. Available at: http://www.dailymail.co.uk/news/article-1102568/French-U-turn-new-Calais-shelter-UK-bound-immigrants-opens-temperatures-plunge.html

Allen, P. (2008b) Mass riot police operation to break up Calais camps full of Brit-bound migrants. *Mail Online*. Available at: http://www.dailymail.co.uk/news/article-1079955/Mass-riot-police-operation-break-Calais-camps-Brit-bound-migrants.html#ixzz2au2DfVfY

Allen, P. (2009a) France sparks diplomatic row after cancelling flight deporting England-bound illegal immigrants. *Daily Mail*. 4. Available at: http://www.dailymail.co.uk/news/article-1086764/France-sparks-diplomatic-row-cancelling-flight-deporting-England-bound-illegal-immigrants.html

Allen, P. (2009b) Nothing will stop us coming to Britain. *Express*.

Allen, P. (2009c) Pictured: New squalid migrant camp pops up in Calais hours after the Jungle is razed. *Mail Online*. Available at: http://www.dailymail.co.uk/news/article-1215568/New-squalid-migrant-camp-pops-Calais-hours-Jungle-razed.html#ixzz2avXFqLTX

Allen, P. (2009d) The UK must open its borders: Calais mayor's demand as riot police tear down illegal camps AGAIN. *Mail Online*. Available at: http://www.dailymail.co.uk/news/article-1216950/Riot-police-destroy-Calais-migrant-camps-AGAIN-mayor-slams-Britain-unable-control-borders.html#ixzz2avbj8LGX

Allen, P. (2009e) The UK must open its borders: Calais mayor's demand as riot police tear down illegal camps AGAIN. *Mail Online*. Available at: http://www.dailymail.co.uk/news/article-1218410/Calais-migrants-flown-home-500-expense-British-French-taxpayers.html#ixzz2avdekaSX

Allen, P. (2011) 'Arab Spring' camp set up in Calais as thousands of North Africans vie to get to Britain. *Daily Mail*. 1389755. Available at: http://www.dailymail.co.uk/news/article-1389755/Arab-Spring-camp-set-Calais-thousands-North-Africans-vie-to-Britain.html#ixzz2b08LOb9k

Allen, P. and Slack, J. (2008) France flies its Afghan migrants home ... and UK taxpayers pick up the bill because 'they were trying to reach Britain.' *Mail Online*. Available at: http://www.dailymail.co.uk/news/article-1086317/France-flies-Afghan-migrants-home–UK-taxpayers-pick-trying-reach-Britain.html#ixzz2au4oR7Tw

Allen, P. and Murray, J. (2009) Pay us £100m or we will let illegals in, threaten French. *Express*. Available at: http://www.express.co.uk/news/uk/82849/Pay-us-100m-or-we-will-let-illegals-in-threaten-French

Allen, P. and Dawar, A. (2012) Loophole gives migrants one-way ticket to Britain. *Express*. Available at: http://www.express.co.uk/news/uk/304899/Loophole-gives-migrants-one-way-ticket-to-Britain

Bhaba, H. (1990) *Nation and Narration*. London: Routledge.

Boswell, C. (2012) How information scarcity influences the policy agenda: Evidence from U. K. *Immigration Policy.* 25(3), 367–389.

Bosworth, M. (2012) Subjectivity and identity in detention: Punishment and society in a global age. *Theoretical Criminology.* 16(2), 123–140. Available at: http://tcr.sagepub.com/cgi/doi/10.1177/1362480612441116 (accessed 25 December, 2013).

Bracchi, P. (2009) Bloody siege of calais: The violent new breed of migrants who will let nothing stop them coming to Britain. *Mail Online.* Available at: http://www.dailymail.co.uk/news/article-1202009/Bloody-siege-Calais-The-violent-new-breed-migrants-let-stop-coming-Britain.html

Brown, M. (2011) We'll end the migrant flood vows Theresa May. *Express.*

Commission for Racial Equality (2007) The Treatment of Asylum Seekers.

Daily Mail Reporter (2009) Razed to the ground: Jungle migrant camp emptied after raid by Calais police (but will it stop asylum seekers flooding into Britain?). *Mail Online.* Available at: http://www.dailymail.co.uk/news/article-1214848/Britain-obsessed-asylum-seekers-let-UK-earliest-convenience-says-Europes-Justice-Commisioner.html?printingPage=true

Davies, N. (2009) None deadlier than the Mail. *New Statesman.* January 24. Available at: http://www.newstatesman.com/media/2008/01/asylum-seekers-mail-report.

Esser, R. (2007) The treatment of asylum seekers.

*Express* (2009a) French are to close 'jungle' camp. Available at: http://www.express.co.uk/news/world/128991/French-are-to-close-jungle-camp

*Express* (2009b) Migrant 'jungle' camp bulldozed. Available at: http://www.express.co.uk/news/world/129163/Migrant-jungle-camp-bulldozed

Fagge, N. (2007) Rival refugees 'bloody battle' to get to Britain. *Express*, January 01 p. 4.

Fagge, N. (2009a) France sets up new camps for migrants sneaking to UK. *Express.* Available at: http://www.express.co.uk/news/uk/144535/France-sets-up-new-camps-for-migrants-sneaking-to-UK

Fagge, N. (2009b) French put new migrants camp...next to lorry park. *Express.* Available at: http://www.express.co.uk/news/uk/131111/French-put-new-migrants-camp-next-to-lorry-park

Fagge, N. (2009c) 'Jungle' migrants freed to try again. *Express.* Available at: http://www.express.co.uk/news/world/130068/Jungle-migrants-freed-to-try-again

Fagge, N. (2009d) Migrants from the Jungle set up a dozen new camps, *Express.* Available at: http://www.express.co.uk/news/world/129467/Migrants-from-the-Jungle-set-up-a-dozen-new-camps

Fernandes, E. (2009) Welcome to heaven, how about a cup of tea? Mail on Sunday special investigation into why asylum seekers head to Britain. *Mail Online.* Available at: http://www.dailymail.co.uk/news/article-1227779/Welcome-heaven-cup-tea-Mail-Sunday-special-investigation-asylum-seekers-head-Britain.html?printingPage=true

Finan, T. and Allen, P. (2010) Stop being so generous to migrants: French plea to Britain after Dunkirk suburb is over-run. *Mail Online.* Available at: http://www.dailymail.co.uk/news/article-1331013/Stop-generous-migrants-French-plea-Britain-Dunkirk-suburb-run.html

Garnham, E. (2009) Police swoop on sprawling immigrant 'jungle.' *Express*. Available at: http://www.express.co.uk/news/uk/129166/Police-swoop-on-sprawling-immigrant-jungle

Geddes, A. (2003) *The Politics of Migration and Immigration in Europe*. Oxford: Oxford University Press.

Giannangeli, M. (2009) Dunkirk beaches shelter army of migrants. *Express*. Available at: http://www.express.co.uk/news/world/130191/Dunkirk-beaches-shelter-army-of-migrants

Greenslade, R. (2004) *Press Gang: How Newspapers Make Profits from Propaganda*. Basingstoke: Pan Macmillan.

Harvey, D. (1973) *Social Justice and the City*. London: Edward Arnold.

Harvey, D. (1990) Between time and space: Reflections on the geographical imagination. *Annals of the Association of American Geographers*. 80(3), 418–434.

Howarth, A. and Ibrahim, Y. (2012) Threat and suffering: The liminal space of 'The jungle', in L. Andrews and Roberts (eds) *Liminal Spaces*. London: Routledge.

Ibrahim, Y. (2011) Constructing 'the Jungle': Distance framing in the Daily Mail. *International Journal of Media & Cultural Politics*. 7(3), 315–335.

Massey, D. (1991) The political place of locality studies. *Environment and Planning*. 23, 267–281.

May, J. (1996) Globalization and the politics of place: place and identity in an inner London neighbourhood. *Transactions of the Institute of British Geographers*. 21(1), 194–215.

Migration Observatory (2013) *Migration in the News: Portrayals of Immigrants, Migrants, Asylum Seekers and Refugees in the National British Newspapers, 2010–12*. Oxford. Available at: http://migrationobservatory.ox.ac.uk/sites/files/migobs/Report – migration in the news.pdf

Millner, N. (2011) From 'refugee' to 'migrant' in Calais solidarity activism: Restaging undocumented migration for a future politics of asylum. *Political Geography*. 30, 320–328.

Park, A., Bryson, C. and Curtice, J. (2014) *British Social Attitudes 31*. London. Available at: http://www.bsa-31.natcen.ac.uk/media/38202/bsa31_full_report.pdf

Rawstorne, T. (2009) Hundreds of illegal immigrants armed with knives and crowbars swarm round Calais trucks heading for Britain. *Mail Online*. Available at: http://www.dailymail.co.uk/news/article-1180180/Hundreds-illegal-immigrants-armed-knives-crowbars-swarm-round-Calais-trucks-heading-Britain.html?printingPage=true

Reid, S. (2007) Return of Sangatte – Countless immigrants plot to slip into UK. *Daily Mail*. Available at: http://www.dailymail.co.uk/news/article-448459/Return-Sangatte–Countless-immigrants-plot-slip-UK.html##ixzz0Wjbx LMHm

Reid, S. (2009) They're back: Mass of migrants queue up at Sangatte to reach 'Promised Land' UK. *Mail Online*. Available at: http://www.dailymail.co.uk/news/article-1161659/Theyre-Mass-migrants-queue-Sangatte-reach-Promised-Land-UK.html

Reynolds, M. (2009) Migrants: Nothing will stop us getting in to UK. *Express*. Available at: http://www.express.co.uk/news/uk/129057/Migrants-Nothing-will-stop-us-getting-in-to-UK

Rygiel, K. (2011) Bordering solidarities: Migrant activism and the politics of movement and camps at Calais. *Citizenship Studies*. 15, 1–19.

Semetko, H. A. and Valkenburg, P. M. (2000) Framing European politics: A content analysis of press and television news. *Journal of Communication*. 50(2), 93–109.

Service, M. F. (2009) Freed to have another go at coming to Britain: French judges release 82 Calais migrants. *Mail Online*. Available at: http://www.dailymail.co.uk/news/article-1216639/Freed-coming-Britain-French-judges-release-82-Calais-migrants.html?printingPage=true

Shields, R. (1991) *Places on the Margins: Alternative Geographies of Modernity*. London: Routledge

Shields, R. (1999) Culture and the economy of cities. *European Urban and Regional Studies*. 6(4), 303–311.

Shields, R. (2013) *Places on the Margin: Alternative Geographies of Modernity*. London: Routledge.

Sibley, D. (1995) *Geographies of Exclusion: Society and Difference in the West*. London: Routledge.

Slack, J. and Allen, P. (2009) At long last, Calais get tough on the people traffickers with massive dawn raid by armed police. *Daily Mail*. Available at: http://www.dailymail.co.uk/news/worldnews/article-1172297/At-long-Calais-tough-people-traffickers-massive-dawn-raid-armed-police.html

Sparks, I. (2009a) French police crack down on migrants in Calais after local young mother becomes victim of sex attack. *MailOnline*. Available at: http://www.dailymail.co.uk/news/article-1185027/French-police-crack-migrants-Calais-local-young-mother-victim-sex-attack.html?printingPage=true

Sparks, I. (2009b) Police swoop on people trafficking network accused of smuggling 5,000 illegal immigrants into Britain. *Mail Online*. Available at: http://www.dailymail.co.uk/news/article-1192110/Police-swoop-people-trafficking-network-accused-smuggled-5000-illegal-immigrants-Britain.html

Sparks, I. (2009c) French police crack down on migrants in Calais after local young mother becomes victim of sex attack. *MailOnline*. Available at: http://www.dailymail.co.uk/news/article-1185027/French-police-crack-migrants-Calais-local-young-mother-victim-sex-attack.html?printingPage=true

Sparks, I. (2010a) Bulldozing of Calais Jungle immigration camp was a 'publicity stunt aimed at placating the British public.' *MailOnline*. Available at: http://www.dailymail.co.uk/news/article-1242854/Calais-Jungle-Bulldozing-immigration-camp-publicity-stunt-aimed-placating-British-public.html?printingPage=true

Sparks, I. (2010b) Controversial French MP praises 'courage' of migrants illegally headed for Britain. *Mail Online*. Available at: http://www.dailymail.co.uk/news/article-1249372/Controversial-French-MP-Jack-Lang-praises-courage-migrants-headed-Britain.html#socialLinks

Sparks, I. (2012) French government to pass law making it ILLEGAL to arrest UK-bound illegal immigrants in Calais. *Mail Online*. Available at: http://www.dailymail.co.uk/news/article-2175441/French-government-pass-law-making-ILLEGAL-arrest-UK-bound-illegal-immigrants-Calais.html

Thomas, D. (2013) *Into the European 'jungle'*. Bloomington: Indiana University Press. Available at: http://books.google.co.uk/books?id=tZoFkV9LqBwC&pg=

PA183&dq=barthes+into+the+european+jungle+calais+migration&hl=en&
sa=X&ei=sGG8UserCsPy7Ab65ICIDQ&ved=0CDQQ6AEwAA#v=onepage&q=
barthes into the european jungle calais migration&f=false
Tristem, A. (2007) The return of Sangatte. 14 January. *Express*.
Trudeau, D. (2006) Politics of belonging in the construction of landscapes:
Place-making, boundary-drawing and exclusion. *Cultural Geographies*. 13(3),
421–433.
Young, J. (2009) EU countries must stop playing pass the human parcel.
*Express*. Available at: http://www.express.co.uk/comment/columnists/jimmy-
young/130275/EU-countries-must-stop-playing-pass-the-human-parcel

# Part III

# Protests and Power

# 10
## Visibility of Protest at the Margins: The Thatcher Funeral Protests

*Katy Parry*

Baroness Margaret Thatcher's death in April 2013, at the age of 87, brought an outpouring of emotion in the UK and beyond, but this was not simply an occasion of national mourning for a retired stateswoman who had long ago exited the political stage. With the rare honour of having a political ideology named after her during her lifetime, Thatcher was a towering figure in UK political culture whose name could inspire hatred as well as admiration. As her official biographer Charles Moore writes in volume one of her biography, the interest in Thatcher's character has not diminished in her death: 'She is someone about whom it is almost impossible to be neutral. People are fascinated, appalled, delighted by her. Many think she saved Britain, many that she destroyed it. The only thing that unites them is their interest' (2013: xvii). So the occasion of Thatcher's funeral on 13 April 2013 was never simply going to present a moment for respectfully marking the passing of a wife, mother and grandmother; it also offered the moment when a nation reflected on how contemporary society has been decisively and divisively shaped by 'that woman'.[1]

This chapter does not intend to rehash the disputed claims over Thatcher's legacy but to focus on the media coverage of the protests which accompanied her funeral. The service was held on 17 April 2013, reportedly costing £1.2 million to stage, despite higher estimations at the time (BBC, 2013), and was broadcast and blogged 'as it happened' across various national media. Where such ritualised media events, especially of the 'coronation' kind (Dayan and Katz, 1992), can bring feelings of reconciliation and national pride to the fore, Thatcher's funeral opened up old wounds and represented a divided UK.

I explore the photographic coverage of the funeral protests in mainstream online news galleries, and especially the 'image politics' (DeLuca, 1999) of those who chose to line the streets alongside the mourners and to quietly express their outrage at the ceremonial event. Following Dayan's proposed 'paradigm of visibility', I analyse how the protesters challenged the narrative offered by mainstream media as 'uninvited intruders' (2013: 145). Media visibility for citizens is often awarded on a conditional basis in mainstream media, but innovative forms of expression attract media attention and subsequent circulation across varied media forms. Thatcher's funeral provided a key moment through which to investigate contentious politics at the margins of a national media event.

The above paragraph hints at a few interrelated research contexts, which in turn provide three questions which guide this chapter. First, in what ways was this a political event and how did the media portrayal work to emphasise or de-emphasise its political nature? One key starting point for political activity is the recognition of who counts as a legitimate political actor, but there is also a consensual understanding of *when* and *where* politics and 'the political' are appropriate (Mouffe, 2005). One way to marginalise the protests is to make the *reasonable* claim that a funeral is not the time for politics. Second, this was an intensely mediated event, but how did the protests appear alongside the ceremonial event? Notions of visibility and visuality are at the heart of an 'image politics' (DeLuca, 1999) which embraces the theatrical and symbolic power of images to challenge notions of control and power. Third, taking a small slice of this national coverage, how do online news galleries tell the story of the day, for mourners and protesters? The use of 'in pictures' photographic slideshows provides a visually focused sample of a condensed form of storytelling. The selected images from both professional and amateur photographers provide at least three layers of visual communication through which to explore how participants perform political subjectivity: the materials prepared by the protesters and their visual display; the content of photographs selected to represent the day 'in pictures' by each media outlet; and the broader narrative offered through the layout and accompanying text. While the analysis is primarily image-led, it is recognised that all media texts are multimodal in nature (Kress and van Leeuwen, 2001; Machin and Mayr, 2013).

The next three sections briefly present the research contexts for the areas listed above: the space for politics; visibility as an expression of citizenship from the margins; and photographic news slideshows as an emerging news genre. Following this, the chapter explores the online news galleries of the BBC, *The Guardian* and *The Telegraph*.

## The place and space of politics and 'the political'

> I think in a way we're all Thatcherites now because – I mean – I think one of the things about her legacy is some of those big arguments that she had had, you know, everyone now accepts. No-one wants to go back to trade unions that are undemocratic or one-sided nuclear disarmament or having great private sector businesses in the public sector.
>
> (David Cameron on the *Today* programme, Radio 4, 17 April 2013)

On the morning of Thatcher's funeral, Prime Minister David Cameron appeared on Radio 4's *Today* programme suggesting that we were 'all Thatcherites now', immediately prompting criticism from both left and right for his use of the term. He was accused of making political propaganda out of the funeral, of exploiting the memory of Thatcher where before he had distanced himself. What this debate reveals is how 'Thatcher' – and what it means to be Thatcherite – still offers a contested term against which we nevertheless identify and measure ourselves. So Cameron's seemingly impromptu remark is particularly provocative given the divisive rhetoric associated with Thatcher – for example, whether a Cabinet colleague was 'one of us', the miners described as the 'enemy within' – so this use of 'we all' and 'everyone' in an off-the-cuff manner ('in a way') is particularly disagreeable for her opponents. Cameron's rhetoric attempts to define the nation together as Thatcherites while simultaneously reminding us of the bygone era of strong party identification and of other collective identities now seemingly diminished in UK political culture.

I include this quotation here because it highlights the ways in which this kind of political talk works to define a consensus, position segments of its audience as included or excluded and possibly constrain debate. But to cast such a divisive figure as some kind of unifying symbol, and Thatcherism an umbrella we can all fit under, only serves to rankle those who blame her for destroying their communities and contributing to a more individualistic society. In stating that 'those big arguments' are behind us, Cameron asks us to put politics aside and commemorate her life. The notions of 'politics', 'the political' and, indeed, the kind of 'post-political' vision as offered cheekily here by Cameron have attracted much academic debate in recent years (e.g. Hay, 2007; Mouffe, 2005). James Martin delineates 'politics' from 'the political', defining 'politics' as the activities and instituted procedures of organised interests, as distinct but dependent on 'the political' dimension: 'the abstract frames or principles that define, for example, who gets represented, and what kinds of issues are legitimate topics of dispute and which social groups are recognized as "acceptable" participants in politics, or not' (Martin, 2014: 4).

Addressing the assembled mourners at St Paul's Cathedral, Bishop of London Richard Chartres said that 'here and today is neither the time nor the place' to debate policies and legacy; that it was instead 'the place for the simple truths which transcend political debate' (Chartres, 2013). As *The Guardian* reported the day before the funeral, Dean of St Paul's Cathedral Dr David Ison said the ceremony was 'not a political demonstration' but rather a demonstration of 'how we respond in the face of death' (cited in Davies et al., 2013: para 2). For both, to engage in political debate would be to debase the Christian service. Those keen to protest were seen by some to be undermining the respectability associated with the solemn occasion of a funeral. We can note here how various authority figures attempt to define the parameters for legitimate contestation, political talk and activity, while presiding over a state funeral in all but name.

## Protest and image politics

For those struggling to gain attention on the political stage, 'image politics' (DeLuca, 1999) offer a striking way to promote a cause and spark imagination. Operating with a freedom of expression that traditional political party politicians are unlikely to risk, the politics of dissent can embrace the symbolic and theatrical. The Thatcher funeral protests are unusual, if not unique, given that they *appear* to be tied up with historical grievances rather than immediate needs or future possibilities. This is not an emergent social movement demanding radical change but rather the creation or re-creation of some kind of transient community of solidarity through which new and old affinities and identities are expressed. The most infamous response to Thatcher's death was the attempt to get the Wizard of Oz song 'Ding Dong! The Witch is Dead' to the top of the charts – a social media campaign which emphasised a deliberately callous celebratory response, along with spur-of-the-moment parties organised across the country (Valentine, 2013). The mode of expression here was through a reappropriation of a popular culture classic which casts Thatcher as the witch, merely through the action of downloading the song. But the funeral itself warranted a different tactical approach and attracted those angry at the perceived harm inflicted on the country by Thatcher's policies, and at the pomposity and expense of the funeral. The day of the funeral was the wrong kind of space and occasion for dissent *vocally* expressed (alongside the funeral procession at least). Instead, protesters held up banners or turned their backs on the funeral procession. Kevin DeLuca and Jennifer Peeples' suggestive idea of a 'public discourse of images' (2012: 133) is relevant here, in that it recognises the performative role of images in bringing the 'public' into being, and the potentials for political agency and citizenship beyond the traditional emphasis on dialogue and voice.

The mediated space for politics and for political performances therefore offers a space to be *seen* acting as a disgruntled or morally disgusted citizen, in addition to finding out about the activities of elite political actors. Rather than thinking about conditions of visibility from the politicians' perspectives, Daniel Dayan's 'paradigm of visibility' (2013) helps us to conceptualise online and physical spaces as contested sites of political meaning, values and identity, in dialogue with other more traditional mediated forms:

> Media are institutions that confer visibility on events, persons, groups, debates, controversies, and narratives. Media make situations visible... You are showing me this? Why are you showing it to me? Why are you showing it this way? What is it? Where is the rest of it? What have you chosen not to show? These are naive questions. These are key questions.
>
> (Dayan, 2013: 146)

In asking these naïve but key questions, we can investigate the different patterns of visible citizen involvement and the kinds of visual display produced and circulated across the mediascape (Parry, 2015).

We might also ask of any protest: What is at stake here? Central to this particular protest is the right to be acknowledged as a politically motivated citizen who is not a mourner, within the *shared public space*, and the right to make visible shared moral objections to the symbolic power of the ceremonial state-sanctioned event. And the involvement of senior figures in the monarchy, military and government along with international representatives places the funeral firmly in the scripting of a reverential coronation media event (Dayan and Katz, 1992). In other words, the protest is about the right to share (mediated) public space without adopting the unified values or narrative offered by the state institutions. In thinking about mediated public spaces in this way, this chapter acknowledges that inclusions and exclusions of visibility are crucially about a political struggle, with first TV (Thompson, 1995) and now the internet shaping the way we see the world and our right to look, and be seen, as citizens (Dayan, 2013; Mirzoeff, 2011).

## 'In pictures': Online news galleries

The selected media genre for this study is the online photographic slideshow, or news gallery. Admittedly this offers only a small window into the intense media coverage that the funeral attracted across many platforms, but it continues the focus on the visual and allows for an analysis of an easily delineated and compact form of storytelling. The study surveys the online news galleries of the BBC, *The Guardian* and *The Telegraph*, noting the degree to which the protests were pictured within the 'in pictures' galleries.[2] In some cases this is about how the protesters appear in the general funeral 'in pictures' coverage, or in the separate slideshow dedicated to the protests, if one exists. Online news galleries as a genre reflect the convergent, multiplatform approach of news organisations and the shift to the visual in online news presentation (e.g. increased numbers of images, video links and infographics). Following Helen Caple and John Knox's detailed overview of various related terms and genres (e.g. picture essay and photo story), I use 'online news gallery' to denote where a news organisation displays a collection of images online which are organised 'through some underlying principle or purpose' (2012: 215).

While other forms of alternative or social media offer the protesters visibility 'on their own terms' (Dayan, 2013), presence in mainstream media still confers a sense of validation or legitimacy. It is the 'subjectivity of the collective, institutional author' of online news galleries (Caple and Knox, 2012: 214–215) which is of interest here. In the news galleries' presentation of the day 'in pictures' they act as performative manifestations of the most significant moments. In terms of journalistic production, the photographic displays are updated promptly on the day while also serving as an easily accessible but lasting archive of a memorable day, collected together for posterity. Similarly, Anna Roosvall's study of global May Day demonstrations uses three influential news slideshows for their 'visually striking and popular' qualities (2013: 56), from Swedish, US and UK newspapers, noting how the genre or subgenre of slideshows offers a 'blatant' example of how pictures accumulate meaning from each other, with images designed to be viewed together 'in a row' (61).

## Multimodal and multilayered visual communication: Notes on methods

The three chosen websites, BBC, *The Guardian* and *Telegraph*, represent popular online UK news sources and a mix of both newspaper and broadcasting organisations (including a left-wing and right-wing broadsheet and a public service broadcaster). In considering how the images individually and collectively accumulate meaning through representational form and mode of address, I follow a multimodal critical analysis approach, exploring layout, image and text, and their interplay in telling the story of the day (Machin and Mayr, 2013). As Caple and Knox (2012) point out, the sequence, spatial organisation and navigation functions of news galleries all work to affect the narrative and rhetorical potentials, and we can note differences and similarities in each news website by exploring such features. In addition to looking into the technical and presentational affordances of the online galleries, a multimodal approach examines the semiotic choices and how they communicate certain ideas. Admittedly we might only be able to claim 'meaning potential', but images are particularly effective in enacting inclusion and exclusion, and in making visible social relations and patterns of legitimation and marginalisation (Machin, 2013).

Finally, while the media genre under investigation is natively digital, the funeral protest itself has significant physical and material attributes to consider. This is clearly not an online protest in the 'Ding Dong' mode but one which exists in a certain time and place (or places), and for which the participants prepared their own signs and banners to hold up. As recent studies of activism in the digital age have argued, the excitement over the potential for mobilisation and organisation enabled by new communication technologies should not distract attention from the importance of embodied, collective, physical gathering and resistance (Gerbaudo, 2012). Indeed, the material objects used by activists possess potent aesthetic and symbolic power, as recently explored in the V&A Museum's exhibition and book *Disobedient Objects* (Flood and Grindon, 2014). Axel Phillips' analysis of protest materials reminds us that even text-based banners have a visual dimension:

> A text is structured and represented in a specific way; thus, the representation and reception of a text is influenced by its composition,

the size of the letters, the space between lines, the type of letters, etc.... Therefore, an examination of visual protest material should take into account *how it is designed.*

(Phillips, 2012: 8)

The following section gives an overview of the multimodal but primarily visual communication at each aforementioned level: the organisation and design of the gallery; the selected photographs; and the protest materials depicted within. Although small-scale and exploratory in nature, this study attends to the nature of visibility afforded to the protesters in the news galleries and how their activities are contextualised within the script of the main media event. Due to space limitations, I present a summary of the galleries' features and analysis of selected recurrent images.

## Patterns of inclusion and exclusion

The design and associated mode of address differs to some degree in each of the galleries. The BBC's main gallery offers 18 images with captions appearing below. The emphasis here is on the ceremonial splendour and ritualised aspects of the day, picturing the coffin draped in the Union Flag on its procession journey and within the funeral service. Along with the Church of England, monarchy, family and government figures, the military role stands out: the three services are each represented and the coffin travels on a horse-drawn gun carriage. This was indeed a 'ceremonial funeral with full military honours', with military bands accompanying the cortege and a gun salute over the River Thames during the procession (also pictured in the BBC gallery). In addition to the formal and sombre rituals, the BBC pictured crowds, with Union Flags featuring heavily within their clothing or draped over, and a close-up on the chest of one supporter displaying a blue rosette and Maggie badges (this is a cropped image of Gloria Martin, whose full image appears in the *Guardian* gallery and shows her wiping a tear (photographed by Kevin Coombs)).

In the BBC's main gallery there is only a single protest image included, taken by Carl Court. The crowd appears as a sea of bobbing heads, out of focus and at the bottom of the frame. In the top centre of the image, a sign is held up in sharp focus; we see only the arm of a woman (with visible nail varnish and large ring) holding aloft a sign which reads 'I am not happy to pay for Thatcher's funeral', spelled out in capital letters in black marker pen, except for 'not', which appears in red and is larger than the rest of the statement. Additionally there are some smaller words in the white space, seemingly penned as an afterthought or with no effort to make them visible from a distance. I cannot be sure but it looks like 'I'm bloody livid'. Is this another voice in conversation with the main slogan (reminiscent of a graffiti conversation scribbled on a toilet door), or a quieter addition which visually whispers this more anger-filled statement? In fact, the published image has also been cropped to omit some of the crowd and strengthen the composition. In making comparisons across galleries we are able to note the repetition of similar images and to document the cropping practices which further work to omit or emphasise elements in the representational form.

Reflecting its 'public value' principles, the BBC website offers a second gallery titled 'Baroness Thatcher's funeral: Your photos', with nine images sent in by members of the public. In terms of subject matter, they offer a similar focus for the day, but without the access to the 'great and good' within the funeral service. Each image is either credited to the named amateur photographer or includes a direct quotation adding context or reflection. There is a degree of visual balance, with a group of protesters pictured in one image and then a supporter in the following image. The selected 'Your photos' generally lack the compositional clarity and artistry of the professional photographers' images, with the single protest photograph depicting a crowd from behind, holding up identical banners produced by the Socialist Workers' Party, rather than the more creative examples in other galleries. The caption also plays down the numbers: 'There were some protests but not the large demonstrations some had predicted.' Another photo depicts a military band with the caption: 'Alan Aiken was watching from Ludgate Circus: He said "Slightly down the road from me a group of protesters were chanting and the crowd around me began clapping to drown them out." ' The direct quotation from the citizen-photographer refers to action not depicted within the frame, so that its inclusion simultaneously affords recognition of the off-screen protest while signalling the disapproval of 'the crowd'. This oblique reference to the protest employs the voice of a named citizen to invoke the disapproval of his fellow crowd members and so works to further diminish the unseen protesters.

In *The Guardian*'s 'Picture Desk Live' gallery, the head and deputy head of photography are named in the byline, making this a more visibly curated page of photographs. It is usual practice in slideshows or galleries for the institutional authorship to be placed in the background. Additionally, rather than a gallery format where the reader clicks through photo by photo, here the images are arranged vertically on a single page, with the option to start from the oldest or the latest image. The timeline feature is much more apparent in this organisation and the 'live' updating of the website highlighted, so that a curated and sequential presentation is brought to the fore: 'The *Guardian*'s award-winning picture team brings you the best photo coverage from today's events in central London.' Another key difference is the openness for comments – and the 328 comments collated during the collection period are still accessible. In contrast, the comments are closed on the *Telegraph* and BBC pages.

*The Guardian*'s approach allows for a larger selection of images and is most inclusive in its presentation of mourners, supporters and protesters in one mediated space. There is also a greater emphasis here on the protests across the country, rather than those in London. These are news agency-sourced images (Getty, the Press Association, Reuters) which provide a sense of narrative and even exact times for each image, while contrasting the sombre but spectacular formalities of the day with the often low-key and low-tech protest materials. This is also a heterogeneous space which includes the more spectacle-driven protests – for example, in the mining town of Goldthorpe, where an effigy of Thatcher is burned in a coffin with a 'Scab' wreath. The pictures of protest beyond Central London provide a critique of the funeral spectacle delivered through the creation of their own counterspectacle: 'Critique through spectacle, not critique versus spectacle' (DeLuca and Peeples, 2002: 134).

Whereas *The Guardian*'s Picture Desk Live integrates the photographs from the funeral procession and service itself; supportive mourners; *and* protesters into a single chronological space, *The Telegraph* provides a separate gallery for the protesters – organisationally enacting a detached mediated public space for the reporting and remembering of the protests. There is a single photograph which connects the two *Telegraph* galleries, appearing in both (Figure 10.1). The image depicts a crowd positioned behind a barrier and a line of Welsh guardsmen in front of them, on the right side of the frame. The foreground is slightly out of focus, with the focal point being a protester's sign which simply reads 'boo!' in large black letters. We can only see a few left-hand fingers of the person holding the sign aloft, its height increased with what look like two bamboo gardening canes as support. In the main *Telegraph* gallery the caption reads 'A protester holds up a banner', while there is slightly more information in the protest gallery caption: 'A protester holds up a banner as guardsmen line the route of the funeral procession.'[3] In the main gallery this image is then countered with

*Figure 10.1* A protester holds up a banner as guardsmen line the route of the funeral procession. Credit: Kevin Coombs/Reuters

the subsequent image which depicts an older man, frontal view, as he squints into the direction of the camera, positioned above the surrounding crowd. His sign, which reads 'But we loved her' in capital letters, appears to be a long piece of white paper with the letters made out of blue tape or plastic, a piece of which is peeling off. He is the central and focal point of the image, with smiling office workers indistinct in the background. In each case the focal length is employed to make the sign appear sharply in the image, with the surrounding crowd cast as bit-players in the scene. It is also worth commenting on the signs themselves. The 'boo!' sign clearly expresses the traditional sound of audience disapproval on an occasion when audible booing would be considered disrespectful. But it also suggests a second meaning – one which is sparked by its positioning in the photo, behind the backs of the guardsmen and with the originator hidden from view, the kind of 'boo!' one shouts in a hiding game. The uncertain-looking crowd and the obliviousness of the guardsmen add to the humour of this image. This is a wry take on the reticence demanded by the occasion and therefore captures something of the mischief which arguably characterises the protests. As Gemma Edwards argues, 'misbehaviour' can offer individuals a politically and culturally significant way to challenge or destabilise authority (2014: 213–234). The Thatcher supporter's banner also offers a poignant image. The inclusion of 'but' at the start of the phrase 'but we loved her' contains a plaintive retort which would not otherwise be apparent in the expression 'we loved her'. This sad recognition of others' hatred or anger is also seen in the man's grimace and his determination to be visible above the crowds.

Whether paying their respects or the opposite, the signs and banners captured by photographers tended to be homemade and basic in aesthetic style. As already noted, these materials express moral outrage at paying for the funeral and often refer to famous aphorisms (e.g. 'If there's no such thing as society, pay for your own funeral'; 'The lady is not returning'; 'Thatcher the Iron Lady; rest in rust'). Others take their representative claims more seriously, such as the two young women with scarfs over their faces holding up a fraying sheet which reads: 'I'm here for the people she killed through poverty, despair, policy and war.' This final image appears in the *Telegraph* protest gallery and reflects a more earnest yet vague claim to political expression, the two women posing for the camera but with their faces partly obscured.

## Concluding remarks

As discussed above, the varying patterns of inclusion and exclusion – the visibility of the protest within the online news galleries, spatial organisations of the websites where the politically contentious expressions of the protesters are separated or sidelined – provide a snapshot of mainstream media coverage on the day. The *Telegraph* website presents an entire gallery dedicated to the protests, but its separation from the *Hello* magazine-style focus on the 'great and good' attending the funeral organisationally and symbolically removes the dissenting politics from the event. The BBC presents its notion of the public through a selection of amateur images, 'Your photos', while concentrating on the military splendour on display. Perhaps not surprisingly given its traditional left-wing inclinations, it is the *Guardian* gallery which presents a heterogeneous collection in a shared mediated space. Here we can most clearly contrast the ceremonial spectacle with the counterspectacle of dissent and the varied efforts to gain visibility. In creating and holding aloft their signs with DIY aesthetics and ironic puns, the protesters aimed to disrupt not the procession itself but the haughty sense of authority which pronounced that this was the time for national mourning and not for political demonstrations. Locating their protests at the site of the funeral potentially attracts ire, but the embodied and situated character of the protests is as vital to this mode of political expression as the media-friendly stylistic choices of visual activism. To politicise the ceremonial event was to claim the right to a form of political participation that not only looked back in anger but also prompted current political leaders to contemplate how the consequences of their policies might be seen in the future.

The Thatcher funeral protests are arguably unique and the broader significations remain unclear. But despite their momentary nature, the protests at least represent a challenge to a state-led definition of the event and its political nature. At both the site of the funeral procession and in local communities, protesters expressed a resistance and brought 'the political' to the event – not the political talk of political leaders but the politics which says we are legitimate social actors who deserve to be *seen* and heard.

## Notes

1. How Ted Heath, among others, reportedly referred to Thatcher. Vernon Bogdanor notes that Conservative Central Office actually referred to her as 'that bloody woman', initialling papers for her with TBW: she thought it was the title of a TV station and did not realise it referred to her (Bogdanor, 2012).
2. The links to the slideshows are as follows:

   > *The Telegraph*, which had both a general 'In Pictures' page with 20 photographs: http://www.telegraph.co.uk/news/picturegalleries/10001 112/In-pictures-Margaret-Thatchers-funeral.html and a protest-specific slideshow with 14 images: http://www.telegraph.co.uk/news/picture galleries/10000692/Protests-during-the-funeral-of-Baroness-Thatcher. html. No comments on either page.
   > The BBC News website had an 'In Pictures' page with 18 photos: http: //www.bbc.co.uk/news/in-pictures-22179697 and a 'Your Pictures' page with 9 photos: http://www.bbc.co.uk/news/uk-22187142. The 'Your Pictures' page had captions written by the editorial team, or quotations from the photographer indicated with quote marks.
   > *The Guardian* had a 'picture desk live' feature with 73 pictures and comments enabled: http://www.theguardian.com/news/2013/apr/ 17/picture-desk-live-the-best-pictures-from-lady-thatcher-s-funeral.

   I also surveyed the *Mail Online* but due to lack of space it is omitted from the discussion. The *Mail Online* has 37 images for the funeral itself in a picture story, with a separate page on the protests including 33 photos, two images from Facebook and two videos.
3. The photograph also appears in the *Guardian* gallery and is credited to Kevin Coombs. The caption here is: 'A protester holds up a very succinct banner as guardsmen line the route of the funeral procession.'

164   *Protests and Power*

# References

BBC (2013) Funeral of Baroness Thatcher cost £1.2m. *BBC News*, 29 July. Retrieved from: http://www.bbc.co.uk/news/uk-politics-23488443 (accessed 1 October 2014).

Bogdanor, V. (2012) Britain in the 20th Century: Thatcherism, lecture at Museum of London, 24 April. Retrieved from: http://www.gresham.ac.uk/lectures-and-events/britain-in-the-20th-century-thatcherism-1979–1990 (accessed 10 October 2014).

Caple, H. and Knox, J. S. (2012) Online news galleries, photojournalism and the photo essay. *Visual Communication*. 11(2), 207–236.

Chartres, R. (2013) The Address given by the Bishop of London at the funeral of Baroness Thatcher. *St Paul's Cathedral*, 17 April. Retrieved from: http://www.stpauls.co.uk/News-Press/Latest-News/The-Address-given-by-the-Bishop-of-London-at-the-funeral-of-Baroness-Thatcher (accessed 10 October 2014).

Davies, C., Watt, N., Dodd, V. and Taylor, M. (2013) Lady Thatcher funeral: Dean of St Paul's accuses protesters of being divisive. *Guardian*, 16 April. Retrieved from: http://www.theguardian.com/politics/2013/apr/16/margaret-thatcher-funeral-protesters-divisive#history-link-box (accessed 1 October 2014).

Dayan, D. (2013) Conquering visibility, conferring visibility: Visibility seekers and media performance. *International Journal of Communication*. 7, 137–153.

Dayan, D. and Katz, E. (1992) *Media Events: The Live Broadcasting of History*. Cambridge, MA: Harvard University Press.

DeLuca, K. (1999) *Image Politics*. New York: Guilford Press.

DeLuca, K. and Peeples, J. (2002) From public sphere to public screen: Democracy, activism, and the 'violence' of Seattle. *Critical Studies in Media Communication*. 19(2), 125–151.

Edwards, G. (2014) *Social Movements and Protest*. Cambridge: Cambridge University Press.

Flood, C. and Grindon G. (eds) (2014) *Disobedient Objects*. London: V&A Publishing.

Gerbaudo, P. (2012) *Tweets and the Streets: Social Media and Contemporary Activism*. New York: Pluto.

Hay, C. (2007) *Why We Hate Politics*. Cambridge: Polity Press.

Kress, G. and van Leeuwen, T. (2001) *Multimodal Discourse: The Modes and Media of Contemporary Communication*. Oxford: Oxford University Press.

Machin, D. (2013) What is multimodal critical discourse studies? *Critical Discourse Studies*. 10(4), 347–355.

Machin, D. and Mayr, A. (2013) Personalising crime and crime-fighting in factual television: An analysis of social actors and transitivity in language and images. *Critical Discourse Studies*. 10(4), 356–372.

Martin, J. (2014) *Politics and Rhetoric: A Critical Introduction*. Oxon: Routledge.

Mirzoeff, N. (2011) *The Right to Look: A Counterhistory of Visuality*. London: Duke University Press.

Moore, C. (2013) *Margaret Thatcher: The Authorized Biography, Volume One: Not for Turning*. London: Allen Lane.

Mouffe, C. (2005) *On the Political*. New York: Routledge.

Parry, K. (2015) Visibility and visualities: 'Ways of seeing' politics in the digital media environment, in S. Coleman and D. Freelon (eds) *Handbook of Digital Politics*. Cheltenham: Edward Elgar, 417–432.

Phillips, A. (2012) Visual protest material as empirical data. *Visual Communication*. 11(1), 3–21.

Roosvall, A. (2014) The identity politics of world news: Oneness, particularity, identity and status in online slideshows. *International Journal of Cultural Studies*. 17(1), 55–74.

Thompson, J. B. (1995) *The Media and Modernity*. Stanford: Stanford University Press.

Valentine, J. (2013) The death of Margaret Thatcher and the question of the media event. *JOMEC Journal*. 3 June, 1–15.

# 11

## 'Pay Your Tax!' How Tax Avoidance Became a Prominent Issue in the Public Sphere in the UK

*Jen Birks and John Downey*

While Habermas' original model of the public sphere has attracted enormous attention from across the humanities and social sciences in the English-speaking world since its belated translation over 25 years ago, his subsequent modifications to the model are much less well known. This is a pity because they provide a much more sophisticated understanding of the complex and dynamic operation of the public sphere that can help scholars explain how changes occur in public discourse and beyond.

In this chapter we will examine, as a case study that informs public sphere theory-building, the work of UK Uncut, a resource-poor anti-austerity group formed in 2010 that campaigns energetically on the issue of tax avoidance by corporations and wealthy individuals in the UK. It has succeeded in intervening in the public sphere to the extent that tax avoidance is now a major issue in mainstream media news and comment, and one that political elites seek to address in policy-making and ultimately contain. This is a remarkable transformation since the issue had been pursued by traditional civil society organisations without much purchase for some years, including a significant investigation by *The Guardian*, which conceded that tax avoidance was a MEGO (my eyes glaze over) issue and difficult to get the public exercised about. We argue that this rise to prominence is not simply down to the actions of UK Uncut but arises because of the coincidence of a complex recipe of causal conditions. On the way we will offer a method to analyse the public sphere in flux (analytical process-tracing) and we will theorise this process, which may be of help to other scholars in their attempts to understand how, when and why marginal protest groups can permeate mainstream public sphere institutions, influence public discourse and affect policy.

## The public sphere in flux

While Habermas' original formulation of his public sphere thesis is widely known, his more recent and much more sophisticated account of the nature of publicness has attracted comparatively little attention (1989, 1996, 2006). In his original formulation, he charts the rise and fall of the public sphere. In the post-Second World War period he sees a 'refeudalisation' of the public sphere. Here, economic and political elites have captured or colonised the public realm and essentially engage in a dance in front of citizens aimed ultimately at winning votes in periodic elections. Habermas' more recent work, in contrast, modifies this theory of elite capture that led in his earlier work to a problematic account of the public sphere in stasis. What impressed him was the ability of new social movements – feminism and the green movement in the 1970s and the 1980s – to make an impact on public debate that ultimately led to some degree of economic, social and political change. These were initially voices from the margins that, subject to modification, became mainstream. Habermas' revisions in this area are influenced greatly by the work of Bernhard Peters and the notion of a 'sluice-gate' public sphere. Peters argues that the control of elites over public discourse is far from complete: 'the centre controls the direction and dynamics of these processes only to a limited degree. Changes can start just as much at the periphery as at the centre' (1993: 340). This presents encouragement to social movements and resource-poor marginal or peripheral groups generally, and a certain amount of succour to elites as they can present themselves as legitimate representatives of citizens and as responsive to society.

Peters' model is made up of a number of concentric circles. On the periphery we have resource-poor groups. Moving towards the centre we have mass-media institutions, such as newspapers and broadcasting, followed by courts and legislatures, with the executive forming the core. Ideas flow towards the centre through the operation of sluice-gates; communication pressure builds up between these different levels at times of crisis, passing through once the pressure has reached a certain point. In previous work we have elaborated upon this model, tracing the process of discursive and political change from the periphery to the centre of the public sphere with respect to the national DNA database in the UK (Downey et al., 2012). We sought to trace the process of discursive and social change by specifying the various ingredients in the causal recipe that led to such change. The ingredients were made up of the presence of 'carriers' or actors in civil society who develop narratives that resonate with broader publics at times of crisis that are then picked up and modified by media and political elites. Here we wish to build on such a causal recipe but also introduce a more sophisticated account of the *mobility* of ideas between different parts of the public sphere (for an elaboration of this argument see Downey, 2014) and the relationship between elites and peripheral publics.

The model of communication flowing from the periphery to the centre via sluice-gates is too linear and it underestimates elite capture. Ideas flow both ways. Peripheral groups pick up, for example, ideas expressed by mass-media institutions. They modify and dramatise them. Then in advantageous circumstances (a crisis of one type or another) these ideas flow back into more powerful institutions of the public sphere as elites become more receptive to new ideas. Elites in turn engage in a process of modification and containment, and these ideas are then disseminated back through the concentric circles of the public sphere. The ability of elites to contain the discursive impulses from peripheral publics depends not only on the ideas themselves (how radical they are) but also on their ability to refashion the discourse and come up with publicly credible responses. It depends also and crucially on the depth and duration of the crisis. What we are proposing therefore is a complex model of discursive change in the public sphere that examines the multidirectional mobility of ideas in a public sphere in flux.

## Methodology

There are special difficulties in devising methods that can capture the mobility of ideas across the public sphere, and no clear methodological toolkit has been developed to do this. Media research methods often entail fixing, isolation and abstraction. Methods of media textual analysis (e.g. content, frame and discourse analysis) will give a 'snapshot' of what a particular sample of media content was at a particular time and place. If we are interested in temporal change then we need a number of snapshots in the manner of time-lapse photography. That will give us, however, only a sense of whether ideas migrate from one place to another over time, but these methods still fix and isolate a moving target and it provides no explanation of *why* ideas might move around –

the economic, political and ideological forces that determine relative mobility. Consequently it is necessary to employ not only methods that fix content but also methods that can capture process.

Process-tracing is a case study small-n method developed and in relatively widespread use in political science and sociology. It has been influential in historicising the study of social science. The basic aim of process-tracing is to discover the causal process, chain, mechanism and conditions that explain the transition from one state of affairs to another. It is particularly useful in cases where there are multiple interacting variables or causal conditions. While process-tracing may have helped to historicise the social sciences, it does not yet appear to have encouraged a consideration of process embedded in space as well as time, but there is no logical reason why this could not be the case. George and Bennett (2005) outline a number of types of process-tracing ranging from the detailed but atheoretical historical narrative to narratives aimed at producing more general forms of explanation at a higher level of abstraction. The type of process-tracing that interests us particularly is somewhere between the two – the 'analytic explanation' variety – which converts:

> A historical narrative into an *analytical* causal explanation couched in explicit theoretical forms. The extent to which a historical narrative is transformed into a theoretical explanation can vary. The explanation may be deliberately selective, focusing on what are thought to be particularly important parts of an adequate or parsimonious explanation.
>
> (George and Bennett, 2005: 211)

If we think of the public sphere as a number of concentric circles with the executive at the centre, surrounded first by legislature and judiciary, then by powerful media institutions, and ultimately by resource-poor groups at the periphery, process-tracing seeks to track the movement of ideas from one arena to the other via sluice-gates. This involves taking snapshots of the state of play of these ideas in the various arenas at different points in time (in this case through media content analysis), and then paying attention to the carriers of these ideas, and the discursive and political opportunity structures that enabled these ideas to be articulated and to take hold. A striking aspect of the tax-avoidance issue is 'multidirectionality' or 'non-linearity' in that it was only through the work of relatively mainstream organisations that those at the margins had something to dramatise and ultimately have an effect on the legislature and the executive in the UK.

## A very brief history of tax-avoidance campaigning in the UK

Tax avoidance is a particularly interesting case study for understanding and developing the concept of sluice-gates because it remained a marginal issue for some years despite some energetic activity in civil society, if not quite on the periphery of the public sphere. In this section, then, we outline the overall timeline of events, before focusing on the role of UK Uncut. It is useful to identify a series of articles written by Nick Davies for *The Guardian* in 2002 as the starting point of sustained attention and investigation by a national newspaper into the issue. Davies' two special reports published in July 2002 explored the Inland Revenue's strategy of accommodation and appeasement towards tax-avoidance practices of multinational corporations and the situation of wealthy 'non-doms' (those resident but not domiciled in the UK) paying little or no tax on their non-UK income and wealth in the UK, and the supposed battle between Chancellor Gordon Brown and the Treasury over this, with Brown wishing to tax this group with the Treasury resisting attempts to do so.

Already established at this point in time was the 'capital and human flight' argument that if the UK government attempts to tax wealthy individuals or, they would simply move their operations overseas, adversely affecting the UK economy. *The Guardian* offers other explanations for previous governments' inaction, including non-doms' donations to the Conservative Party (though the Lakshmi Mittal scandal had already established that Labour was not immune to this). A lack of leadership, resources and skilled inspectors meant that banks, accountancy firms and tax lawyers advising multinational corporations kept ahead of the state, resulting in a loss to the Treasury of £25 billion per annum (24 July 2002: 11). By October, however, Davies noted that non-doms were beating off government interest in their wealth (14 October 2002: 14), and public interest in the story waned.

The next significant encounter with the issue on the part of *The Guardian* was its reporting of the Tax Justice Network's establishment of an office in London, a year after it was founded (Duncan Campbell, 21 September 2004: 21). Here, however, the focus was not on the cost of tax avoidance to the UK Treasury but rather on how multinationals were avoiding taxes on profits earned in developing economies, due to founder John Christensen's work with Oxfam on the issue. The Tax Justice Network was again cited the following week, by George Monbiot, in support of his criticism of Gordon Brown's inaction on the issue (28 September 2004: 21), but the issue failed to gain momentum. *Guardian* articles over the following two years included criticisms of the legal but highly dubious moral practices of accountancy firms that help firms to avoid taxes (Prem Sikka, Professor of Accounting at Essex University, 5 September 2005: 15), the UK's 'cash in hand' culture (Richard Adams, 12 August 2006: 25), and praise for the Institute for Fiscal Studies review of the UK's tax system, which bemoaned the explosion of the tax-avoidance business (Polly Toynbee, 15 September 2006: 35). In 2007, coinciding with Gordon Brown becoming prime minister, there was a relative flurry of articles about tax avoidance, hoping (forlornly as it proved) that his ascendancy would now mean that the Labour government would pursue tax avoiders with more vigour, including one in which John Christensen argued once again that 'the time has come to confront the tax-haven monster' (30 May 2007: 28).

In 2008 *The Guardian* returned energetically to the story with a report erroneously claiming that Tesco used offshore companies to avoid paying corporation tax on property sales in the UK, whereas, it transpired, it had been avoiding stamp duty (though *Private Eye* subsequently alleged that it was avoiding corporation tax after all). Tesco issued a libel writ, along with three other actions globally. *Guardian* editor Alan Rusbridger commented at the time: 'To use the law of criminal libel – which they are using in one of the other actions – seems to me incredibly menacing and seems to be done with the purpose of inhibiting criticism' (*Press Gazette*, 2008).

Undeterred, in February 2009 *The Guardian* launched an investigation, The Tax Gap, examining the tax affairs of more than 20 companies on the front pages of the newspaper over two weeks. Investigations editor David Leigh led a team of seven journalists dedicated to the task, including Richard Brooks from *Private Eye*. It drew repeatedly on the Trades Union Congress's (TUC) recently published Touchstone pamphlet *The Missing Billions: The UK Tax Gap* (2008) by Richard Murphy, estimating the cost of tax to the UK Treasury at £25 billion per annum. Rusbridger told the Culture, Media and Sport Select Committee in May that year that prepublication legal work on the investigation had cost £90,000, and that legal costs were deterring investigative journalism.

Despite receiving support from Liberal Democrat MPs, including the deputy leader, Vince Cable, who contributed an article arguing that the crisis should be an occasion to confront tax-avoiders (3 February

2009: 26), and Matthew Oakeshott, who used parliamentary privilege
to undermine the high-court injunction Barclays obtained against *The
Guardian* in relation to documents obtained by a whistleblower,[1] and
despite the financial crisis, public concern over tax avoidance remained
low. Truly tax avoidance had proved to be a MEGO issue.

Over the course of almost a decade, then, *The Guardian* together with a
number of pressure groups (Tax Justice Network) and NGOs (e.g. Oxfam,
Action Aid) had campaigned against tax avoidance by both wealthy
individuals and corporations. These campaigns, however, failed to ignite
public anger or to persuade the government to make a step-change
in its efforts to collect tax. Why was this the case? Reasons for this
can be divided into three areas: an unpromising ideological environment; an unhelpful political environment; and an infertile economic
environment.

*Ideologically*, *The Guardian* and pressure groups were battling against
the prevailing neoliberal ideology that regarded increased government
action to collect tax owed as either anti-business (and thus harming
the interests of UK Plc) or as resulting in endless bureaucratic red tape.
*Politically*, calls for greater action on the part of the Labour government
were seen as being potentially divisive and it was easy to categorise tax
campaigners as being 'old Labour', with associated fears for the party
of being characterised as anti-business, and as under the thumb of the
unions. Divisions within the labour movement, therefore, tended to act
as a brake on the development of political momentum behind the campaign. It was left to the Liberal Democrats to seize tax avoidance as a
political issue prior to the 2010 General Election campaign. *Econom-
ically*, the UK was experiencing a period of growth, however illusory
that turned out to be. While the public finances were in good shape,
the estimated £25 billion per annum tax gap did not appear to matter.
With the onset of the financial crisis, collecting more tax from corporations was seen to be inopportune, and public expenditure was being
boosted to stave off economic collapse. By late 2010, however, all of
these conditions had changed.

## Evidence that the tax issue became present in the mass-media public sphere

While as a consequence of the *Guardian* campaign in early 2009 there
was a spike in national newspaper coverage of tax avoidance, this was
fleeting. It was not until September 2010 that we can see the gates of
the sluice slowly rising (see Figure 11.1). That month saw widespread

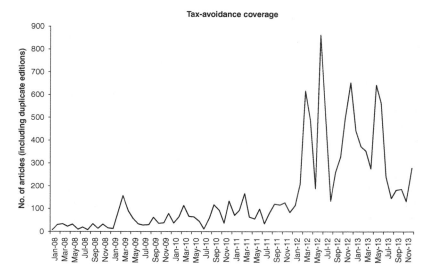

*Figure 11.1* Graph showing tax avoidance coverage in selected UK newspapers, 2009–2013

coverage of the Her Majesty's Revenue and Customs (HMRC) deal with Vodafone, in which it reportedly negotiated its tax bill down by £6 billion. This story was broken by Richard Brooks in *Private Eye*, and, as he says, its particular significance was that it 'coincided with the Tories announcing their programme of spending cuts', and that 'UK Uncut was formed as a direct result' in October 2010 (interview, October 2014). Making use of social media, UK Uncut dramatised the issue of tax avoidance by holding protests outside and within high-street stores that were associated with tax avoidance. Their message was not new, having been firmly established by Richard Murphy's work for the TUC. As Murphy says, 'they had a ready-made narrative, in a sense, and I'd written a lot of that narrative, and they picked it up and ran with it. And they ran with it very successfully. Sitting outside Vodafone, and saying 'pay your tax' got headlines' (interview, August 2014). UK Uncut effectively amplified the alternative narrative to austerity where others had failed.

In the seven months prior to September 2010 there were 377 articles that mentioned tax avoidance in 12 UK national newspapers. This was during a General Election period where tax avoidance was part of the Liberal Democrats' manifesto and where there were revelations of Lord Ashcroft's non-dom status (the largest and most prominent

Conservative Party donor). In the seven months from September 2010 the issue was mentioned in 627 articles. UK Uncut was mentioned explicitly by national newspapers for the first time in November 2010, but in the following five months it was mentioned 364 times. To give some indication of comparative visibility, the TUC and the Tax Justice Network had been mentioned in relation to tax avoidance in national newspapers 136 and 139 times, respectively, from 2007 to 2010.

The issue was then subsequently picked up by political elites. Margaret Hodge, for example, the chair of the Public Accounts Committee of the House of Commons, was mentioned only three times in relation to tax avoidance in 2010, but in 2012 and 2013 was mentioned a total of 834 times. As the issue was picked up by political elites, mentions of UK Uncut fell. It played a part in the initial opening of the sluice-gates but as the water started running through, the issue was picked up by established resource-rich elites who then attempted to steer the issue according to their own interests.

Having provided evidence of the sluice-gates opening, we will now discuss the complex coincidence of causes that resulted in this discursive shift.

## Resonant narratives: Pay your tax!

The anti-austerity protest agenda needed to create a powerful alternative narrative to challenge the established narrative that cuts were regretfully necessary. The government's sleight of hand in shifting the financial crisis caused by bad mortgage debt traded by banks to a fiscal crisis of public debt was, and is, successful, an example perhaps of how neoliberal policy-makers capitalise on crisis, diagnosing the cure for the ills of neoliberal capitalism with a purer version, with lower corporate taxes and a smaller state. UK Uncut saw this as 'a matter of rhetoric, and we had to challenge that rhetoric, and we did that by talking about tax' ('Jo', UK Uncut, interview, November 2014). It presented austerity as 'ideological', and proposed a crackdown on tax avoidance as an alternative to cuts, much as the TUC had two years earlier, but also succeeded in dramatising and popularising the argument. The particular significance of this is that it managed, at least initially, to avoid the trap between the spectacular but typically delegitimised and the socially legitimised but typically disregarded (Juris, 2011). As Jo says, 'we didn't want to be portrayed as a marginal group, the thing we were really keen to avoid was the sense that there are political activists and there is the rest of the public and there's something dividing them'. UK Uncut achieved this both by anticipating the delegitimising news frames routinised in protest reporting and by reproducing and repurposing legitimising news frames.

The emergence of UK Uncut through a Twitter hashtag forms an important part of its legitimating narrative, as is evident on the 'About UK Uncut' section of the group's website.[2]

> At that point [the initial Vodafone shop protest], UK Uncut only existed as #ukuncut, a hashtag someone had dreamed up the night before the protest. As we sat in the doorway, chanting and handing leaflets to passers by, the hashtag began to trend around the UK and people began to talk about replicating our action. The idea was going viral. The seething anger about the cuts had found an outlet. Just three days later and close to thirty Vodafone stores had been closed around the country.
>
> (UK Uncut, n.d.)

This emphasises the spontaneity of their origins, as something that grew without direction from above – avoiding the accusation of being instrumentalised by vested interest (which, for much news media, would include trade unions) – and its basis in an emotional prepolitical response, as an anger that pre-existed and was already seeking an 'outlet'.

Because the organisers saw the need and the potential to build a critical mass, they took what Rucht (2013) calls an 'adaptation' orientation to mainstream media, drawing on members' experience of working with the media in NGOs and previous activism to appeal to dominant news values. A filmmaker known to organisers through environmental activist networks responded to the callout for that first action and produced a film that, hand-held camera aside, uses the visual language of broadcast news, including sped-up video, filler shots focusing in on storefront signage, and on-the-street vox pops. The video was broadcast on *Newsnight*, one of the BBC's flagship news programmes, in January 2011, and members of UK Uncut appeared on the programme several times during 2011.

Both voiceover and activist interviewees use similar frames: a straightforward connection between tax avoidance and public sector cuts, and the solution as similarly uncomplicated. The connection is simply made through the juxtaposition of clauses, or their temporal or sequential connection: 'the government's allowing corporations like Vodafone to get away with not paying taxes then cutting our public services', 'at the

same time he's making these huge cuts to welfare'. The policy alternative
to public spending cuts is presented as equally obvious: 'a simple one is
just getting everyone in society to pay their fair share and that means the
corporations stop dodging tax and pay what they owe'. It is notable that
they talk of 'fairness' rather than 'social justice' or 'equality', appealing
to news media frames of 'fairness to taxpayers' more typically associated
with stories initiated by the Taxpayers Alliance and against public-sector
pay disputes (Birks, 2014).

The moral justifications are left for bystanders to make in vox pops, in
an interesting reversal of the established role of the bystander in news
reporting of protest, whereby they stand in for the public disapproval
of the protesters. Here is it used to demonstrate public disapproval of
corporate tax avoidance among a demographically diverse selection of
individuals – not only an angry denunciation of 'fat cats' but also a nice
elderly lady agreeing that 'it is all wrong', and two young men, typically
assumed to be disengaged from politics. Two of the contributors object
that ordinary people owning small sums to HMRC are pursued aggressively with additional charges, so it cannot be fair that Vodafone should
be allowed to negotiate its debt down. In a way, this is the commonsense reversal of the false analogy that the government makes between
the public finances and balancing the family budget.

## Receptive media and political elites

The personal authenticity of protesters' outrage was surprisingly broadly
recognised, not just in *The Guardian* and *The Observer*, but also in the
*The Times*, *The Sunday Times*, *The Daily Mail* and *People*. In some cases
this took the form of vague assertions of the public mood, describing
big business as the 'focus of rising anger', 'growing disquiet' (*Observer*,
5 December 2010: 20) and 'legitimate public anger' (David Wighton, *The
Times*, 15 December 2010: 23). However, the diversity of protesters was
also frequently noted, and more often than not in direct reference to the
spontaneous viral spread of the movement through social media, suggesting that UK Uncut's self-legitimising narrative was directly picked
up, simultaneously a testament to dominant understandings of 'social
media'.

The epidemic of students and grandmothers lying on pavements to
bar access to global brands is just the latest example of the way in
which Twitter and other social media websites are being used to mobilise
loose coalitions of ordinary but angry citizens (*Independent*, 18 December
2010: 8).

Similarly, *Times* commentator Stefanie Marsh (18 December 2010: 8) defined them as both a 'grassroots organisation' and 'without doubt the most successful example of "viral activism" in the country', referring to supporters as 'followers' and 'fans' in social media terms. One of the quotes from elderly protesters demonstrates an awareness of dominant media-framing, and even of their own legitimating role: 'And don't let anyone say this protest is hijacked by anarchists. If anything, it's hijacked by pensioners!' (*Observer*, 5 December 2010: 20). Echoing UK Uncut's video, *The Guardian* described bystanders as 'fairly sympathetic' (4 December 2010), while Polly Toynbee (*Guardian*, 7 December 2010: 29) went as far as to say that 'many were supportive and a few joined in'.[3] The porous boundary between protesters and bystanders undermines the typical definition of the public in contradistinction to protesters, but also problematised their treatment. Both *The Sunday Mirror* and *The Sunday Times* (5 December 2010) reported the aggressive removal of protesters by Top Shop security guards, including one who said she was a shopper. Even *The Sunday Express* quoted a protester describing how security guards carried her out by her ankles and hair and describing the experience as 'quite scary' (5 December 2014: 12).

There was *some* evidence of traditional delegitimisation, but initially it was limited to a smattering of references to disruption and inconvenienced shoppers. It was only after the second student anti-tuition fee protest march, when a branch of Top Shop plastered with UK Uncut signs had its window broken and Prince Charles's car was jostled nearby, that *The Telegraph* was able to characterise UK Uncut as a violent mob of anti-capitalists and anarchists (*Telegraph* blog, 10 December 2010; *Daily Telegraph*, 11 December 2010). *The Mirror* (10 December 2010), too, described 'panic-stricken and angry' shoppers barricaded (by security) inside a branch of Top Shop due to a UK Uncut protest (although the panic seems to have been caused by the impression that it was a bomb scare).

Interestingly, the corporate perspective was rather muted, but primarily because the companies implicated decided on a strategy of silence, presumably to avoid adding fuel to a fire that they hoped would die out quickly. While Arcadia told *The Sunday Times* (5 December 2010) that the protests were 'highly irresponsible' as their demands would only 'stop business, stop employment', and claiming their own social responsibility on the basis of being 'one of the largest employers in the country', they declined to comment to *The Mail on Sunday* or *People* (5 December 2010). Other than a widely reported terse dismissal that the £6 billion tax bill was an 'urban myth' (a soundbite also, interestingly, attributed to HMRC), Vodafone made no comment. Vodafone's head of communications explained to *The Independent* (17 December 2010, Business: 34) that the company had 'decided against a direct confrontation with the protesters' because 'getting into a debate with protesters would be counter-productive'.

Newspaper commentators and business editors similarly muted their prior assertion of business interests as being identical to the national interest. The capital flight argument appeared in Tracey Corrigan's business column in *The Daily Telegraph* on 19 November, but by 8 December she conceded: 'Business needs to win the popularity contest; Protests against tax-dodging may be misguided, but they have caught the public mood'. David Prosser in *The Independent's* business pages (11 December 2010: 54) similarly admitted that there was 'much to admire about the campaign group UKuncut', objecting only that government is the appropriate target for protest, rather than businesses, which are not going to pay more than they have to. Prosser also drew a moral equivalence between corporate schemes and tax arrangements available to married couples in a piece representing 'the business view' alongside 'the protesters' view' from a UK Uncut member pointing out, among other things, that the distinction is marked by the *spirit* rather than the letter of the law (18 December 2010: 8). Even incoming Confederation of British Industry president Roger Carr was quoted making a distinction between 'efficient' tax planning and 'artificial' arrangements (*Observer*, 12 December 2010, Business: 43). Polly Toynbee (*Guardian*, 7 December 2010: 29) suggested that it was the material presence of Arcadia shops and Cadbury factories in the UK that made it clear that they were clearly based in and making their profit in the UK (in comparison with a 'flighty finance company'), drawing on a commonsense notion of fairness, but also hinted at a more populist angle, which was picked up by *The Daily Mail*.

It was moves by Kraft, the Swiss firm that had controversially acquired Cadbury's, to make the brand a subsidiary and thereby reduce its UK tax liabilities that attracted the attention of *Daily Mail* city editor Alex Brummer (6 December 2010). He introduced a nationalistic tone with an article headlined 'This plunder of our heritage'. Lamenting the way that 'the Government has stood by while huge chunks of Britain...have been sold to foreign buyers', the article was peppered with references to the nation, including 'hard-working, tax-paying Britons', 'the British brand', 'Britain's industrial base' and 'the nation's tax revenues'. Brummer acknowledged the neoliberal argument that the 'financial sacrifice' was made to attract inward investment, 'But when the economy collapsed and manufacturing output fell by 10 per cent, these foreign owners' cynical and deliberately planned tax avoidance strategies left Britain's corporate tax base horribly exposed.' The distinction between the interests of corporations and citizens (or 'taxpayers', in the paper's more clientalistic terms) was transferred into an 'us and them' discourse about Britons and foreigners, to better suit the editorial ideology of the newspaper.

The first evidence of a political response was as early as Monday 6 December, when the treasury minister, David Gauke, announced plans to close loopholes in corporate tax law and to consult on further proposals. Both *The Guardian* (13 December 2010, leader column: 28; 7 December 2010, Polly Toynbee: 29; Alex Hawkes, 7 December 2010: 23) and *The Independent* (6 December 2010, Business: 34) concluded that UK Uncut was instrumental in forcing, amplifying or accelerating governmental action regarding tax avoidance. However, Hawkes quotes a UK Uncut spokesman remarking that it was 'great to see the process works so quickly', but that this would prevent a fraction of total annual tax avoidance.

More significantly, however, Margaret Hodge was prompted to ask questions of HMRC at hearings of the Public Accounts Committees, which Richard Brooks credited as 'essentially the big political change' (interview, October 2014) and Richard Murphy credited for placing the issue on the agenda at the 2013 G8 summit at Lough Earne, for the introduction of an anti-avoidance principle and ultimately for a drop in tax avoidance (interview, August 2014).

> UK Uncut exists within a kind of ecosystem of other activist groups and people doing work, and the fact that there were already people out there who had done all this fantastic research on tax, it laid the groundwork. It meant that we, direct action and activists, we were the kind of wedge, we helped to open this space up, and it was great that there were people there that were ready to fill that space who could talk about it. We never pretended to be experts, we never tried to be, and it's so good that there were people out there who were doing that. And what I think is happening now with the tax issue is that other people are now pushing it forward in a way in which a group like UK Uncut never could.
>
> ('Jo', UK Uncut, interview, November 2014)

## Conclusion

At first sight the case of the rise to prominence of tax avoidance in the UK's public sphere is an example of Peters' sluice-gates in operation. The actions of a group at the margins resulted in a discursive shift in mainstream media and in how the core institutions of the public sphere sought to deal with the issue. We have added two modifications to the sluice-gate model: first, we see this discursive and policy shift as the product of a complex causal recipe where the actions of UK Uncut were a necessary but not sufficient cause; second, we argue that discursive shifts need to be understood not as linear processes but as multidirectional. Without the prior work of mainstream public sphere actors such as Oxfam, the TUC and *The Guardian* to establish the evidence and arguments, UK Uncut would have had nothing to dramatise. This points not only to the continued importance of investigative journalism, which is under threat in UK broadcast and print journalism, but also casts doubt on the idea suggested by the sluice-gate model that marginal actors can bring about change unaided. Key to understanding this is process-tracing over time and space: tracking the migration of ideas from the mainstream to the margins and then back again in a different set of circumstances that affect both political and discursive opportunity structures.

## Acknowledgements

The authors would like to thank 'Jo' from UK Uncut, Richard Murphy and Richard Brooks for agreeing to be interviewed and for their valuable contributions.

## Notes

1. The writ obliged them to remove documents detailing the bank's involvement in tax avoidance provided by a whistleblower from their website and prevented them from publicising their availability elsewhere on the internet.
2. http://www.ukuncut.org.uk/about/ukuncut.
3. Jo reports that Polly Toynbee quietly joined several UK Uncut actions in London and was very supportive.

## References

Birks, J. (2014) *News and Civil Society*. Farnham: Ashgate.
Downey, J., Stephens, M. and Flaherty, J. (2012) The 'sluice-gate' public sphere and the national DNA database in the UK. *Media Culture Society*. 34(4), 439–456.

Downey, J. (2014) Flux and the Public Sphere. *Media Culture Society.* 36(3), 367–379.

George, A. L. and Bennett, A. (2005) *Case Studies and Theory Development in the Social Sciences.* Cambridge, MA: MIT Press.

Habermas, J. (1989) *The Structural Transformation of the Public Sphere.* Cambridge, MA: MIT Press.

Habermas, J. (1996) *Between Fact and Norms.* Cambridge: Polity/Blackwell.

Habermas, J. (2006) Political communication in media Society: Does democracy still enjoy an epistemic dimension? The impact of normative theory on empirical research. *Communication Theory.* 16, 411–426.

Juris, J. S. (2011) Mediating and embodying transnational protest: Internal and external effects of mass media global effects of mass global justice actions, in S. Cottle and L. Lester (eds) *Transnational Protest and the Media.* Oxford: Peter Lang, 98–108.

Peters, B. (1993) *Die Integration Moderner Gesellschaften.* Frankfurt am Main: Suhrkamp.

*Press Gazette* (2008) Tesco out to gag me with a £1.6m action. *Press Gazette,* 25 April 2008. Retrieved from http://www.pressgazette.co.uk/node/40949

Rucht, D. (2013) Protest movements and their media usages in C. Bart, M. Alice, and M. Patrick (eds) *Mediation and Protest Movements.* Bristol/Chicago: Intellect.

TUC (2008) *The Missing Billions: The UK Tax Gap.* Touchstone Pamphlets. Available at: www.tuc.org.uk/sites/default/files/documents/completedownload.pdf

# 12
## UGC in the Newsroom: How BBC Journalists' Engagement with Internet Activists Has Altered Newsroom Practices

*Lisette Johnston*

This chapter examines how BBC journalistic practices have changed to incorporate UGC and activist voices during the Syrian uprising that began in March 2011. The research proposes that limited access to the country since that time has led to greater interaction with citizens and activists within Syria, whose voices were marginalised at the start of the violence. As the conflict continues into its fourth year, more than 100,000 people are believed to have been killed, many journalists have been captured or murdered, and the country is arguably becoming unreportable. This means that those seeking to cover events in Syria must engage with citizens on the ground. Some of these voices went largely unheard initially, yet media activists, arguable non-elite sources who were once at the margins of reporting, are now perceived to be something akin to 'correspondents', and news organisations' relationships with them are evolving.

The study uses newsroom observations and qualitative interviews to also examine how BBC journalists' engagement with Syrian activists has changed from when protests began in Deraa in March 2011 right up to the chemical attacks in Ghouta on 21 August 2013. An understanding of how BBC journalists engage with activists inside and outside Syria is important, not least as the world's biggest broadcaster continues to strive to achieve accuracy and impartiality in its news reporting. The latter aspect has proved crucial to BBC teams as they continue to cover Syria without a continuous presence in the country. At times the relationships between journalists and activists not only dictates the content used in news programming but can also impact on future programming through the snowball effect of gaining new contacts via existing ones. By examining the BBC's engagement with activists in Syria, and how this has impacted on journalistic practice, it is hoped those working on the conflict in the future can develop best practice in dealing with this challenging situation, yet continue to give a voice to the those who are 'voiceless' and are at times at the margins of society in Syria. The guiding questions this chapter seeks to address are: How has UGC helped BBC newsrooms to understand developments surrounding the conflict? How have journalists engaged with citizens and activists within Syria? And have BBC journalistic practices changed to incorporate this content and these voices?

## The debate about UGC

Any non-professional visual content submitted to the BBC must be verified before being put 'on air'. That job rests with the BBC newsroom team known as the UGC Hub, which harvests content posted online and processes text, videos and photographs submitted to the BBC, often from audience members. The Hub arguably had its watershed moment when the 7/7 bombings took place in London in 2005. Within six hours of the attack, the BBC had received more than 1,000 photographs, 20 videos, 4,000 SMSs and 20,000 e-mails (Sambrook, 2005), marking a point where journalists' relationships with the audience evolved to become more like a conversation (Gillmor, 2006). All of this content, usually created by 'the audience', is considered by the BBC to be UGC. Given that the participation of audiences is not something new, UGC is in some ways a contested term. Journalists may have processed such content previously but not considered it to be UGC. After all, audience comments are very different from eyewitness footage in terms of how they are dealt with. The term also assumes a certain use of technology and engagement, but there are different levels of engagement depending on the nature of the content. Also, is it content only sent directly to the BBC and only by audience members that comes under this title? Much has been written about the BBC using UGC amid calls to more clearly define what UGC actually is, but this has often related to online platforms and blogs (Barkho, 2011; Fornaciari, 2012; Hermida and Thurman, 2008).

One of the most comprehensive studies of UGC in news is Wardle and Williams (2008) work, 'ugc@thebbc'. The research used staff interviews and participant observation to understand how UGC is used by the BBC and journalists, and how the audience perceive it (Wardle and Williams, 2008). The study covered many elements of UGC, ranging from phone-in interviews, comments under online stories and video initiatives with the public, as well as 'snow pictures' sent in by viewers. These varied elements were all considered to be types of 'audience material', high-lighting that 'the complexities are sometimes lost because of the reliance of the catch-all term "UGC"' (Wardle and Williams, 2008: 10). For the purposes of this chapter, UGC will refer to visual content as well as eye-witness testimonies not gathered by the BBC or journalists working for traditional agencies such as Agence France-Presse, the Associated Press or Reuters. Most agencies have a social media feed of content they find online, which they redistribute, but this chapter seeks to focus mainly on UGC the BBC gathers itself rather than agency-sourced material, though inevitably there may be some overlap.

## Understanding Syria

The uprisings which began in the Middle East in 2011 have unsurprisingly garnered great attention. There has been huge debate about the extent to which social media platforms played a role in incit-ing protests in various countries (see Castells, 2012; Howard et al., 2011; Khondker, 2011; Tufekci, 2011). This has also prompted studies of how social media platforms such as Facebook and Twitter have been used as sources of information or content for activists, citizen journalists and professional journalists (Goodman, 2012; Hermida et al., 2013), as well as examinations of how old and new media can work in partnership with each other (Robertson, 2013).

It is clear that UGC has played a key role in helping the BBC cover crises and conflicts in recent years. Hänska-Ahy and Shapour (2012) believe journalists at BBC Arabic and Persian first acknowledged the importance of UGC during the Iran elections in 2009. At that time staff reported feeling 'uneasy about how best to use UGC', (2012: 6). By con-trast the BBC journalists they later interviewed in 2011 'seemed far happier, more confident and at ease about using UGC than journalists interviewed 16 months earlier in 2010' (2012: 7). Results also indi-cated that some journalists felt changing practices could shape the news agenda and 'output [ ... ] changed markedly, and UGC has become far more prominent within that' (2012: 12).

To put this research into context, in terms of events in Syria, access to the country has been challenging during most of the conflict. Journalists have been severely restricted in their movements in the country, and for the first six months of the conflict Western journalists were not given government visas. News organisations have therefore relied heavily on content generated inside the country by citizens, in particular activists. In this respect, citizens have become producers, or 'produsers' – both users and producers (Bruns, 2003). This is important because previously those critical of the government were unlikely to have their views aired by either domestic or international news media.

In other breaking news situations, 'citizen journalism' has been employed in addition to scrambling news crews to the location – for example, following the 2010 Christchurch earthquake, or the aftermath of Hurricane Sandy (Thorsen and Allan, 2014). However, in Syria, media organisations are frequently relying on their audience to be newsgatherers. As a result the ability to engage with activists and tap into their expertise has been harnessed by journalists trying to cover the conflict.

## A changing media ecology?

Journalists' jobs appear to be changing: the news products they create are now published and consumed across a variety of interactive platforms. Meanwhile, social media platforms help producers reach a wider range of sources and content, including that created by citizens. Understanding how these developments are altering newsroom practices and roles is essential, not only to safeguard the future of journalism but also to help define what these roles will be in the future. Do journalists continue to be the gatekeepers of the news that people access, or are they remediating and curating content and conversations that citizens are having anyway?

The hypothesis of this chapter is that while a news editor may have the final say, certain ways of working with outside content have changed and will continue to evolve, so this research proposes that journalists' goalposts have moved: 'the journalist's role as gatekeeper will be eroded by some forms of audience material' (Wardle, 2008: 43).

## Methodology

The study incorporates semistructured qualitative interviews with 16 BBC staff. These include correspondents, TV producers, UGC Hub staff and journalists from interactive programmes covering TV and radio. Some potential respondents were contacted through BBC editors and others personally via e-mail. Some were selected as the researcher knew they had experience relevant to the study, whereas others were recommended by fellow members of staff. In a bid to ensure a more active response rate, interviews were made anonymous by coding transcripts. This was important because some might consider the work to be ethically or politically sensitive, and to put the respondents at ease they were first asked to give a brief history of their BBC employment and to talk about what their current job involved.

As a result, some questions were revised, taking into account the different roles and responsibilities journalists have within the BBC, and also their level of involvement in covering events in Syria. For example, one interviewee was very experienced at getting guests on air from Syria and developing a rapport with activists but had very little to do with accessing footage. Another respondent was hugely experienced in terms of working at the UGC Hub but had not been tasked with getting content from Syria to a great extent. The final interviews were audio recorded, then transcribed and coded using NVivo software, which allowed the researcher to identify any emerging themes.

The interviews were complemented by newsroom observations, mainly taking place at the UGC Hub in New Broadcasting House in London. It was decided not to audio record the observations, which largely involved shadowing journalists during their shifts, but rather to ask questions when appropriate and make notes as staff went about their daily routines.

The current Syria conflict began in March 2011 and for the first six months foreign journalists were unable to enter the country. Since then, foreign correspondents from the BBC and other organisations have sporadically been able to enter Syria, yet the risks in doing so are high. The death of *Sunday Times* correspondent Marie Colvin in Baba Amr in February 2012, and the beheading of US freelancer James Foley by Islamic State in October 2014, highlight how dangerous a Syria assignment can be. While journalists do still report across parts of the country, UGC showing events on the ground and the voices of those marginalised in the conflict, as well as media activists, is now a vital tool in telling the story, particularly where there are no journalistic 'boots on the ground'.

## Results: New measures

All of those interviewed believed that they had experienced a steep learning curve in developing new practices and measures to ensure non-BBC content could go to air. For example, while some content continues to be sent into the BBC directly, BBC journalists are increasingly harvesting visual content from social media platforms such as Facebook and YouTube. As one journalist argued,

> If someone [in Syria] is going to get their content seen, they will smuggle it to an FSA commander and they'll decide where it goes, probably YouTube. They won't come onto the BBC website, see a post and send us their clip.
>
> (Interviewee 10)

BBC journalists were frequently in contact with groups such as the Local Coordinating Committees (LCC) across Syria, and Shaam News Network. Many conversations began with BBC journalists tracing the owners of YouTube accounts who had uploaded content, in some cases via interaction on Facebook. Events depicted by these groups would be triangulated with reports from agencies and other sources' interactions; journalists would not solely rely on such content, and LCC footage goes through the same checks and balances as any other piece of UGC. That said, LCCs have become well established online and their content has frequently been proved to be accurate. As a result, certain groups' footage, contributors and intelligence have been used more regularly as the conflict goes on. This in turn raises questions of balance, which will be discussed below.

Other relationships developed after BBC Arabic staff contacted people they trusted inside Syria. Conversations would snowball, resulting in journalists speaking with other 'trusted' individuals, including activists. In other situations, members of Syrian diaspora in the UK helped locate individual activists via phone, e-mail and social media. There are obvious problems in relying on such individuals, such as the fact they may exaggerate reports of deaths or violence in a bid to highlight their cause. Like the UGC posted by activists, any claims were checked. Individuals' viewpoints given on air were 'held to task' by the news presenter interviewing them in a bid to maintain some level of impartiality.

## Moving towards signposted content

Throughout the Arab Spring the type of content submitted and encountered by the BBC has also altered. Journalists covering Syria reported that rather than a long video clip being posted online it was common to see sequences edited together, or for it to include signposting such as date stamps, or in-video commentary. This finding echoes the work of Hänska-Ahy and Shapour (2012), who cited the filming of key landmarks as an approach taken by activists to show where they were.

Staff also revealed that activist groups became more organised by cataloguing content posted on their Facebook pages. The LCCs provided both English and Arabic descriptions of the videos they uploaded. However, journalists have become conscious that some of those sharing content are doing so along political lines, and activists may arrange content in a certain way to push a particular narrative. It is for the journalist, using the skills they have learned, to try to make sense of it and ensure where possible there is a degree of balance. Findings from the period of participation suggest that the UGC Hub is all too aware of the risks associated with using UGC. The high-profile hoax of the blog 'Gay Girl in Damascus' where a US-Syrian lesbian blogger turned out to be an American man writing from Edinburgh University is 'emblematic of the more fundamental challenges facing journalists reporting the Arab Spring' (Bennett, 2011: 193).

### Striving to achieve balance

BBC staff said they did try to engage with Syrians from across different groups, and there was an active effort to get pro-Assad voices on air to try to balance coverage of an increasingly complex and fractured conflict. In fact, one journalist suggested that when communication security became a concern it was often only pro-Assad voices that could be reached as they were the only ones still contactable by landline.

However, as time went on, civilians and government officials were either harder to research or unwilling to speak. Therefore activists, keen to engage with the media, became a regular voice, and relationships between those activists and BBC producers further developed. As the dangers inside Syria grew, so did the reliance on these people, and the BBC employed new coping strategies to maintain engagement amid concerns about security of communication with contributors. The journalists interviewed frequently mentioned a 'duty of care' to contributors, which might be another reason why later on the voices on air were predominantly activists. Strategies were constantly evolving and guidelines on the best method of approach could change daily. Today BBC policies remain under review but the following sections outlines key changes which have been put in place since the start of the conflict.

UGC Hub editors decided to amend their copyright policy (BBC, 2013), which previously dictated that a producer should always speak to the uploader of content as per previous events. Managers realised by its very nature it was almost impossible to get hold of the original source of Syria videos, so relaxed that rule in terms of getting copyright permission. Producers were also given clear guidelines as to phrases to use when contacting people in Syria by telephone so as not to arouse suspicion – for example, opening a phone call with 'This is Ben in London' not 'This is Ben from the BBC' (Interviewee 8).

UGC producers said there were concerns that landlines and even satellite phones could be tracked. A ban on routinely calling satellite phones was imposed at the Hub amid fears about the safety of those using them. However, this was not a blanket BBC ban as correspondents may still use such devices when 'in the field'. However, it was recognised there could be risks involved; some attribute Marie Colvin's death to her phone being tracked (Rayner and Spencer, 2012). As a result there was increased reliance on the Voice over Internet Protocol service provided by Skype, which is now the preferred medium for contacting people inside Syria. Producers use anonymous Gmail and Skype accounts which do not mention the BBC in a bid to ensure anonymous contributors will not be linked to the organisation.

Having to rely on intelligence and content from activists inevitably has some pitfalls, and, as with any non-BBC content, including social media footage from agencies such as Storyful and Reuters, UGC from Syria goes through a verification process. Meanwhile, intelligence about developments on the ground is vetted and corroborated with other sources. However, producers stated that some contributors became trusted sources over time. As a result, a rapport built up between journalists and activists both in the country and among Syrian diaspora.

The research identified that the expertise of the Syrian diaspora has been harnessed by BBC journalists to assist with on- and off-air issues. As well as groups such as the Syrian Observatory of Human Rights, individual members of the Syrian community have become go-to sources for information, with many becoming 'trusted' contributors that journalists were be happy to put live 'on air'. Off screen, producers continue to engage with Syrians abroad, whether they are helping establish contacts within Syria, or providing information which helps confirm that certain events have happened in the country such as barrel bombing or attacks on certain area. This was a type of engagement that was not previously seen at the BBC. One reporter spoke about a Syrian editor from an Arab TV channel who came into the BBC's London office late at night at short notice. As well as going on air to speak to BBC TV News, he stayed on and helped BBC producers to verify their content when there was no one else available.

### Evolving with social media

As the scope of the work done by the UGC Hub has evolved, the research suggests that the way its journalists perform their jobs has become much more forensic in nature. Journalists have had to become 'part detective, part librarian' (Interviewee 1). As well as the usual contact with contributors, BBC producers have further harnessed social media skills: tracking lists of Skype addresses, joining Skype conversations with activist groups and eyewitnesses to garner information while cataloguing valuable on air contributors and off air contacts, often going back to them later if their information has been of value or proved to be true.

UGC Hub staff developed a checklist detailing the processes journalists go through in a bid to find out if content and contributors are what they claim to be (Murray, 2011), which goes further than the usual 'common sense, journalistic questions' (Interviewee 9) that someone involved in newsgathering might go through. Examples of this could include asking contributors about the weather, or what they could see from the location they filmed in, and correlating their response and content with Google Maps, picture-reversal software and weather reports.

Perhaps acknowledging the changing media ecology, the BBC introduced new social media guidelines in 2011 with the aim of helping all staff understand the steps that both content and contributors should be put through before being transmitted on air. This is further evidence that journalistic practices have altered, as well as there being a reliance on outside sources, particularly UGC from non-elite groups since the start of the Arab Spring.

While there have been some pan-BBC changes in approach, this research documents more extensive structural and organisational changes within the UGC Hub itself. The interviews and observations in particular highlight various changes to UGC roles in response to the way content related to Syria is being accessed, and also the need to engage with eyewitnesses, particularly activists in areas where English was not widely spoken.

## Conclusion

During the course of the Syria conflict, the way journalists access UGC, engage with activists and the way the BBC newsroom is structured have all altered, and these changes extend to roles in the newsroom. The research presented here found that throughout the Arab Spring, BBC news teams called on the skills of BBC Arabic. In relation to Syria specifically, BBC Arabic staff were 'embedded' within the UGC Hub, particularly on Fridays when protests frequently followed prayers. As well as being able to bridge language barriers with people sending in content or possible contributors, these staff analysed accents and language, which plays a massive part in verifying UGC.

The need for these skills as the crisis in Syria continued was apparent, and this resulted in the creation of an attachment programme. This allows a BBC Arabic producer to work for three months at the UGC Hub, learning relevant skills while providing expertise. The benefit of having a dedicated Arabic speaker on the team is obvious – no more so than in August 2013 when that producer was working the night of the Syria chemical attacks:

> That was a moment on a professional level and a personal level for UGC, and it kind of proved the point of having someone from Arabic there, in the same building. The material I verified that day was sent to [Middle East editor] Jeremy Bowen, and all the videos that he used were ones that I verified. So yeah, it worked out very well on that day. Horrific story but in terms of newsgathering it was great.
>
> (Interviewee 3)

UGC Hub editors also understood the importance of continually being aware of all the video material related to Syria which came into the BBC from agencies or from other sources such as activists. Rotas were made 'more fluid and flexible', and dedicated Syria producers were appointed to allow consistent handovers. These new roles, guidelines and organisational structures give an idea of how staff are covering events in Syria with few journalists available on the ground, while processing a huge amount of UGC posted to social media platforms or sent into the BBC.

The media landscape has undoubtedly become more collaborative and interactive, and audience participation at all levels is now a consideration for journalists who harvest content from websites, Tweet the audience directly and encourage contributions to their programme in a variety of forms. Engaging with the audience is not new, but new technologies are allowing this to happen more quickly, and at the most basic level this is allowing everyday people to capture content and for it to be taken, shaped and used by journalists. The benefit of being able to engage with citizens and activists has been highlighted, and, as Allan (2013) argues, the reliance on these individuals is often most apparent in relation to crisis events, or the aftermath of events happening where there is limited or no journalistic presence.

While one cannot generalise, it seems the relationship between BBC journalists and people within Syria has changed throughout the course of the conflict and there is a need to engage with the audience, including previously unheard voices, on a much deeper level and for extended periods of time. There is rarely a BBC presence in Syria, and producers must gather footage and intelligence from other online portals rather than relying on it being sent to them. In this respect it could be argued that staff are engaging in 'gatewatching' (Bruns, 2003), with the journalist becoming more of a facilitator for news.

However, as has been documented in this chapter, BBC journalists still decide what UGC they want to include in their final reports, which footage they put through the verification process and which, albeit limited, Syria voices they wish to hear from. Therefore the reality is that only a fraction of what would-be contributors and media activists put out will ever make it into a BBC news report. Put simply, 'journalists have remained journalists and audiences are still audiences' (Williams et al., 2011: 96).

## Are activists new correspondents?

There are, of course, exceptions, and numerous interviewees spoke about the fact that existing contacts were particularly good for case studies, and would write or assist in creating pieces to appear online. For example, one journalist took down a testimony from an Arabic-speaking man living under rebel control in Damascus. This was translated into English and BBC staff added the written article as a side panel to an existing online story. Another contributor relayed his personal experience of living in Homs during the shelling in March 2012 (BBC, 2012). This took the form of an online diary documenting the difficulties of living in a place full of military checkpoints. Both these pieces showcase the benefits of developing a rapport with individuals to get a human-interest story and 'colour' about the conflict, rather than reporting specific news events.

Despite this, overall coverage of the Syria conflict is not truly collaborative and this research suggests a change in the relationship between BBC journalists and people in Syria, with a certain degree of trust developing with various non-elite sources whose intelligence proved to be good over time. Moreover, roles and structures within the BBC Hub have altered to reflect this changing dynamic. However, the fact is that as an international broadcaster the BBC must adhere to certain rules, and its values of truth, accuracy and, where possible, impartiality should be maintained. As such, newsroom practices may have altered but this content continues to come with health warnings and caveats from BBC staff, both on air and off.

Put differently, there has undoubtedly been greater engagement and interaction with Syrians – in particular media activists – and detailed newsroom policies and new coping mechanisms have been put in place to deal with a fairly unique conflict in the Middle East. The findings reported here indicate that this engagement has to a certain extent informed newsroom changes. However, in a situation where certain narratives may be posted, and where facts cannot be verified fully, information and content cannot be taken at face value and must be filtered in a way that traditional journalistic content is not. In this respect the relationship with activists has altered the way BBC staff work, but these 'new correspondents' in Syria cannot truly be considered as such. They are more akin to a valuable news source in what at times is a journalistic black hole.

## References

Allan, S. (2013) *Citizen Witnessing: Revisioning Journalism in Times of Crisis.* Cambridge: Polity Press.
Barkho, L. (2011) The Discursive and social paradigm of Al-Jazeera English in comparison and parallel with the BBC. *Communication Studies.* 62(1), 2011.
BBC (2012) Life in Homs is 'checkpoint hell', *BBC News Website*, 03 March 2012. Retrieved from: http://www.bbc.co.uk/news/world-middle-east-17243085 (accessed 4 January 2014).
BBC (2013) User-generated content FAQs. Retrieved from: http://www.bbc.co.uk/terms/faq.shtml (accessed 4 November 2013).
Bennett, D. (2011) A 'Gay Girl in Damascus', the Mirage of the 'Authentic Voice' and the Future of Journalism, in R. Keeble and J. Mair (eds) *Mirage in the Desert, Reporting the Arab Spring.* Abramis, 187–195.
Bruns, A. (2003) Gatewatching, not gatekeeping: Collaborative online news. *Media International Australia Incorporating Culture and Policy: Quarterly Journal of Media Research and Resources.* 107, 31–44.
Castells, M. (2012) *Networks of Outrage and Hope: Social Movements in the Internet Age.* Cambridge: Polity Press.
Fornaciari, F. (2012) Framing the Egypt Revolution: A content analysis of Al Jazeera English and the BBC. *Journal of Arab & Muslim Media Research.* 4(2–3), March 2012.
Gillmor, D. (2006) *We the Media: Grassroots Journalism by the People, for the People.* Sebastopol, CA: O'Reilly Media Inc.
Goodman, E. (2012) Harnessing the power of social media at Al Jazeera', Editor's weblog, 11 September. Retrieved from: http://www.editorsweblog.org/2012/09/11/harnessing-the-power-of-social-media-at-al-jazeera (accessed 9 January 2013).
Hänska-Ahy, M. T. and Shapour, R. (2012) Who's Reporting the Protests? Converging practices of citizen journalists and two BBC World Service newsrooms, from Iran's election protests to the Arab uprisings. *Journalism Studies.* 14(1), 29–45.
Hermida, A. and Thurman, N. (2008) A clash of cultures: The integration of user-generated content within professional journalistic frameworks at British newspaper websites. Reprint in *The Future of Newspapers.* Routledge, 2009.

Hermida, A, Lewis, S. and Zamith, R. (2013) Sourcing the Arab Spring: A Case Study of Andy Carvin's Sources During the Tunisian and Egyptian Revolutions. *Journal of Computer-Mediated Communication.*

Howard, P. Duffy, A. and Freelon, D. (2011) Opening Closed Regimes What Was the Role of Social Media During the Arab Spring? Working Paper, Project on Information Technology & Political Islam. Available at: www.pITPI.org

Khondker, H. H. (2011) Role of the new media in the Arab spring. *Globalizations.* 8(5), 675–679.

Murray, A. (2011) BBC processes for verifying social media content. BBC Blog. Retrieved from: http://www.bbc.co.uk/blogs/blogcollegeofjournalism/posts/bbcsms_bbc_procedures_for_veri (accessed 13 June 2013).

Rayner, G. and Spencer, R. (2012) Syria: Sunday Times journalist Marie Colvin killed in 'targeted attack' by Syrian forces. *Daily Telegraph.* Retrieved from: http://www.telegraph.co.uk/news/worldnews/middleeast/syria/9098175/Syria-Sunday-Times-journalist-Marie-Colvin-killed-in-targeted-attack-by-Syrian-forces.html (accessed 5 January 2014).

Robertson, A. (2013) Connecting in crisis: "Old" and "New" media and the Arab Spring. *The International Journal of Press/Politics July* 2013. 18(3), 325–341.

Sambrook, R. (2005) Citizen Journalism and the BBC. Nieman Reports, Winter 2004. Retrieved from: http://www.nieman.harvard.edu/reportsitem.aspx?id=100542 (accessed 29 October 2013).

Thorsen, E. and Allan, S. (eds) (2014) *Citizen Journalism: Global Perspectives Volume 2.* New York: Peter Lang.

Tufekci, Z. (2011) Tunisia, Twitter, Aristotle, Social Media and Final and Efficient Causes. Retrieved from: http://technosociology.org/?p=263 (accessed 6 August 2013).

Wardle, C. and Williams, A. (2008) ugc@the bbc: Understanding its impact upon contributors, non-contributors and BBC News. Cardiff School of Journalism, Cardiff 11.

Williams, A. J. Wardle, C. and Wahl-Jorgensen, K. (2011) "Have they got news for us?" Audience revolution or business as usual at the BBC? *Journalism Practice.* 5(1), 85–99.

# 13

## Police, Protester, Public: Unsettling Binaries in the Public Sphere

*Pollyanna Ruiz*

During public demonstrations, protesters seek to instigate social and political change by bringing people and ideas that they perceive to have been marginalised into mainstream public spaces (Ruiz, 2014). This move from the margins to the mainstream is frequently both materially and symbolically fraught. However, demonstrators who are happy to move within officially sanctioned parameters are generally recognised as being an important part of a fully functioning democracy (Cottle, 2006; Della Porta et al., 2006). Indeed, such gatherings could be interpreted as the embodiment of Habermas' normative notion of the public sphere – a rational, deliberative and self-organising space in which private individuals congregate in order to reflect upon how best to achieve the greater good.

Demonstrators who challenge this normative model on the other hand tend to be perceived very differently. These protesters tend to be treated by mainstream organisations such as the police, news providers and the wider public as a disruptive and potentially dangerous threat to democracy (Della Porta et al., 2006; Juris, 2005; Williams, 2007). Moreover, when demonstrations spill over into conflict, the police are required to distinguish between members of the public exercising their right to protest and those engaging in criminal activity (Waddington, 1999). In this way the police 'patrol the boundaries of citizenship', deciding on a case-by-case basis whose respectability is to be secured and whose is to be denied (Waddington, 1999: 41).

The distinction between 'good' and 'bad' protesters drawn by the police on the ground is invariably echoed by journalists in the news (Hewson, 2005). This is because journalists have traditionally relied heavily upon official news sources when constructing the news

(Chomsky, 2002; McChesney, 2008). Such practices symbolically reproduce the material distinctions made by the police and justify the
exclusion of 'bad' protesters from mediated public spaces. In this way
the policing of popular protest on the ground, and the representations
of popular protest in the news, *together* enable and constrain the wider
public's engagement with the political.

The fact that most citizens' engagement with public demonstrations
is heavily mediated requires us to think carefully about the everyday
practices and processes that construct the relationship between what
happens on our streets and what happens in our news. For example,
Williams points out that when members of the public see images of the
police in riot gear, it is easy for them to assume that 'the crowd they are
monitoring is dangerous or even criminal' (2007: 193). Such assumptions can deter 'good' protesters from attending public demonstrations,
especially those that appear to be potential sites of conflict (Klein, 2001).
Thus while one cannot claim that the media have the power to construct
reality per se, one can suggest that they constitute one of the spaces in
which power is decided (Castells, 2007).

Furthermore, mediated spaces continue to construct wider public understandings of protest long after a demonstration has ended
and protesters have dispersed. News narratives will unfold through
legal proceedings, official inquiries and possibly beyond. Moreover, as
Waddington points out:

> The shifting sands of respectability make policing itself rather precar-
> ious; for it cannot be guaranteed that those upon whom 'respectable'
> values are imposed are, at the time of the encounter, one or other
> side of the citizenship line; or that later their citizenship will not be
> redefined and police conduct regarded as impermissible.
>
> (1999: 61)

Waddington's analysis here is highly significant. It draws attention away
from the categorisation of protesters as good or bad by the police and
requires us to consider the way in which the police can themselves be
categorised as right or wrong by the wider public. This sense of uncer-
tainty over time creates a space in which the ability of the police to act
as 'de facto arbiters' (Waddington, 1999: 41) and legitimately exclude
protesters from both material and, by extension, mediated space can be
challenged.

In this chapter I will bring together a number of scholarly fields
in order to examine the way in which the police force's ability to

categorise protesters as 'good' or 'bad' on the streets is being under-mined by the existence of new information flows in the papers. I will suggest that the information flows opened up by the widespread use of smartphones are posing a particular challenge to the police's ability to exercise lasting control over news narratives as they unfold. I will con-clude by suggesting that the public are consequently being called upon to make retrospective distinctions between 'good' and 'bad' public order policing.

These issues will be discussed with reference to 104 broadsheet arti-cles covering the death of Ian Tomlinson on 1 April 2009. These were taken from a range of national broadsheets (*The Guardian*, *The Independent*, *The Times* and *The Telegraph*) published between 12 March 2009 and 29 April 2009. In other words, they offer a range of ideological affiliations and include news articles, editorials and commentary pieces published in the month before and the month after Tomlinson's death. A lexis search of the month before Tomlinson's death and using the keywords 'police' and 'G20' drew a sample of 31 articles. A second lexis search of the month after Tomlinson's death and using the keywords 'police' and 'Tomlinson' drew a sample of 83 articles. Before going on to analyse this coverage, it is helpful to pause for a moment and recollect the circumstances surrounding the death of Tomlinson.

## The death of Ian Tomlinson

Tomlinson was a news vendor who collapsed and died during demon-strations called in response to a G20 meeting in Central London. Initial reports suggested that he was a protester who had fallen and conse-quently died of a heart attack. However, it quickly became clear that he was not an activist but a passing member of the public. Moreover, witnesses claimed that Tomlinson had been struck on the legs and later pushed over by an unidentified police officer. These alternative accounts were denied and then downplayed by the authorities, which eventu-ally launched an internal inquiry. The inquiry was led by the City of London police – who had also been responsible for the policing of the G20 demonstration – and initially concluded that Tomlinson had died of natural causes.

The case recalled the death of Blair Peach. As in the case of Peach, there were multiple eyewitness accounts of Tomlinson's death, all of which contradicted the police's version of the narrative. As in the case of Peach, these were not enough to unsettle the police's traditional role as the primary definers in the production of news. However, while it took

30 years for an incomplete account of Peach's death to finally enter the public domain, it took just over two years for an inquest to find that Tomlinson had not died of natural causes but been unlawfully killed by PC Simon Harwood. As has been generally recognised in the mainstream press, 'the difference between the Peach and the Tomlinson case, of course, is that the latter was captured on video' (*Independent*, 2011).

Seminal works such as those of Halloran et al. (1970) and Gitlin (1980) (which were published in the period before and immediately after Peach's death) have found that the mainstream media's coverage of demonstrations places a disproportionate emphasis on acts of violence. This body of work suggests that the everyday practice of news management often constructs coverage that is so hostile to protest that it could be viewed as anti-democratic. Within this context, Hall et al. maintain that the police have an 'exclusive and particular "double expertise" ' based on their combined professional and personal experience of crime (Hall et al., 1978: 68). They go on to argue that this position enables the police to act as primary definers in the production of news.

However, the parameters of mainstream mediated spaces are increasingly being opened up by new and unexpected informational flows (Castells, 2009). Consequently, coverage of conflict during public demonstrations is increasingly less uniform (Cammaerts, 2013) and has occasionally been sympathetic (Cottle, 2006). In particular, the ubiquity of the mobile phone means that protesters and other members of the public are in a position to record instances of conflict during public demonstrations and then distribute the footage via websites such as YouTube. This has unsettled traditional relationships between protesters, police and journalists (Bennett and Segerberg, 2012), and opened up mediated spaces to new forms of contestation. The following two sections will examine the ways in which the police's 'exclusive and particular "double expertise" ' (Hall et al., 1978: 68) is being undermined by these new technological flows in mainstream print spaces.

## Police/public binaries immediately before and after Tomlinson's death

The atmosphere of the coverage during the build up to the G20 meeting in London in 2009 was characterised by an expectation of conflict. The press releases issued in advance of the demonstration, and the articles that communicated them to the wider public, positioned protesters as at best unruly and at worst downright dangerous. For example, the broadsheet press ran a series of stories in which the police advised bankers to dress down in order to avoid being targeted by potentially violent protesters (Fox, 2009; Jenkins, 2009), warned hotels in the area to prepare for guerrilla raids (O'Neill, 2009a) and advised hospitals to prepare for an influx of patients (*The Times*, 2009). Preparations for the meeting and subsequent demonstrations were described by the police and widely reported by journalists as 'unprecedented' (Hughes and Taylor, 2009; O'Neill, 2009b), 'huge' (Edwards, 2009) and 'feverish' (Hope et al., 2009).

This chaos and disorder frame was further emphasised by the fact that many of the bylines named crime correspondents rather than political correspondents. These editorial decisions further depoliticised the upcoming protests and, in doing so, closed down the spaces in which protesters might have been hoping to articulate their dissent. They can be read as part of a wider process that leads to the criminalisation of protesters in anticipation of particular demonstrations (Della Porta et al., 2006). This was also the case in newspapers that had a history of being supportive of the left (Cammaerts, 2013), such as *The Guardian*, as well as in more traditionally hostile papers, such as *The Times* and *The Telegraph*. However, the unexpected death of a man assumed to be a protester unsettled this frame and created a moment in which the dynamics of public order policing rather than the 'criminal' behaviours of activists could eventually become the focus of public scrutiny.

The representation of protesters in the days immediately after Tomlinson's death extended the definitional frame established during the buildup to the demonstration. Most notably, a police statement was released within hours of Tomlinson's death, stating that a number of missiles – believed to be bottles – were thrown at police officers as they attempted to call the London Ambulance Service. This narrative trope was reproduced and amplified in the tabloid coverage of the demonstration. Consequently, the following day *The Evening Standard* published an article which claimed that 'the police were bombarded with bricks, bottles and planks of wood' as they tried to revive the unconscious Tomlinson (Davenport and Brierley, 2009). Similarly, *The Mirror* maintained that the police were 'pelted with bottles by a screaming mob' and *The Daily Mail* suggested that the police were 'pelted with bottles as a medical team tried to revive a demonstrator' (cited by Campbell, 2009). As *The Guardian* later recounted, these accounts turned out to be 'colourfully reported' untruths (Orr, 2009).

Characterisations of the police as defenders of the weak and vulnerable against the strong and unruly rely upon a particular perception of the police and their relationship with the public. This perception is rooted in a Hobbesian tradition in which criminals deny the rights of others and the police re-establish 'civic order' by restoring those rights (Amatrudo, 2009: 52). This theoretical position places the police in a binary alongside the wider public and against those who are not acting in the common interest. It's a position that can be heard in the words of Sir Ian Blair, the former Metropolitan police commissioner, in a lengthy article published in *The Times*.[1]

Blair identifies what he describes as a 'British way' of public order policing which he contrasts favourably with other countries' use of water cannons, plastic bullets and chemical munitions. He states:

> The British tradition of controlling disturbances was, and is, designed to emphasis police legitimacy, as citizens in uniform struggle with other citizens without recourse to specific weaponry. (2012)

He goes on to assert that officers on the UK mainland 'have policed disorder toe to toe with demonstrators' (2012).[2] In doing so he ignores the police's power to forcibly detain members of the public. Police officers at the G20 demonstration 'routinely' had speedcuffs, extended batons and CS gas spray, and they were supported by officers with 50,000 volt Taser stun guns (Leppard and Swinford, 2009). This view of the police as citizens engaged in a battle of equals partially elides the police and the public. It presents them as both 'of us and also not of us' (Amatrudo, 2009: 47). This is a categorisation that is fraught with unacknowledged complexity (McLaughlin, 2007) and is underpinned by the need for legitimacy in the eyes of the wider public.

## Police/public binaries in the weeks after Tomlinson's death

The coverage immediately after the death of Tomlinson constructed a social imaginary (Taylor, 2003) in which the police acted as a protective barrier between a vulnerable member of the public and a disordered and violent mob of protesters. According to this understanding, the interests of the police and the public coincide in response to the aggression of the protesters. This understanding of events in material space continued to define the news narrative in the tabloids and the majority of the broadsheets. However, it was soon called into question within mediated spaces by certain sections of the media, most notably papers from the Guardian Media Group.

Two days after Tomlinson's death on 1 April, *The Guardian* published photographs showing a stricken Tomlinson being aided not by the police but by protesters. These pictures visually challenged the police's verbal description of disruptive protesters throwing bottles. Four days after his death, on 5 April, *The Observer* published a series of eyewitness accounts that contradicted the police narrative in a number of important ways and challenged the criminalisation of protesters as a bottle-throwing mob. Three witnesses suggested that the police had had contact with Tomlinson prior to his death, despite their claims to the contrary. However, these accounts did not find traction in the wider news coverage until 7 April, when *The Guardian* received video footage of Tomlinson being struck and then pushed over by a masked police officer. *The Guardian* posted the video on its website and it quickly found its way onto YouTube and went viral.

The video footage was taken by an American businessman, Chris La Jaunie, who happened to be passing through the city of London on 1 April. As a result, the apparent balance between police as 'citizens in uniform' standing 'toe to toe' with protesters (Blair, 2012) was unsettled by the introduction of a third party – the public. This separated out the previously collapsed notion of the police and the public creating a space in which the relationship between the police, protesters and the public could be reconceptualised. La Jaunie's position within both material and mediated public spaces will be returned to shortly.

Despite this evidence, the view of the police as defenders of the vulnerable continued to be developed in some sections of the press in the days immediately after Tomlinson's death. Indeed, a new social imaginary began to emerge in which the police acted as a protective barrier between a traumatised family and a prurient and intrusive group of journalists. Journalists had been told that the Tomlinson family were relying upon the police to keep them 'informed of any developments' (*Guardian*, 2009) and were now told that they 'were not surprised to hear what happened' (Laville and Lewis, 2009). The implication was that Tomlinson's lifestyle had made him peculiarly vulnerable. Thus, according to *The Guardian*, a combination of 'official guidance, strong suggestion and press releases' implied that Tomlinson was a homeless, long-term alcoholic whom the police had been unable to save from the disordered actions of protesters.

As *The Observer* noted, 'the proliferation of images from mobile phones and cameras on the internet' was inevitably 'helping to push the case of critics' (McVeigh et al., 2009). The multiplying plethora of counternarratives welling up from below led the police to attempt to 'kettle' information in mediated spaces in much the same way as the police attempted to kettle protesters in material city spaces (Hyde, 2009). For example, the police asked *The Guardian* to remove the video from its newsfeed and prepared an injunction against Channel 4 designed to prevent it from showing a second piece of mobile-phone footage. Moreover, journalists were actively discouraged from asking questions about the emerging counternarrative on the grounds that 'speculation upset the family' (Laville and Lewis, 2009). A week after the protest, and under the guidance of their liaison officer, Tomlinson's family put out a public statement that read:

> we know that some people who were at the protest may not feel comfortable talking to the police. People are putting pictures on the internet, writing on blogs and talking to journalists. But we really need them to talk to the people who are investigating what happened.
>
> (*Guardian*, 2009)

In this way the police attempted to stem the flow of unofficial information and regain the position they had formally enjoyed as filtering gatekeeper of news narratives.

However, as eyewitness accounts began to be substantiated by still images taken in the vicinity, and, finally, moving images showing the assault itself, a new trope began to appear in the broadsheet coverage. An understanding of the police as a protective barrier was replaced by an understanding of the police as an impeding barrier. This trope began to crop up across all the broadsheets. Protesters who had gone to Tomlinson's aid when he first fell maintained that the police had prevented them from passing information on to the London Ambulance Service (*Guardian*, 2009). Photographers covering the G20 protests announced that they had been physically prevented from documenting the demonstration (*Guardian*, 2009). Journalists who had been warmly received by the family at a memorial service were prevented from contacting them again for a 48-hour period (Laville and Lewis, 2009).

On 9 April the counternarrative that had been emerging through the pages of *The Guardian* was taken up by the other broadsheets and became the widely accepted account. *The Times*, *The Telegraph* and *The Independent* all published lengthy articles (over 1,000 words) about Tomlinson's death. As a direct consequence of the publication and wide distribution of such 'incontrovertible' evidence (Lewis, 2009), the elision of public and police on one side of a binary against protesters became unsustainable. Thus while the coverage of the traditionally right-wing papers were still unsympathetic to the demonstrators, describing protesters at the scene as 'a mob of between 20 and 25 violent protesters' (Brown, 2009) or as 'bent on violence' (Riddel, 2009), all the papers acknowledged that the video footage raised serious issues which had to be addressed.

*The Independent* described the police as 'unaccountable, secretive and out of control' (2009), and *The Daily Telegraph* went as far as describing the police as 'thuggish and ill-tempered' (2009). Within days of Tomlinson's death, the description of the police's role in events as they unfolded moved from 'misleading' (*Independent*, 2009) through 'sanitised' (Graef, 2009) to 'substantially false' (Davies, 2009) and 'crude deceit' (Randall, 2009). Even the usually reliably supportive *Times* piously noted that 'although the police had footage from the streets, they did not admit to concerns over his death until amateur film was given to the media' (O'Neill, 2009c).

## News narratives, mobile technologies and citizen journalism

Both *The Times* and *The Guardian* highlighted the police's initial claim to have come 'under attack from missiles' while administering first aid to Tomlinson, pointing out that an 'analysis of television footage and photographs shows just one bottle, probably plastic, being thrown in the area' (Brown, 2009). This trope quickly became the new frame constructing wider understandings of Tomlinson's death. Moreover, the popular understanding of the police as misleading at best and deceitful at worst continued to shape the news narrative as it unfolded through botched post mortems, inadequate internal inquiries, critical inquests and, finally, legal proceedings. While these narrative strands fall beyond the scope of this particular chapter, it is clear that the public's confidence in the police's ability to act as arbiters of citizenship (Waddington, 1999) had been fatally undermined within days of Tomlinson's death.

The speed with which the news narrative moved from headlines reading 'Police pelted with bricks as they help dying man' (Davenport and Brierley, 2009) to 'Revealed: Video of police attack on man who died at G20 protest' (*Guardian*, 2009) is enormously significant. While Peach's death at the hands of the Metropolitan Police went publically unacknowledged for 30 years, the death of Tomlinson was on the verge of being acknowledged a 'mere' eight days after the event. This intensification of the news cycle is rooted in the advent of mobile technologies and has far-reaching consequences. The work of Philo and

Berry (2004) has demonstrated the way in which initial news frames linger in the public's mind long after their factual basis has been undermined or exposed. However, in this instance all the dynamics of a scandal (Thompson, 2005) were speeded up and the police narrative had barely been established before it was revealed to be untrue.

This chapter has offered a timely and necessary lens through which to better understand the mechanisms that shape the public engagement with the politics of contentious protest. It has done so by examining police/protester binaries before the video appeared, as the video was appearing and after it had appeared. In doing so it has suggested that the advent of mobile technologies is undermining the police's ability to exercise lasting control over news narratives as they unfold. It has argued that the consequently problematised representation of the police in the broadsheet press is unsettling many of the binaries that have traditionally defined the coverage of mass demonstrations.

This interdisciplinary examination raises some broader issues about the role of new communications technologies within the public sphere. Such issues exist within an environment characterised by a deeply critical audience, which is losing confidence in traditional institutions (Norris, 1998). This sense of distrust has extended to include a loss of faith in mainstream journalism, which has been described as a 'growing disconnect (and alienation) between the journalist and his or her audience' (Deuze, 2009: 256). Within this context many commentators have invested their hopes in the work of citizen journalists. This hope is rooted in the belief that new communications technologies can empower individuals and grassroots movements challenging the authority of those in positions of institutional power (Castells, 2012).

Others are more cautious about the ability of technology to radically alter power (Morozov, 2011). Despite these carefully considered scholarly critiques of the role played by the mobile phone and social networking sites during the so-called Arab Spring (Ali and Fahmy, 2013), popular news narratives still champion the emancipatory potential of mobile technologies (Mason, 2013). This trope is particularly prevalent in the coverage of those resisting repressive regimes but can also be found in stories about authority within more mature Western democracies. For example, we have news narratives around individuals such as Salam Pax, who began blogging from Baghdad and went on to become a correspondent for *The Guardian*, and Matt Drudge, who made 'no pretence of being a journalist' (Allan, 2009: 22) but nevertheless become well known for his revelations in the US.

Goode describes the term 'citizen journalism' as 'nebulous and potentially unwieldy' (2009: 1288), but argues that it includes both a range of web-based activities and a wider range of social practices, such as eye-witnessing and breaking news stories. According to this definition, La Jaunie could be read as a citizen journalist. However, while many individual citizen journalists have become well known for their revelations, La Jaunie remains a curiously underdeveloped figure in the news narratives that constitute the coverage of the death of Tomlinson. As has been previously discussed, the video footage of Tomlinson's death was not taken by a member of the police force, nor by a G20 protester, but by a visiting American businessman – a bystander.

La Jaunie's social role as a bystander complicates more common understandings of citizen journalism in two ways. First, his decision to film the policing of the G20 demonstrations was not part of an ongoing set of activist-orientated practices. Indeed, it was a single act – one which was hugely impactful but also largely serendipitous. Second, his actions were not motivated by a desire to challenge the status quo or even to expose the excessive nature of public order policing in the UK. His decision to hand his footage over to a UK newspaper was prompted by his belief that 'the family were not getting any answers' from the authorities in charge of the investigation (cited in *The Guardian*, 2009). Consequently, his behaviour is more in keeping with Rosen's far looser definition of citizen journalism in which 'the people formally known as the audience employ the press tools in their possession to inform one another' (2008).

Having (anonymously) borne witness to the death of Tomlinson, La Jaunie quickly faded from public view. His lack of an explicitly defined political position in relation to the protest (he neither supported nor condemned the G20 demonstrations) and his distance from events as they unfolded on the ground (he contacted *The Guardian* from his home in the US) cut through the cynicism which often permeates public reactions to breaking news stories. As such he escaped the tension identified by Goode between 'modernist heroic' understandings of citizen journalism and 'more postmodern' interpretations that emphasise collective processes of circulation, reworking and interpretation (2009: 1290). Instead La Jaunie can be read as occupying a far quieter social role – not necessarily a citizen journalist but 'a person like me' (Edelman, 2008); a citizen bystander. Moreover, it would appear that in a world suspicious of spin, neither a classical emphasis on sincerity (Johnson, 2001) nor an alternative emphasis on authenticity (Atton, 2002) can guarantee truth as well as a more casual disinterest.

## Notes

1. This letter was not drawn from the lexis sample. It was published two years later, after the legal process had been exhausted.
2. One should note Blair's casual use of the word 'Mainland' and recognise that his characterisation of UK policing would be completely unrecognisable to those being policed in Northern Ireland during the Troubles.

## References

Ali, S. and Fahmy, S. (2013) Gatekeeping and citizen journalism: The use of social media during the recent uprisings in Iran Egypt and Libya. *Media War and Conflict.* 6(1), 55–69.

Allan, S. (2009) Histories of citizen journalism, in S. Allan and E. Thorsen (eds) *Citizen Journalism Global Perspectives.* AL: Peter Land, 17–32.

Amatrudo, A. (2009) *Criminology and Political Theory.* LA: Sage.

Atton, C. (2002) *Alternative Media.* London: Sage.

Bennet, L. and Segerberg, A. (2012) The logics of connective action: digital media and the personalisation of contentious politics. *Information Communication and Society.* 15, 739–768.

Blair, I. (2012) Ian Tomlinson is Our Rodney King moment. *Times,* 21st July 2012.

Brown, B. (2009) See you Tomorrow Barry, if I'm still alive and breathing. *Times,* 9th April 2009.

Cammaerts, B. (2013) The mediation of insurrectionary symbolic damage: The 2010 UK student protests. *The International Journal of Press/Politics.* 18, no. 4, 525–548.

Campbell, D. (2009) A man has died. Now we must find out why. *Guardian,* 8th April 2009.

Castells, M. (2007) Communication, power and counter power in the networked society. *International Journal of Communication.* 1, 238–266.

Castells, M. (2009) *Communication Power.* Oxford: Oxford University Press.

Castells, M. (2012) *Networks of Outrage and Hope: Social Movements in the Internet Age.* MA: Polity Press.

Chomsky, N. (2002) *Media Control: The Spectacular Achievements of Propaganda* (2nd edn) New York: Seven Stories Press.

Cottle, S. (2006) *Mediatised Conflict.* Open Berkshire: University Press.

Davenport, J. and Brierley, D. (2009) Police pelted with bricks as they help dying man. *Evening Standard,* 2nd April 2009.

Davies, N. (2009) Under attack: Why did it take 6 days and citizen journalism to shed light on Ian Tomlinson's death. *Guardian,* 27th April 2009.

Della Porta, D., Peterson, A. and Reiter, H. (2006) *The Policing of Transnational Protest.* Aldershot: Ashgate.

Deuze, M. (2009) The future of citizen journalism, in S. Allan and E. Thorsen (eds) *Citizen Journalism Global Perspectives.* AL: Peter Land, 255–264.

Edelman (2008) *Edelman Trust Barometer.* London: Edelman.

Edwards, R. (2009) Record pounds 10m costs for G20 security. *Daily Telegraph,* 21st March 2009.

Fox, I. (2009) How not to look like a banker. *Guardian,* 27th March 2009.

Gitlin, Todd (1980) *The Whole World Is Watching: Mass Media in the Making and the Unmaking of the New Left.* Berkeley, CA: University of California Press.

Goode, L. (2009) Social news, citizen journalism and democracy. *New Media and Society.* 11(8), 1287–1305.

Graef, R. (2009) The met in the spotlight. *Guardian,* 15th April 2009.

*Guardian, The* (2009) New G20 video compounds doubts over police's account of Tomlinson's death. *The Guardian,* 9th April 2009.

*Guardian, The* (2009) Police name man who dies at G20 protest. *The Guardian,* 2nd April 2009.

*Guardian, The* (2009) Policing: death and denials. *The Guardian,* 9th April 2009.

*Guardian, The* (2009) Video reveals G20 police assault on man who died. *The Guardian,* 7th April 2009.

Hall, S., Critcher, C., Jefferson, T., Clarke, J. and Roberts, B. (1978) *Policing the Crisis: Mugging, The State and Law and Order.* New York: Palgrave Macmillan.

Halloran, J. Elliott, P. and Murdock, G. (1970) *Demonstrations and Communications: A Case Study.* London: Penguin.

Hewson, P. (2005) 'It's politics stupid'. How neo-liberal politicians, NGOs, and rock stars highjacked the global justice movement at Gleneagles . . . and how we let them, in D. Harvie, K. Milburn, B. Trott, and D. Watts (eds) *Shut Them Down! The G8, Gleneagles 2005 and the Movement of Movements.* Leeds and New York, NY: Dissent!/Autonomedia, 135–150.

Hope, C. Edwards, E. and Gregory, O. (2009) 5,000 police on streets for G20. *Daily Telegraph,* 14th March 2009.

Hughes, M. and Taylor, J. (2009) G20 protesters 'will try to bring London to a standstill'. *Independent,* 21st March 2009.

Hyde, M. (2009) Put enough cameras on the police and even the serially deferential wake up. *Guardian,* 11th April 2009.

*Independent, The* (2009) A vital step towards accountability. *The Independent,* 25th May 2009.

*Independent, The* (2009) *Unaccountable, secretive and out of control. The Independent,* 9th April 2009.

Jenkins, A. (2009) Eat the bankers? That sounds yummy to me. *The Independent,* 28th March 2009.

Johnson, J. H. (2001) Versailles, meet les Halles: Masks, carnival and the French revolution. *Representations.* 73, 89–116.

Juris, J. S. (2005) Violence performed and imagined: Militant action, The Black bloc and the mass media in Genoa. *Critique of Anthropology.* 25, 413–432.

Klein, N. (2001) They call us violent agitators. *Guardian,* 23rd March 2001.

Laville, S. (2009) Police try to forestall 'innovative' G20 summit protesters. *Guardian,* 21st March 2009.

Laville, S. and Lewis, P. (2009) Bland statements and quiet briefings – how police tried to manage a death. *Guardian,* 9th April 2009.

Leppard, D. and Swinford, S. (2009) Police to use stun guns on G20 protesters. *Sunday Times,* 29th March 2009.

Lewis, P. (2009) G20 death Now officer may face manslaughter charge. *Guardian,* 18th April 2009.

Mason, P. (2013) From Arab Spring to global revolution. *Guardian,* 5th February 2013.

McChesney, R. (2008) The political economy of mass media: Enduring issues, emerging dilemmas. *New York Monthly Review Press.*

McLaughlin, E. (2007) *The New Policing.* London: Sage, 37.

McVeigh, T. Syal, R. and Hinsliff, G. (2009) How the image of UK police took a beating. *Guardian,* 19th April 2009.

Morozov, E. (2011) *The Net Delusion: How Not to Liberate the World.* UK: Penguin.

Norris, P. (1998) *Critical Citizens: Global Support for Democratic Government.* Oxford: Oxford University Press.

O'Neill, S. (2009a) Summit police fear attacks on hotels used by G20 leaders. *Times,* 18th March 2009.

O'Neill, S. (2009b) *City told to expect weeks of protests. Times,* 21st March 2009.

O'Neill, S. (2009c) New broom fails to make clean sweep of the yard. *Times,* 10th April 2009.

Orr, D. (2009) The catalogue of incidents that tell the Met is out of control. *Independent,* 9th April 2009.

Philo, G. and Berry, M. (2004) *Bad News from Israel.* London: Pluto Press.

Randall, D. (2009) The man who was trying to get home. *Independent on Sunday,* 12th April 2009.

Riddel, M. (2009) Our society is indeed broken: But at the top, not the bottom. *Daily Telegraph,* 9th April 2009.

Rosen, J. (2008) A most useful definition of citizen journalism. *Press Think* 14th July.

Ruiz, P. (2014) *Articulating Dissent: Protest and the Public Sphere.* London: Pluto.

Taylor, C. (2003) *Modern Social Imaginaries (Public Planet).* Durham, NC: Duke University Press Books.

Thompson, J. (2005) *The New Visibility, Theory Culture and Society.* London: Sage.

*Times, The* (2009) Hospitals on alert as police prepare for G20 violence. *The Times,* 27th March 2009.

Townsend, M. and Lewis, P. (2009) Police 'assaulted' bystander who died during G20 protests. *Observer,* 5th April 2009.

Waddington, P. A. J. (1999) *Policing Citizens.* London and New York: Routledge.

Williams, K. (2007) *Our Enemies in Blue: Police and Power in America.* Cambridge, MA: South End Press.

# Afterword

*Stuart Allan*

Things fall apart; the centre cannot hold.

W. B. Yeats (1921)

To what extent does our sense of marginality prefigure the mainstream, the interior centre that anchors a projection of exterior boundaries or limits? Much will depend upon who shares 'our' vantage point, of course, and thereby who is likely to be excluded accordingly. Everyday life is permeated with social divisions and hierarchies, many of which appear perfectly normal or ordinary, imperceptibly engendered by time-worn conventions to the point that they are taken for granted, ostensibly inevitable if not desirable. As the contributors to *Media, Margins and Civic Agency* have shown us on these pages, however, there is nothing intrinsically normal or necessarily ordinary about these inequalities. Rather, what's at stake is the seemingly 'commonsensical' imposition of power relations in the hallowed name of tradition, helping to encourage an emotive attachment to the status quo as a natural embodiment of 'the past'. To challenge convention, it follows, is to risk censure, to be found wanting as an outsider – someone who does not belong, whose very presence poses a lurking threat to social order and stability.

In seeking to elucidate this drawing and redrawing of 'us' and 'them' dichotomies for the purposes of critique, researchers have long recognised the centrality of the news and entertainment media in upholding, even inviting, 'appropriate' forms of identification widely perceived to be consistent with preserving social cohesion, particularly in the face of rapid technological change driven by the unrelenting imperatives of globalisation. 'After three thousand years of explosion, by means of

fragmentary and mechanical technologies, the Western world is implod-
ing,' the celebrated media theorist Marshall McLuhan boldly declared in
1964. 'Today, after more than a century of electric technology, we have
extended our central nervous system itself in a global embrace, abolish-
ing both space and time as far as our planet is concerned' (McLuhan,
1964: 19). This emergent 'global embrace', increasingly discernible in
the 'simultaneous happenings' of the compressed planet left in the wake
of the receding 'mechanical age', represented dramatic new potentials
for human connectivity. The 'globe is no more than a village,' McLuhan
continued. 'Electric speed in bringing all social and political functions
together in a sudden implosion has heightened human awareness of
responsibility to an intense degree.' Clarifying his contention in a language sadly typical of the times, he proceeded to argue that it is this
'implosive factor that alters the position of the Negro, the teen-ager,
and some other groups. They can no longer be contained, in the political sense of limited association.' In other words, he added, 'They are
involved in our lives, as we in theirs, thanks to the electric media'
(1964: 20).

This cultural politics of othering, whereby 'the position of the Negro,
the teen-ager, and some other groups' is counterpoised with 'our lives',
underscores seriously problematic tensions in McLuhan's inquiry, which
reverberate further in speculative assertions made about the demise of
'tribal cultures' in this new, globalising electronic environment. It is
regrettable to note the extent to which his efforts to describe what
he perceived to be the imminent collapse of 'traditional' dichotomies
effectively reasserted related ones based on prejudicial assumptions
warranting close criticism. While it is important to acknowledge that
McLuhan (1969) made apparent his awareness of how 'the white political and economic institutions mobilize to exclude and oppress Negroes',
today's reader will be struck by the ways in which this tacit othering
persisted nonetheless in his writing. Due care needs to be taken with
his conception of how 'electronic media' underwrite the 'global village',
it follows, so as to clarify its investment in affirming as self-evident
stratified norms and values consistent with certain Western academic
conventions of the time.

Bearing this in mind, the reader may well remark positively nonetheless about McLuhan's prescient assessment of how the 'global-village
conditions being forged by the electric technology' would aspire to
enhanced interdependence and mutual understanding, thereby facilitating 'creative dialogue' to help reduce conflict. Given that this chimerical

image of a global village was being posited decades before the internet became widely available (let alone mobile digital technologies, or social networking platforms familiar to so many of us today), credit is deserved for envisioning how these 'electro-magnetic discoveries' might one day bring together 'the entire human family into a single global tribe' (McLuhan, 1962: 8). In recognising how the normative values of the global village have helped to lend shape, in part, to current debates about virtual communities in a global public sphere, our analytical purview widens to consider how fluid, uneven discourses of citizenship otherwise constrained by time, space and place may be imagined afresh. For those prepared to listen, it is readily apparent that the subaltern have found new ways to speak across digital mediascapes.

Few would dispute that the globalisation of media forms, practices and epistemologies is crucial in this regard, even if attendant public spheres, as John Keane (2003) argues in *Global Civil Society?*, 'are still rather issue-driven and more effective at presenting effects than probing the intentions of actors and the structural causes of events' (2003: 169; see also Chouliaraki, 2012; Papacharissi, 2010; Spivak, 1988). Echoing McLuhan, at least to my ear, he suggests that global audiences are frequently being taught lessons in 'flexible citizenship', where boundaries between 'native' and 'foreigner' blur, just as a sense of ethical responsibility converges with a cosmopolitan affectivity (2003: 170). In his words,

> by witnessing others' terrible suffering, at a distance, millions are sometimes shaken and disturbed, sometimes to the point where they are prepared to speak to others, to donate money or time, or to support the general principle that the right of humanitarian intervention – the obligation to assist someone in danger, as contemporary French law puts it – can and should override the old crocodilian formula that might equals right.
>
> (Keane, 2003: 171)

Related issues associated with 'distant suffering', a recurrent theme in pertinent scholarship, assume an added complexity when considered in relation to how journalistic mediations of what I have termed elsewhere 'citizen witnessing' (Allan, 2013) encourage (as well as dampen, or dissuade) a shared sense of pathos – the 'politics of pity', as Hannah Arendt (1990) described it, or news 'saturated with tears and trauma', as Carolyn Kitch (2009) contends – among those looking on from afar.

Whether or not McLuhan's proposition that the 'globe is no more than a village' resonates, one of the intriguing issues that remains concerns how to make good his conviction that the 'aspiration of our time for wholeness, empathy and depth of awareness is a natural adjunct of electric technology' (1964: 21). *Media, Margins and Civic Agency* succeeds in placing the presumed alignment between media and citizenship squarely on the agenda, at once alert to the conceptual intricacies for academic scholarship as well as the wider strategic implications for reimagining human connectivity – and social responsibility – across digital mediascapes, near and distant. Time and again I was reminded of the oft-borrowed line from Yeats's poem, 'The Second Coming', quoted above, when reading my way through the chapters. Each contributor, in different ways, brings to life what social exclusion looks, sounds and feels like, and why it matters. Viewed from the perspective of those on the margins of public life, there is impassioned hope that that the centre cannot hold, that it is a matter of time – and concerted effort – before things fall apart. Acutely ideological questions thus arise over how, when and in whose interests they will be rebuilt again, thereby demanding careful interrogation of emergent configurations of centre and periphery striving to claim their purchase on political legitimacy. In prompting a search for answers to such pressing questions, *Media, Margins and Civic Agency* shows us why critical understandings of mediated citizenship are invaluable to progressive thinking about social change, promising to inspire dialogue and debate about how best to enrich democratic cultures in the name of equality.

## References

Allan, S. (2013) *Citizen Witnessing: Revisioning Journalism in Times of Crisis*. Cambridge: Polity Press.
Arendt, H. (1990) *On Revolution*. London: Penguin.
Chouliaraki, L. (2012) *The Ironic Spectator: Solidarity in the Age of Post-Humanitarianism*. Cambridge: Polity Press.
Keane, J. (2003) *Global Civil Society?* Cambridge: Cambridge University Press.
Kitch, C. (2009) Tears and trauma in the news, in B. Zelizer (ed) *The Changing Faces of Journalism*. New York: Routledge, 29–39.
McLuhan, M. (1962) *The Gutenberg Galaxy: The Making of Typographic Man*. Toronto: University of Toronto Press.
McLuhan, M. (1964) *Understanding Media: The Extensions of Man*. New York: McGraw-Hill.
McLuhan, M. (1969) The playboy interview: Marshall McLuhan, *Playboy Magazine*, March, Vol. 16, No. 3, 26–27, 45, 55–56, 61, 63.

Papacharissi, Z. A. (2010) *A Private Sphere: Democracy in a Digital Age.* Cambridge: Polity Press.

Spivak, G. C. (1988) Can the Subaltern Speak?, in C. Nelson and L. Grossberg (eds) *Marxism and the Interpretation of Culture.* Urbana, IL: University of Illinois Press, 271–313.

Yeats, W. B. (1921) 'The second coming,' in R. J. Finneran (ed) (1989) *The Collected Poems of W.B. Yeats* (rev. edn). New York: Scribner, 187.

# Index

Printed and bound by CPI Group (UK) Ltd, Croydon, CR0 4YY